PAINLESS PUBLIC SPEAKING

Takes the fear and anxiety out of public speaking whether you have to speak formally to many or informally to a few. This book helps you plan, rehearse and put across your ideas in a compelling and persuasive manner.

PAINLESS PUBLIC SPEAKING

SHARON BOWER

Elizabeth:
Here's to Painless Performances!
Sharon Bower
Jan 12-1994

THORSONS PUBLISHING GROUP

First published in the United Kingdom 1982
This edition first published 1986

Original American edition published by Prentice-Hall, Inc.,
Eaglewood Cliffs, New Jersey, U.S.A.

British Library Cataloguing in Publication Data

Bower, Sharon
Painless public speaking
1. Public speaking
I. Title
808.5'1   PN4121

ISBN 0 7225 2414 5

*Published by Thorsons Publishers Limited, Wellingborough,
Northamptonshire NN8 2RQ, England*

Printed in Great Britain by William Collins Sons & Co. Ltd, Glasgow

1 3 5 7 9 10 8 6 4 2

Contents

Preface

Why *not* speak effectively when it *is* possible for you to gather your courage and develop your skills without reading weighty tomes or taking costly courses? If you want to speak better and more easily, then this book is for you. If you are ready to break out of your scared-to-death frame of mind, then get ready, because here are some ways to boost your budding courage and consolidate your waking wits. If you are standing impatiently behind your public-speaking barriers, aglow with the desire to break forth and be heard, then this guide is intended for you. In fact, these methods are so easy to learn that in no time you can teach them to your spouse, children, colleagues, and friends. So, if you have had enough of running scared, then read on—and later on you will speak more easily and effectively.

In the past several years I have taught hundreds of students these fear-reducing methods. The most frequent complaint of student speakers goes something like this: "I'm so scared of the speech that for days ahead I can't think. My notes are scattered all over the house, my brain is scrambled into fragments, my body feels beaten, and I know I'm going to blank out and die when I have to get up there and speak." When I ask them what they would like to get out of a speech-fright course, many of them say, "Just give me confidence that I can know what I'm going to say before I say it, so I don't feel like dying up there."

And that's what this handbook aims to do: Help you stay alive and alert in front of an audience. To accomplish those goals, I shall suggest some ways for you to take charge of your courage, to develop self-confidence through no-nonsense train-of-thought steps, and to practice your speech in a way that won't bore you to death by the time you give it.

To learn any skill takes some investment of your time and energy. Your first experience with the train-of-thought method will be the longest, because you will read and complete worksheets, as well as prepare a train-of-thought outline. Be ready to work for several hours over a period of days the first time you use this method. However, after you know the method, you can speed up according to your experience, needs, and time schedule.

Try the train-of-thought method and notice how it helps you decide where you're going with a speech and how you'll get there in a quick and lively manner. I think you'll find preparing and practicing your speech a pleasant and rewarding experience, and I'll bet you'll discover new confidence the next time you speak before a group. I hope this book will help you find out what works best for you, so that you can experience the confidence and pleasure of speaking effectively *before* you have to give that speech!

ACKNOWLEDGMENTS

I wish to thank the people who have supported me in careers of speech communication, theater, and counseling. These careers have culminated in this book, which aims at helping people deal more successfully with stage fright. The following people encouraged me through the years: as a speech and theater major at Gustavus Adolphus College in Minnesota—my acting teacher, Evelyn Anderson; as a graduate student in theater at Northwestern University—my teachers, Lee Mitchel and Marie Carr; as a speech teacher and theater director—colleagues Waldo Braden, the late Giles Grey, Claude Shaver, and Owen Peterson of Louisiana State University's speech department; as a graduate student in Stanford University's counseling psychology program—my professors, John Krumboltz and Carl Thoresen, and my supervisor, Beverly A. Potter. I wish to thank Beverly for her important contributions involving the train-of-thought mnemonic.

As a consultant-trainer for the past nine years, I have been especially encouraged by Vicky Katz-O'Brien, Director of Community Services for DeAnza College in Cupertino, California, in developing new communication courses. I also thank Judy Moss and Bea Tracy of Stanford University's personnel and training program, and Richard Henning, Director of Short Courses at Foothill College, Los Altos Hills, California, for their continuous promotion of my courses.

I especially appreciate Mary Munter, coordinator of the communication skills program at the Graduate School of Business at Stanford University, who expertly and enthusiastically edited the first draft of *Painless Public Speaking* in the spring of 1979. I'm grateful to Maria Carella, College Book Production Editor at Prentice-Hall, who used her unusual skills in helping me deliver my train-of-thought. I also wish to thank Philip Zimbardo for his enthusiastic interview, as well as all the authors who have permitted me to quote from their writings. These are acknowledged in notes at the end of the book. I appreciate my husband, Gordon Bower, who encouraged me and helped me when I needed it. I thank our daughter, Julia, who carefully drew the original train-of-thought. Finally, I wish to thank our friends who were unusually supportive—Joyce Lockwood, Georgia Meredith, Carol Becker, and Naomi Kline, who urged me to "Hurry up! Lots of people need your book!"

Sharon Anthony Bower, M.A.
Stanford, California

Courage comes from *wanting* to say it well.
Security comes from *knowing* you can say it well.
Confidence comes from *having* said it well.

Introduction: The Train-of-Thought Method for Public Speaking

It has been said that good speakers have a way of moving audiences; great speakers have a way of moving generations. What is the way, the style, that moves an audience? I think the winning way is pretty much what Lincoln used to say he liked about a talk. It should be "as personal and familiar as a chat between two people riding along in a buckboard." Speak *with* people, not *at* them or *to* them. The train-of-thought practice sessions in chapters 10 and 11 will help you to develop your own confident style of speaking.

Public speaking is a skill. To become good at it, you must be as determined as a marathon runner. You must want to be good, to be so alive with a need to reach your audience that you forget yourself. Like the marathon runner, you spend hours in practice to run the last mile because you want to go all the way.

This book will guide you step by step, but it cannot serve solely as inspiration. You must slave for your own slave master. You must drive and inspire yourself. Similar to the learning of any skill, the preparation and practice required make for a lonely journey. There may be few rewards or reinforcements while you wonder about your organization or practice again and again to an empty room. All I can tell you is that the satisfaction of giving a good speech, one that can move people to think and act, is a great builder of courage, self-confidence, and a purposeful life.

Will you take some time for yourself? I suggest that you reserve an hour a day for a week or two to learn how to use the train-of-thought method. Isn't the thought of being able to speak well and be proud of yourself worth a little of your time right now?

This book will help you to systematically develop and practice a five-minute talk. Although an informative talk is easiest to organize, and deliver, you may need to develop a persuasive talk (chapter 6 will help you to understand some elementary rules of argumentation).

For best results, follow the program step-by-step beginning with the Introduction chapter. However, you may want to read certain chapters, such as "Imagine Speaking with Ease," "Speaking Up in the Meetings," or "Avoid Last Minute Panic" because you need help right *now* and time is short. Read whatever chapters may be immediately useful to you, and then return to the first page and read each chapter in succession to learn the entire train-of-thought method step-by-step from beginning to end.

The train-of-thought method is not intended as the only way to organize a speech. More sophisticated approaches are certainly available, and on many occasions, when presented by experienced speakers, they may be highly desirable. However, the train-of-thought method is an easy, practicable program that will help many speakers to take charge of their courage, so they can present their ideas in a meaningful and lively way without being scared to death.

Appendix 1 contains helpful relaxation exercises while Appendix 2 has suggestions for speech topics that are appropriate starters for developing a speech with the train-of-thought method. Appendix 3 lists sources for additional information on public speaking and speech anxiety. Appendix 4 illustrates a train-of-thought outline made from a news article. This appendix presents an easy way to begin the train-of-thought method: Simply choose a short, interesting article from a newspaper or magazine and organize it into a speech step by step, as chapters 1 through 7 suggest. Of course, if you already have a topic you wish to research and develop for a speech, proceed. However, if you think you have "nothing interesting to say," then why not say in your own words what someone else has written about? Many students report that reworking an article into a speech gets them "off the fence." Of course, be sure to tell your audience the source of your information.

Many students get an unexpected payoff from learning to organize a short talk: They notice an improvement in their willingness to share information in casual conversations. These individuals make good use of their new speaking skills and put them to use easily and quickly in everyday conversations. These skills are useful not only for "speechifying" but for communicating with an audience, whether that audience is one person or hundreds.

How to Use a Speech Route for Your Preparation

Before starting a journey people should have a roadmap. My roadmap for preparing a speech is diagrammed on page 4, which describes the steps to be taken, with alternative routes for easy or hard talks prepared by experienced or novice speakers. Novices or beginners should begin by learning relaxation procedures in order to control their fears of public performance. Next you should organize your upcoming speech using the train-of-thought method, which is presented as nine steps in chapters 1–7. You then revise and polish your first outline. The next step depends on whether your talk is to be easy or difficult for you. It's easy if it is short (less than 10 minutes) or requires no novel technical knowledge on your part: it's a "piece of cake," like telling us what you ate for dinner. The speech is difficult if it is long, your future hinges on its outcome, it involves unfamiliar items, lots of details, or requires careful or precise formulations: an example would be a description of a legal opinion from the Supreme Court.

If your talk will be easy, take the left branch of the roadmap (diagram); if you are a novice, pick up the desensitization program in chapter 8 to conquer your fear, and then learn the memorization techniques in chapter 9 before going into practice sessions with your speech (chapters 10–11). Once you are already familiar with the desensitization and memorization techniques, you will use them automatically before proceeding from your revised outline to the practice sessions.

Suppose, however, that you decide this upcoming speech will be difficult for you. Then you should follow the right-hand branch of the diagram. From your revised outline, write out your speech in detail, getting the technical details or exact wording you want. Then make up a new outline (your third!) from that written speech. This final outline will be used for practicing your speech. After this, you learn and use the desensitization and memorization techniques in chapters 8 and 9 before moving on to the practicing methods described in chapters 10 and 11. But even for difficult speeches, you should not try to memorize your speech word for word. The train-of-thought method will help you remember what you want to say without memorizing your speech word for word. Instead, you'll learn to communicate your ideas with enthusiasm and spontaneity.

How to Estimate Your Preparation Time

People wonder how much time is required to prepare a good speech. The time obviously depends on which route you take through the speech roadmap. The time depends at least on the following:

- □ The complexity of the subject
- □ Your skill in speaking fluently
- □ The length of the talk
- □ The importance of the speech to you

If you consider all of these items, preparing and practicing a five-minute talk can take minutes for already experienced speakers or five hours for the inexperienced.

A person with *average* experience and skill who is preparing a five-minute talk on a simple subject to a *receptive* audience could follow the shorter route with an *estimated* time schedule such as the following:

ALTERNATIVE ROUTES FOR PREPARING EASY AND DIFFICULT SPEECHES

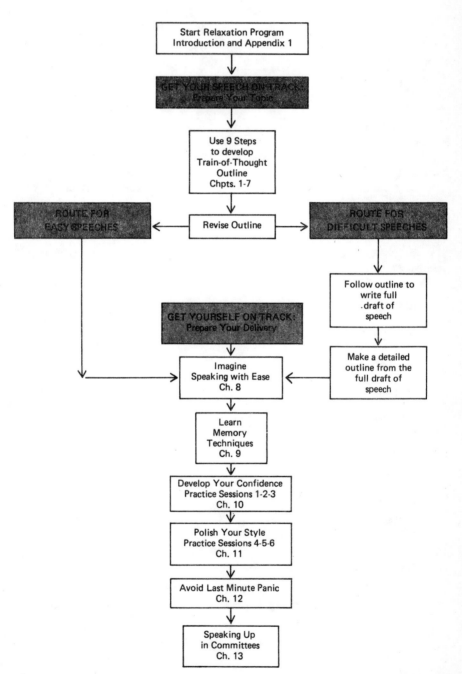

Start Relaxation Program
Introduction and Appendix 1

GET YOUR SPEECH ON TRACK:
Prepare Your Topic

Use 9 Steps
to develop
Train-of-Thought
Outline
Chpts. 1-7

ROUTE FOR
EASY SPEECHES ← Revise Outline → ROUTE FOR
DIFFICULT SPEECHES

Follow outline to
write full
draft of
speech

GET YOURSELF ON TRACK:
Prepare Your Delivery

Imagine
Speaking with Ease
Ch. 8

Make a detailed
outline from the
full draft of
speech

Learn
Memory
Techniques
Ch. 9

Develop Your Confidence
Practice Sessions 1-2-3
Ch. 10

Polish Your Style
Practice Sessions 4-5-6
Ch. 11

Avoid Last Minute Panic
Ch. 12

Speaking Up
in Committees
Ch. 13

- To complete the nine train-of-thought steps: twenty minutes to one hour
- To revise the first train-of-thought outline: ten to thirty minutes
- To practice a five-minute speech: thirty minutes to two hours

Total estimated preparing time: one to two hours for a simple speech. However, many speakers prepare one hour for every minute of performance—thus a thirty-minute speech can take thirty hours of preparation and practice—or longer!

WHY PEOPLE ARE AFRAID OF PUBLIC SPEAKING

People are not born afraid of public speaking. They learn to be afraid. They learn their fear in different ways. Jim learned his fear of public speaking because his father was terrified of public speaking, and he conveyed that terror to his son. Jim also suffered watching his father gasping for breath to keep from fainting when he finally forced himself to speak to the PTA group. So, some people learn to be afraid by adopting and imitating the speech fears of others, all without having made a speech themselves.

Some people learn their fear by a direct traumatic experience with public speaking. In high school, Ann had a very minor problem with stammering and occasional blocking on a word. For a class assignment she was urged to give a brief monologue during a play the class was to present to the entire high school assembly. When time arrived for her speech, Ann spoke the first two lines clearly and then blocked. She tried to start again, stammered, panicked, and then became absolutely dumbstruck, and speechless. To a strained silence in the auditorium, she walked off the stage in panic and complete humiliation. That traumatic experience associated anxiety and voice-blocking in Ann's mind with speaking before a group. In Ann's case, her anxiety spilled over from the large assembly monologue and spread so that she avoided speeches before her class, or was afraid to ask questions in class or in any large social group. She said, "My anxiety came to be sparked by that ultimate moment when I'd get attention to speak so that everyone looked at me waiting for me to say my piece. Then my throat would stop my breath and I'd block—and I couldn't even speak up to tell people to 'never mind.' "

Ann's failure experience was catastrophic for her. Others usually don't have such spectacular foul-ups—just moderate embarrassments and unpleasantries. You might have prepared an informal talk for 5 people only to find that 50 showed up unexpectedly and one was your boss. You flubbed it badly. Or you gave a talk that bored the audience and put them to sleep. Or you prepared a talk for supervisors and vice-presidents turned-up. We all seek approval, and the public performer is saying, "Look at me and love me." But we fear disapproval from an audience. Psychologists call these types of bad outcomes "punishments." Speech fear usually starts with the person having some bad punishments associated with public speaking.

Occasionally the bad things that happen are all inside the mind of the speaker. You may judge yourself too severely, using higher standards then anyone in the audience would. The perfectionist says: "Yes, they liked me but I know I stunk, and I hate myself for it. To try it again will just make me miserable."

A common flaw of fearful speakers is to overreact to the slightest hint that someone in their audience might be disinterested. Thus, in a class of 500, Clive, a popular lecturer, will recall "that one student in the 43rd row left, reading the newspaper." But looks of disinterest are often misleading. People fall asleep for many reasons. Jane, a teacher, was distraught and blamed herself for boring a class of 75 in which a particular student seemed frequently to fall asleep. Screwing up her courage, she finally asked the student about his sleeping in class. The student apologized, explained this morning class was the one he attended after working at an all-night job, and that he was already practically asleep when he walked into class. He said he "was sorry to miss so much of your fascinating lectures." The point is that we shouldn't overreact, shouldn't draw the worst possible conclusions from some apparent disinterest. Such punishment only creates later discomfort and desire to avoid speaking again.

Whatever starts a person's fear of public speaking going, it is a fear that feeds on itself: it grows and spreads like a cancer throughout many parts of one's life. Speech-phobics refuse all requests to present themselves and their ideas before a group. Their fear often causes them to lose out in professional advancement or personal fulfillment. They sit at the back of the room, rarely speak up at a public meeting, and escape exposure. They avoid careers such as teaching or politics where they would have to speak in public a lot. Often, they are upset to find that advancement in their career or job requires that they speak in public despite all efforts to avoid it. Such people are frequently among those who come to my classes to learn painless public speaking techniques.

Students who enter my speaking class begin at all stages of avoidance. A few come when they first feel their senses flying apart at the podium, others when they realize they can't get anywhere in their jobs without knowing how to speak persuasively. Most people come because a lifetime of silence has proved more painful and distressing than learning to give a speech. They often admit that they were injured by an early traumatic speaking experience, but they are determined not to be crippled by the unfortunate event any longer. Much like people who have experienced the trauma of an automobile accident, they have learned that in order to control their fears and their lives they need to get back in the driver's seat and take charge of their courage.

These people frequently complain that they feel they have become "too anxious" or that they "can't control" their emotions. In distressing speech situations they allow their emotions to misuse them. To speak easily when you want to, you must learn how to cope successfully with fear and tension and to use your skills productively to deal with frightening feelings. In this chapter and in Appendix 1 I will explain some specific techniques for learning to relax so that you can look forward to speaking without having your muscles in a bundle of knots. With this information and a few weeks of daily practice, you can look forward to acquiring the skill to speak with more ease and confidence.

Here are some questions to ask yourself to test the strength of your desire to learn how to control your speech anxiety:

- ☐ Do you have a desire to speak well?
- ☐ Are you willing to read and think about your speech material for a number of hours?
- ☐ Are you willing to practice, both silently and aloud?
- ☐ Are you willing to *act* confident, even though you may not feel confident?

HOW YOUR EMOTIONS CAN KEEP YOU FROM BECOMING AN EFFECTIVE SPEAKER[1]

A learned emotional reaction (such as speech anxiety) has four aspects: the environmental situation, your bodily reactions, your overt (observable) behavior, and your covert (silent) behavior. For instance, suppose the situation is that you are giving a report. Your physical reactions may be shallow breathing and heart palpitations, your overt behavior may be shaky hands and wobbly knees, and your covert behavior may be that you are saying to yourself, "I'll fail" or "I can't remember," or seeing yourself fainting or sweating or gasping for air. The relationship of these factors are diagrammed in the chart below.

The important thing to keep in mind is that your emotional reaction to public speaking has been learned. The current performance stimulates an emotional reaction because it resembles past situations where you felt fearful. Your imagination then triggers a physical response such as perspiration, weakness, or dizziness. Because emotions are learned behaviors, undesirable emotions can be unlearned or modified.

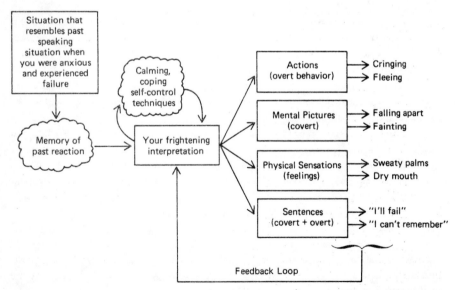

Dynamics of a learned emotional reaction. (From *Asserting Yourself* by Sharon A. Bower and Gordon H. Bower. Copyright © 1976. Reprinted by permission of Addison-Wesley Co., Reading, Mass.)

Ordinarily we think of behavior as actions (such as facial expression, gestures, posture, or movement) or as spoken words. But the definition of behavior goes beyond what we can see and hear. Our silent thoughts, the pictures we hold in our imaginations, and our internal physical sensations or feelings are also behaviors. It is these internal behaviors that help form our attitudes toward people, things, ideas, and situations (such as public speaking). These attitudes, then, trigger a physical response, such as dizziness, heart palpitations, "lumps" in the throat, and "cotton-mouth." Once we have these feelings, we say we're scared. An example adapted from *Asserting Yourself*[1] will show you how your internal behaviors can dictate your actions. Suppose you are giving a report. You are reminded that the last time you gave a report, you felt anxiety and humiliation. That old picture of embarrassment, revived from memory, causes mild physiological reactions along with an "interpretation" of what is happening, what you predict will happen, and how you feel about the experience. This interpretation—which depends largely upon your emotional training and emotional habits—shapes your reactions.

Here is what can happen when emotions get the best of you while you are waiting to address a small audience: While you are being introduced, you notice that your mouth is dry and your head is hot. You feel dizzy and weak as you are walking to the speaker's stand. You may feel physical signs of tension, which result in tight shoulders and a rigid, tight jaw. As you begin to address the audience, you may say negative sentences to yourself ("I can't express myself" or "What will happen if I forget my ideas?"). You may be assailed by negative images—of some metaphor relevant to the current scene ("I see myself as a simple homemaker trying to speak to a sophisticated audience") or of a feared outcome or consequence of the current scene ("I see the audience falling asleep or walking out"), or you notice that you can't concentrate because of your "dizzy" physical feelings ("I can't remember; I'm stupid"). You can't focus your eyes or stop your frequent blinking, and your audience becomes a sea of faces ("This audience is too fearsome for me to speak to; they must think I'm a bore—I'll pretend I'm ill and excuse myself").

Note that when you experience these negative emotions, you make interpretations about your inability to win; they cancel out your potential speech power. Also, in some cases noticing signs of slight tension can cause even further anxiety in an accelerating spiral. When you allow these emotions to happen, you can easily become self-conscious, distracted, and forgetful. Under these circumstances, it's nearly impossible to speak in a lively, enthusiastic manner.

If you have experienced emotions like this, you have overreacted to the symptoms of mild tension anyone feels before a public performance. Effective speakers tell themselves the tension is due to the slightly stressful situation, so they carry on, knowing that they are aroused, alert, and prepared. Inexperienced speakers tell horror stories to themselves about their disabilities and likely failure. These increase tension and exaggerate the physical signs of arousal. Experiencing these increased physical signs sets off another cycle of increasingly frightening self-evaluations, ending with the strong urge to flee from the situation. If you do, you will look back upon this disaster as evidence that you "never could speak before a group." Clearly you are the victim of your own horror movie, having sold yourself a self-defeating belief. You have mistakenly exaggerated your interpretation of normal tension. You defeated yourself before getting to the podium.

How, then, can you change your emotional reactions? You can develop new coping skills to change your attitudes so that you are more positive about yourself and, specifically, about your speaking before a group. By learning specific coping skills you can develop new attitudes. Skills in learning how to cope with stress are a scientific application of "willpower training." For many, changing negative attitudes toward public speaking is a crucial first step.

Right now, pinpoint those behaviors that spell stage fright for you. Then you will know where to concentrate your efforts to change. How can you systematically identify what it is that hinders your peace of mind about public speaking?

Remember that a learned emotional reaction (such as speech anxiety) is expressed by your actions, your mental pictures, your physical sensations, and both your spoken and your silent sentences. Your reactions or behaviors can be easily remembered by using the acronymn AMPS, which can help you become more aware of the source of your negative emotions.[2] Use AMPS to pinpoint your various behaviors—both good and bad ones:

Actions: body movements, which include eye contact, facial expression, posture, movement, and gestures which others can see

Mental pictures: the images you carry in the "theater of your mind." *Examples:* tall, straight, graceful, squatty, slouched, awkward

Physical sensations: physical reactions that tell you how you feel. *Examples:* blushing, dry mouth, shakiness, dizziness, heart palpitations, weakness, nausea, numbness

Sentences: *Spoken.* For example, saying to your audience, "I haven't had time to prepare" or "I only have a couple of things to say" or "I'm not sure how to say this." *Silent.* For example, "I'm no good," "I'm inferior," "I never could express myself," and other silent interpretations.

In the following awareness exercise, use AMPS to identify behaviors that stifle your personal development, those behaviors that make you feel nervous and unsure of yourself when speaking before a group. After each exercise a number of behaviors are listed. Check off those that apply to you.

Monitor Your AMPS:
An Awareness Exercise

Instructions:

Remember the last unpleasant time you spoke before a group. Can you recall your nervousness? Can you or anyone else recall your *actions?* Do you have a *mental picture* of your performance? What were your *physical feelings?* Was your voice forceful and expressive as you spoke the *sentences?* Did you talk negatively to your self?

Monitor Your Actions.

Actions or body language are instantly communicated to others. Have others commented on a distracting or annoying speech mannerism? Use a mirror to get reliable feedback or, if available, a video playback of a short speech. A sympathetic critic can give you important feedback instruction and encouragements. Which of the following actions define your body movement, posture, facial expression, gestures?

___ awkward as you approached the podium?

___ pacing aimlessly? standing with feet too close or too far apart?

___ gesturing needlessly? wringing hands? cracking knuckles? hiding hands?

___ freezing like a statue? standing cross-legged?

___ looking at everything except the audience? the ceiling? the floor?

___ scratching in unseemly places? pulling ear or nose?

___ fiddling with your keys? jewelry? pencil? clutching skirt?

___ slouching like a prisoner? hands in pocket?

___ moving mechanically like a toy soldier? rocking back and forth from heels to toes?

___ somber as if you had lost a friend? wetting lips?

___ grasping the podium for dear life?

___ leaning on the podium for support? rocking backward and forward?

___ handling your visual aids clumsily? folding and unfolding notes?

___ standing in front of your blackboard, flip chart, or slide?

___ writing so small the audience needs a magnifying glass?

___ any other actions that detract from you and your message?

Which one is most bothersome for your audience? _____

Which one is most bothersome for you? _____

CHANGE AWKWARD, INAPPROPRIATE ACTIONS

Actions can be changed for the better! As you practice your speech, you will be eliminating distractions and mannerisms and developing a forceful delivery. During your practice sessions (see chapters 10 and 11), you'll be encouraged to try special exercises designed to help you develop more expressive body language. Meanwhile, start changing in everyday living one or two of your bad habits. For example, deliberately change your slouching posture, stop tinkering with your jewelry or massaging your beard, and so forth.

Monitor Your Mental Pictures

Next, take a look at the image you have of yourself as a speaker. How do you picture yourself? What is your self-image? Do you see yourself as appearing

—— too old, tired, or "over the hill" to be believed?

—— too young, naíve, or innocent to be taken seriously?

—— to fat? too thin?

—— too plain? too ordinary?

—— too unintelligent?

—— too flippant, silly, vacuous?

—— too dull, "heavy," and uninteresting?

Which is the worst image from your point of view? _____

Name other negative ways in which you see yourself: _____

CHANGE A NEGATIVE MENTAL PICTURE

Negative mental pictures create a negative self-image that can damage your confidence. Instead, amplify what's good about you. Ask good friends and relatives what they think are your best physical characteristics. What is most noticeable? What can you do to enhance your best features? Do you need to work on your figure, wardrobe, haircut, makeup? How do you want to look? How do you fall short of your best image? What can you do to change yourself so that your real image approximates your ideal version of yourself? Do you need help with the colors you choose for your clothes? Your makeup? Could you use a wardrobe expert? Does your haircut suit your face?

If you can, seek professional help with your physical image. By altering your physical image you can often feel a new "lift" and enthusiasm. As a speaker, it is especially important to feel confident about how you look. If you feel you don't look good, you'll be preoccupied with your poor image and be distracted from your speech. Don't be self-conscious about your looks; such distractions can cause stage fright.

Monitor Your Physical Sensations

A third aspect of behavior is your physical sensations. When you react to a threat, such as speaking before a group, your muscles might tighten, literally causing you to feel uptight, scared, unable to move. By learning to identify and release the knots of muscle tightness in your body, you can gain control of a large part of your fear. Check off those sensations that apply to you:

—— sweating

—— dry mouth

—— rapid heartbeat

—— blushing

—— short breath; unnatural breathing pattern

—— inability to speak loudly

—— tense, tight throat

___ tense face, inability to control facial expression

___ tense body, inability to move easily

___ sickish, nauseous feeling

___ butterflies in stomach

___ coldness

___ twitchy sensation

___ itchy sensation

___ any other signs of physical arousal? _____

Which are your worst physical sensations? _____

When do they occur? _____

CHANGE PHYSICAL TENSION INTO RELAXATION

Through a technique called progressive relaxation thousands of people have learned to control formerly "uncontrollable" tension.[3]

Because tension is specific and physical you can easily experience it and learn to control it. Try this experiment: Make a tight fist and notice the feelings from the fist muscles as you tense them. That is the sensation of tension. Now let your fist become limp; the feeling as your hand loosens is relaxation. Now try to produce the same experiences with other parts of your body. For instance, make as big a smile as you can, squinching up your face—feel the tension in the jaw, lips, and throat. Now let it go and feel the sensations of relaxation.

With repeated practice sessions you can learn to monitor, identify, and control even small tensions such as those in the neck, eye muscles, or forehead, as well as other muscle groups in your body. Many people have unnoticed tension in their eyes (squinting at an audience), or in their forehead (wrinkling of forehead when trying to remember a point in their speech), in their shoulder muscles while they are leaning on a podium, in their neck muscles when holding their head steady to speak into a microphone, or in their jaw and throat muscles while straining to project their voices. Your goal is to detect and eliminate such muscle knots, because those tight muscles in your throat, lips, shoulders, and stomach can ruin your chance to speak effectively.

Start your relaxation program now. Turn to the progressive relaxation exercise in Appendix 1 (pp. 204–206) for daily practice.

Monitor Your Spoken Sentences

Both spoken and silent sentences account for a large part of our behavior. The spoken words communicate the content of our communication. Do you speak concisely, clearly, and concretely? Or do you occasionally clutter your communication with distracting words and phrases? Did you (or a friendly critic) notice any of the following things about your speech?

___ long, complicated sentences?

___ inappropriate slang language?

___ offensive sexist or racist terms?

___ abstract, boring platitudes?

___ hackneyed clichés?

___ disfluencies, such as "ah," "uh," "okay?"

___ passive verbs instead of active ones?

___ too many involved qualifying phrases?

___ terms that are private "shop talk"?

___ any other bad spoken-word habits? _____

Which is your worst habit? _____

How often and when does it occur? _____

CHANGE INAPPROPRIATE EXPRESSIONS

Keep a record of your own (and others') disfluencies and examples of complicated phrases, boring abstractions, jargon, and so on. Make a special effort to eliminate these distractions from your speaking.

It is important to identify strong and appropriate use of language, too. Sometimes an ordinary sentence can gain emotional impact through the voice. Is your voice strong and expressive, colorful and varied? Is it interesting, clear, resonant? It should be if you want your sentences to convey special meaning. A voice without variety means a delivery without emphasis. Special exercises to help you develop an expressive vocal delivery are contained in chapter 11.

Monitor Your Silent Sentences

Our silent sentences are a powerful part of our inner life. We can literally talk ourselves into a bad case of nerves by saying negative things to ourselves, such as "I'm scared to death" or "I never could talk" or "I'll forget everything." What sort of things do you say to yourself, before, during, or after a speech? Check off the sentences that are similar to yours. Check off your negative sentences first, then read on.

Negative Self-Statements   *Write a Positive Version*

___ "I'm always disorganized."   Example: "I can organize when I spend extra

                                   time at the job."

___ "I never could express myself." _____

___ "I'm not really prepared." _____

___ "I look stupid and awkward." _____

___ "Everyone knows more than I do." _____

___ "What am I doing talking to experts?" _____

___ "Who would listen to me?" _____

— "I must look too young (too old) to be believed." _____

— "I think I'll faint." _____

— "I'll *never* talk again." _____

Do you have other monstrous statements that you repeat to yourself? Write them down here: _____

CHANGE NEGATIVE SELF-TALK

If you are putting yourself down with negative back talk, get yourself on a different track. Deliberately work out new sentences you can say to yourself so that you don't scare yourself to death before you reach the audience. Develop some positive statements that you can really believe. Don't kid yourself; do not say "I can organize" if you really can't. As with your mental pictures, you don't want to make up lies.

Also, make sure that you are positive. Say, "I have something to say that I know is useful for people" instead of "I *hope* I have something useful to say." Take out the *hopes* and *wishes*, because they are not affirmative; substitute assertive words such as *know* and *is useful*.

Look at the sentences you checked above and write a positive self-statement to replace the old negative ones. Memorize the positive statements and say them to yourself as you organize your speech. This is a good beginning for developing your confidence. Chapter 8 (pp. 114–119) offers additional help in changing your negative silent sentences, particularly as you move close to performance time.

SUMMARY

Now that you have used AMPS to identify some of the self-defeating actions, mental pictures, physical sensations, and sentences that undermine your courage and self-confidence, it is time to outwit your annoying habits and fears. For example, do not overreact and interpret any physical sign as an emotional attack. A blush does not mean that you must be embarrassed, nor a dry mouth that you can't learn to speak convincingly. The same physical symptoms are not debilitating for everyone. For example, skilled speakers use physical symptoms to give them energy and expression. Do not let a negative self-image or a negative expression overcome you. Skilled performers learn to replace negative views and debilitating self-talk with positive pictures and statements about themselves. Likewise, this book will teach you additional ways to use your emotions productively and not allow those negative emotions to misuse you destructively. Continue to use AMPS as a guide to help you pinpoint those "fear buttons"—both the physical and mental behaviors, which trigger your emotions and defeat you. Strike a positive note with yourself. Take charge of your courage by getting yourself in shape physically and mentally.

GET
YOUR SPEECH
ON TRACK:
PREPARE
YOUR TOPIC

1

Assemble
Your
Train-of-Thought

PARTS OF A SPEECH

A typical speech has three major parts: a beginning introduction, a middle discussion, and an ending conclusion. Each part accomplishes certain purposes. If you leave out any part, your speech will not present your message in a logical or memorable way. You will be "off track," and your audience may feel confused and irritated because they can't follow your train-of-thought.

The beginning of a talk is referred to as the introduction. A good introduction accomplishes three things:

1. It gains the attention of the audience
2. It makes the subject relevant to a particular audience by relating to their needs (it appeals to them as useful)
3. It introduces the central thought, sometimes called the "purpose statement"

The second major part of a speech—the middle and longest section—is most often called the discussion, body, or argument. A good discussion has one major purpose: It presents facts and sound reasoning to make the central thought understandable and memorable.

The last part of a speech is called the conclusion or closing. A good conclusion summarizes the highlights of a speech by doing at least five things:

1. It alerts the audience that you are concluding
2. It repeats an appeal to the audience's needs
3. It repeats the central thought
4. It summarizes only the main points (not the subpoints)
5. It concludes with a memorable final statement

Following the 9 steps in this book, you will learn to put together the parts of your speech quickly and efficiently. The steps provide an easy method for organizing. However, the way you organize a speech is not the order in which you deliver your speech. The sequence for delivering your ideas is set down in your speech outline. Most people are flustered by both tasks; they don't know how to organize material step by step, and they don't know how to remember the ideas in the right order so that they can deliver them according to plan.

USE A TRAIN-OF-THOUGHT

One of the best ways to feel self-assured is to understand where you are going with a speech, both in the preparation and in the delivery stages. If you know your overall plan, then you can easily locate the information you are searching for in your memory. But how do you help yourself remember your speech plan? Memory experts and research have shown that the best way to remember any information—ideas, facts—is to associate or link the new idea to something else you already know. And the strongest form of association occurs when you visualize in imagination a concrete object representing your idea doing something dramatic to link it to the known, familiar thing. Let's call this the "mating game" for learning a new idea.

Now, a speech has a *series* of ideas. How to learn their order? The answer is to play the mating game using a *known series* or train of familiar objects as pegs upon which to hook the successive ideas of your speech, pairing off the first idea of your speech with the first object on your familiar list, the second speech idea with the second familiar object, and so on to the end. Later, to recall the speech, you go through the train of familiar objects, letting each object in turn remind you of the idea that comes at that place in your speech. Laboratory research has shown that such methods improve people's memory two to five times, so it is strongly recommended.[1]

What familiar series of objects should we use as memory pegs? I have found that speech students are most helped by using their common idea of a train (yes, a choo-choo) with its several parts arranged in familiar order. So I recommend that the parts of a train be used as the familiar objects for mating up with (associating to) the ideas in your speech. The advantage of the train metaphor is that we can select parts that suggest the nature of the part of the speech to be associated there, and that really helps. Also, the train is a metaphor for organizing the speaker's "train-of-thought." Details will be given shortly, and the metaphor is used throughout this book. The metaphor is not just a fanciful gimmick but an integral part of my recommendation for learning a speech. And the technique of using the train metaphor really does improve memory for a speech, regardless of whether it strikes you as a bit unnatural. Even the best speakers use some private memory aids like the train metaphor. The proof of the pudding is in the eating, and students testify that the method works wonders. Will you take it seriously too?

To follow your train-of-thought, that is, to remember the sequence of your ideas, you should actually see parts of the train in order (engine, then boxcars, then caboose). The picture of the train should help you remember the parts of your speech and the components of each part in an ordered sequence. For example, associate the introduction of your speech with a train engine.

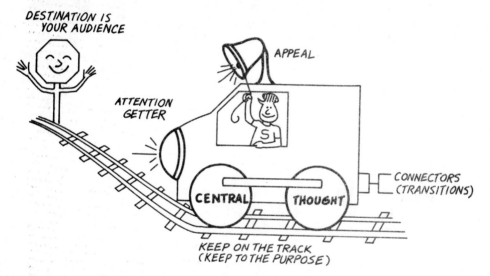

The engine is the Introduction in your train-of-thought.

The stop sign is the audience. Associate it with your destination for your train-of-thought; the stop sign reminds you of your audience, whom you want to reach. The bright headlight represents your attention getter, which should light up your audience. The bell pealed by the engineer reminds you to appeal to your audience's needs. The strong wheels represent the central thought, which supports and moves your train-of-thought forward. The central thought keeps your train-of-thought on a purposeful route or track that extends to your audience. The engine contains three objects to remind you of three components of an introduction:

 is the *attention getter* (The bright spotlight is the attention getter that focuses on the audience.)

is the *appeal* (The bell is pealed to let the audience know you are attending and appealing to their needs.)

 is the *central thought* (Wheels carry the train-of-thought just as the central thought carries the overall message.)

In addition, put your train-of-thought on tracks leading to an audience:

 is your *purpose* (Your train-of-thought must stay on track—stick to its purpose—in order to reach the audience.)

 is your *destination* (Your goal is to reach the audience.)

Close your eyes. Reconstruct the engine: Remember these symbols and associate them with the parts of an introduction: the attention-getting headlight comes first, then the bell, which appeals to the needs of your audience, and third, the strong wheels of the central thought. On a speech outline these symbols are sequenced like this:

INTRODUCTION (Engine)

 First, you say the *attention-getting* sentence(s).

 Second, you show how your subject will *appeal* to the audience because it helps fulfill one or more of their needs.

Third, you say the *central thought* (purpose statement) of your speech.

For now, simply remember these three objects and associate them with the three components of a simple introduction: the light with the attention getter, the bell with the appeal, and the wheels with the central thought. Later in this book you'll learn to develop a good attention getter, appeal, and central thought for your speech.

Next, think of the main points of your talk (the boxcars in your train 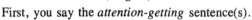) hooked together with strong rods and bolts (the transitional links between points ⊐⊏). These boxcars make up your discussion section. Each boxcar represents one main point in your discussion.

In addition, each boxcar has its own distinctive top, symbolizing different material in each boxcar. These distinctive tops ▭ ◠ △ mean that each car on the train contains the specific cargo (the subpoints) that belong to specific boxcars (main points). Empty boxcars are not included. (Empty cars are like main points without backup materials; they are barren and useless.) Your train-of-thought now has an engine carrying several cars, each with its own supply of good ideas linked together with connecting transitions.

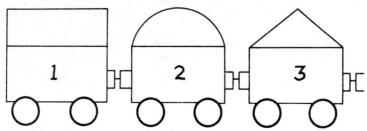

The boxcars and cargo are the Discussion in your train-of-thought.

On an outline, the discussion points are symbolized by boxcars with cargo and look like this:

DISCUSSION (Boxcars)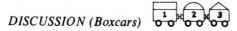

Boxcar 1 represents *main point* 1 in the discussion section of your speech.

The rectangle represents the cargo in boxcar 1. This cargo indicates *subpoints* for your first main discussion point.

The nodes and bolts represent a *transition sentence* connecting point 1 to point 2.

Boxcar 2 represents main point 2 in the discussion section of your speech.

The half-moon symbolizes the cargo (subpoints) for main point 2.

Connecting, transitional link to point 3.

Boxcar 3 represents main point 3 in the discussion section of your speech.

The triangle symbolizes the cargo (subpoints) for main point 3 in your discussion section.

Connecting, transitional link to conclusion.

If you have additional points and subpoints, continue numbering successive boxcars and create additional symbols for their subpoint cargo, such as .

The caboose is the Conclusion in your train-of-thought.

The caboose, or the conclusion, ends the train-of-thought. It contains an attention getter, appeal, repetition of the central thought and main points, and a final statement. After your final statement, you are ready to jump off your train-of-thought and sit down (now a "trained" speaker!). Here's a picture of the concluding caboose.

On your train-of-thought outline, the caboose symbols will tell you what to say first, second, third, and so on in this way:

CONCLUSION (Caboose)

First, *gain the attention* of the audience again.

Second, *appeal* to your audience's needs (again, remind them how your subject fulfills a need they have).

Third, remind them of your *central thought*.

Fourth, repeat your *main points* (no subpoints).

Fifth, end with a memorable *final statement*.

SUMMARY

Identify parts of your speech with parts of a real train. As you remember your speech, simply move along from the front engine to the caboose. Here is a train-of-thought with each part representing important parts in a speech. Read from left to right starting with the engine and moving toward the caboose.

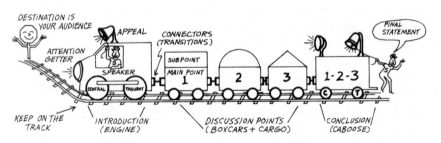

Train-of-thought for organization of a speech.

Now let's take apart the entire train-of-thought symbol by symbol and put it into a chronological listing of what you will say first, second, third, and so forth, until you wind up the speech with a final statement. Pages 26–29 contain a train-of-thought outline. Associate each part of your outline with the appropriate part of your train-of-thought—the introduction with the engine, the discussion with the boxcars, and the conclusion with the caboose.

Familiarize yourself with the symbols and what they stand for right now. Whenever you make these associations, you stand a better chance of remembering the sequence of ideas in your speeches.

STEPS FOR ORGANIZING YOUR TRAIN-OF-THOUGHT*

Organizing a speech can be an exciting, creative adventure if you move along systematically, doing one step at a time. Starting with step 1 in this chapter, each of the following nine steps will be explained in the next seven chapters. Each one of these nine steps will help you organize your train-of-thought quickly and clearly.

Step 1. Aim toward your audience.

Step 2. Get on track with a central thought.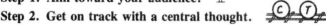

Step 3. Appeal to the needs of your audience.

Step 4. Light up your audience with an attention getter.

Step 5. Choose your main-point boxcars.

Step 6. Fill your boxcars with subpoint cargo.

Step 7. Connect your boxcars with transitions. ⊐—⊏

Step 8. Conclude your train-of-thought with a caboose.

Step 9. Jump off your train-of-thought with a final statement.

While the train-of-thought steps are designed to help you decide what to say and how to say it, the outline sequence spells out the order in which you deliver the information. Notice on the outline that the steps for organizing your speech are numbered to the right of the train symbols.

To show you how this method of organization works, pretend that you are in a class to reduce speech fright, and you must prepare a speech for the class. Your purpose is to inform your new classmates about yourself as a speaker (step 1). To do this, you might speak briefly about your speaking assets, your deficits, and which behaviors you want to change. The following example shows Karen's answers. These answers provided the train-of-thought for her speech.

*Expanded from *Speakeasy Guide* by Sharon Anthony Bower. Copyright © 1977 by Sharon Anthony Bower.

Train-of-Thought Outline*

Introduction (Engine)

Organizing
Step

4. Gain our attention by telling us how to remember your name: _I'm Karen who is carin' about my stage fright._

3. Relate to the audience; suggest (appeal) to what we have in common: _Many of us have jobs which require us to give reports or introduce others at meetings._

© Ⓣ 2. State your central thought: _I'd like to tell you about myself as a public speaker._

⊐⊏ 7. Connect the Introduction to the discussion (engine to the boxcars): _By pinpointing my positive & negative habits as a speaker, I can decide what behaviors to change._

Discussion (Boxcars)

5. Main Point 1: Tell us about your speaking assets and deficits: _I'd like to speak about my assets, then my deficits._

6. What do you feel you do well as a speaker (assets)? _I feel I have a strong voice - folks can hear me! I like to find good examples & stories._

*Expanded from *Speakeasy Guide* by Sharon Anthony Bower. Copyright © 1977 by Sharon Anthony Bower.

What do you feel you do poorly as a speaker? (deficits)? *I'm scared to look at my audience. I feel stiff / frozen & don't move.*

7. Connect Main Point 1 to Main Point 2: *Knowing I can do some thing right helps me think I can change whats wrong.*

5. Main Point 2: Which changes do you want to make first? *I want to begin my new public speaking habits by:*

First change: *looking at my listeners at least half the time, and*

6. Second change: *looking more lively by moving at least once during the introduction.*

7. Connect your discussion to your conclusion (boxcars to caboose): *So, like everyone here, I'm ready to start eliminating the weaknesses because*

Conclusion (Caboose)

8. Use an attention getter to remind us of your name: *I'm carin' about my job advancement & my self image.*

Remind us of how we share common interests (appeal to our needs, interests, goals): *I hope that you are as eager as I am to correct poor speaking habits.*

Repeat your central thought (same as in the introduction): *I've told you about me as a speaker.*

Repeat main points (not subpoints):

1. *I have strengths to be happy about & weaknesses to change.*

2. *I have specific goals to meet in this class.*

9. Make a memorable final statement: *Together I hope we can bolster each other's courage so that speaking will be painless & pleasureable*

By making a simple copy of this outline with symbols and step numbers, you can practice the train-of-thought method. To organize a speech similar to Karen's, simply follow the steps in numerical order (they are numbered next to the train symbols). Remember, these steps are your *methods of organizing* your train-of-thought; the steps tell you when to fill in the various parts of your outline. In other words, you will "jump around" your outline as you complete each step. Answer the questions by *following the numbers* of the steps and see how quickly you can put together a speech. (Remember, your purpose is to inform a speech class about yourself as a public speaker.) Complete your outline now by beginning with step 2 (get on track with a central thought) and then complete step 3, step 4, and so on, in numerical order. Refer to Karen's speech and answer the questions step by step on your own outline.

Train-of-Thought Outline

Now that you are more familiar with the train-of-thought outline, you can learn how to develop an outline step by step for your own personal speech. Use the following outline form below to try out the train-of-thought method with your speech material. If you need more space, simply make your own outline by drawing the symbols and corresponding numbers on your own sheets of paper. For example, use one paper for the introduction, individual sheets for each discussion point, and a separate sheet for the conclusion. When you are ready with the outline form you intend to use, begin reading step 1, which follows this outline.

Introduction (Engine)

Organizing
Step

4. _____

_____

ATTENTION
GETTER

_____

_____

_____

_____

APPEAL

3. _____

_____

_____

_____

_____

_____

C **T**

**CENTRAL
THOUGHT**

2. _____

_____

_____

_____

DEFINE, IF NECESSARY: _____

_____

**CONNECTING
TRANSITION**

7. _____

_____

_____

Discussion (Boxcars)

1

MAIN POINT

5. _____

_____

SUB POINTS

6. _____

_____

_____

_____

_____

7. _____

_____

2 5. _____

_____

6. _____

_____

_____

7. _____

_____

_____

3 5. _____

_____

6. _____

_____

_____

7. _____

_____

_____

4 5. _____

_____

6. _____

_____

_____

7. _____

_____

Conclusion (Caboose)

ATTENTION
GETTER
8. _____

_____

_____

_____

APPEAL

8. _____

_____

_____

CENTRAL THOUGHT

8. _____

_____

_____

REPEAT MAIN POINTS

8. 1. _____

_____

2. _____

3. _____

4. _____

FINAL STATEMENT

9. _____

_____

_____

_____

ASSEMBLE YOUR TRAIN-OF-THOUGHT

Step 1: Aim Toward Your Audience

This first skill is one that speakers often overlook. Speakers fail to size up their audience; therefore, they do not understand their audience's needs, hopes, and aspirations. Instead, they have the notion that if they have something to say and know their subject, the audience will be eager to hear them. This is like saying that if I serve a cake that I like and can make well, my guests will be eager eaters. However, guests may not like my favorite recipe and may prefer a new concoction. Similarly, make sure that what you serve up in a speech is within your audience's capacity to digest and enjoy. Nothing is so unsavory as long-winded speakers forcing their listeners to try their recipes, their point of view, without any consideration for the audience's desires or needs.

"Know your audience" is advice to be taken seriously. Misjudging your audience can spell disaster to you as a speaker. For example, suppose your audience is knowledgeable about conservation bills up before the legislature. You would bore them if you simply inform them about those same proposed bills. Very likely they would expect arguments for and against the various bills, and they would be disappointed and annoyed with you for talking about facts without giving your opinions. You would be considered an irrelevant speaker, someone who repeats everything they already know.

Aim your train-of-thought toward your audience. To do that you need to size up the group carefully before you start organizing your topic. If you will be speaking before a familiar audience, such as a speech class, you might make some reasonable guesses about their interests without gathering systematic data. However, if you will be speaking to an unfamiliar audience, you should systematically gather information about your audience and draw some conclusions about what they might want to learn from your topic. If you have questions about your audience, it is always a good idea to check with the person who invites you to speak. Frequently the best ideas for a speech topic come from asking your host, "Why do you think your group would be interested in hearing me speak?" Don't be afraid to be direct. Hosts are generally enthusiastic about their group and can tell you a lot about your unseen audience.

To size up your audience systematically, take an inventory of the audience. This audience inventory will help you gather all the necessary information so that you can make reasonable conclusions about their needs and aspirations. It will help you decide who will be in your audience and why. Use this inventory to help you assess your audience in an organized way.

Step 1: Worksheet

Audience Inventory

Think specifically about the *interests, values, goals, age, sex,* and *race* of your audience. Next, consider the *occasion, time limit,* and *physical conditions* where you will speak. The unstarred questions ask for factual information about your audience; the starred questions require you to make value judgments about your audience so that you can talk about your topic in a meaningful way that relates to their special needs.

INTERESTS?
What occupations do your audience have in common? _____

Are they at the same (or different) levels of expertise? _____

What kinds of leisure activities do they share? _____

*Will you alter your language to make it more (or less) sophisticated or technical?

_____

*What aspect of your topic might help them solve their problems or fulfill the needs they have? _____

_____

VALUES?
What ideals do they hold most important? _____

_____

*How can your subject touch on those values? _____

_____

GOALS?
What might these people want to accomplish professionally and/or personally in the next few years? _____

_____

What might be their lifetime goals? _____

_____

*How can your subject help them reach their goal(s)? _____

_____

SEX? AGE? RACE? CULTURE?
Generally, speaking to one sex or the other will not make a difference in your speech, but in some circles, it does mean you will need a slightly different speech with different kinds of examples.
Which is the predominate sex? _____
*How does the predominance of men (or women) affect your speech, especially choice of examples for illustrating a point? _____

_____

What is the predominant age? _____

*Will their age affect your speech? _____

*What language adjustments will help your audience understand more easily? (For example, could you use the buzz words or shop talk of your craft or profession without explaining their meaning?) _____

Is this audience mixed racially? culturally? _____

*How might these mixtures change your speech? _____

OCCASION?
Is your audience meeting for a special reason? _____

*How might your subject relate to the occasion? _____

*How might the occasion dictate the specific topic, purpose, and style of your speech? _____

TIME LIMIT?

Do you have five minutes or fifteen minutes or fifty minutes? Always know exactly how long you should speak. Because delays and mechanical mishaps generally use up allotted time, it is wise to prepare a shorter speech than the one requested.

*How long should you speak? _____

_____

ASSESS THE PHYSICAL CONDITIONS

A topic should be delivered in a style that meets the requirements of the audience, as well as the time, place, and format. Deciding whether you should be informal or formal, brief or detailed, depends not only on knowing who is in your audience but also on assessing some physical conditions that determine the style of your speech and kinds of visual aids. It is natural to put off settling such details as format, setting, publicity, introductions, fees, and expenses. It is *very* important to get these arrangements settled with your host so that you can choose a style in tune with the occasion and the environment.

Below are some items to talk over with your host when you first agree to speak.[2] Usually these items are discussed at the same time you inquire about your audience. They definitely need to be settled before you start preparing your speech.

SIZE OF AUDIENCE AND LOCATION OF SPEECH

- □ Size of audience?
- □ Location of speech?
- □ Ask your host for clarification. You can be shaken if you are expecting to chat informally with thirty people in armchairs and three-hundred turn up in a hotel ballroom.
- □ Will the size of the audience and the location of the speech determine your organization and style?

FORMAT

- □ Formal or informal setting?
- □ Will you be the only speaker or will you be part of a team of speakers?
- □ Will you sit on the dais with exposed legs or will you sit behind a draped table? Your choice of long dress, pants, or skirt might depend on whether you are fully exposed.

SETTING

- □ Where will you speak? From a podium? platform? armchair?
  If you rely on a podium to hold your notes, you need to emphasize that fact to your host! If you are on a dais as part of a symposium, ask for a straight-backed chair that improves your posture.

□ What kind of microphone will you have? A lavolier mike that strings around your head is easiest to use.

SEATING

□ Suggest ways you would like people seated. Semicircles and circles are friendlier than straight rows, because people can see each other more easily. Audiences as large as seventy-five people can be intimately arranged in rows, semicircle fashion.

PUBLICITY

□ Are you using brochures, flyers, posters, TV spots, radio announcements? Send your publicity with directions (or suggestions) on how it can be used most effectively. Would a photo help? A biographical sketch with your exact topic is a necessity.

□ Ask that copies of all publicity be sent to you for your files.

INTRODUCTION

□ If you want to be introduced in a certain way, write out a short paragraph to e sent to the person who will introduce you. Make it easy for people to get the facts straight. See chapter 12 (pp. 162–163) for instructions on writing your own introduction.

FEE

□ Confirm amount and pay arrangement *in writing*.

□ When will it be paid? If it isn't paid, whom do you contact? (especially important for governmental agencies and big business)

□ Assert yourself and ask to be paid immediately after you speak. It saves time and energy.

□ If you are an expert, consider charging a fee.
Women speakers are often passive about charging, and the world (including other women) often expects women to donate their time to nonprofit organizations. If you put in hours to prepare a speech, you cannot afford to speak for nothing. Even nonprofit groups, who can pay five to ten dollars for their luncheons, can be assessed an extra one dollar per person for their speaker.

□ If you are donating your honorarium to the group, ask your host to print it in the program.

□ Does the fee include handouts? Who will runoff and collate the materials?

EXPENSES

□ What expense-account arrangements are made?

□ Who pays for materials (handouts)?

□ If you speak at a hotel, what is it and what is the address?

- ☐ How should you get to the hotel? limousine? cab? airport bus? private party?
- ☐ Who picks up the hotel bill? If you do, are you reimbursed? When?
- ☐ Who pays for meals? How?

Make final arrangements for distribution of handouts, equipment, and other special needs with your host a week or more before you talk. Chapter 12 (pp. 163–167) includes a short list of items you should check off with your host the last week. Assert yourself! Get the very best of conditions you possibly can both now and later.

After you have information about your audience and have made basic arrangements, it is time to prepare your speech. Move on to chapter 2, which will help you choose an appropriate subject and central thought for your audience.

2

Choose the Best Topic

STEP 2: GET ON TRACK WITH A
CENTRAL THOUGHT

When an old mountaineer was carving a beautiful horse, a young boy asked him,
"How come you can carve such beautiful horses?" Hesitating for only a moment, the
old man replied, "It's easy, I just cut away what ain't horse!" If only speakers could
follow this advice, audiences would not become bewildered by rambling orators who
never seem to get to the point. Many speakers do not "carve the horse" because they
fail to whittle a specific topic out of a general subject. If they are asked to talk about
racehorses to racetrack enthusiasts, they will bore their audience by talking about
horses in general or, worse, about workhorses. Following are a few examples of how
the general subject (the block of wood) can be carved to a specific topic (the horse).

General Subjects (pieces of wood)	Carved To Specific Topics (figures or images)
The hope for peace in the Middle East	→ Sadat's visit to Israel in 1978
The improvement of personality	→ The usefulness of self-help books
The responsible citizen	→ Preparations to be a community volunteer
Philosophy of life	→ Psychological implications of abortion

WHAT SHOULD YOU TALK ABOUT?

To decide what you should talk about, you must first narrow down one general subject to a specific topic until you can come up with a suitable central thought. (For those who would like to try the train-of-thought method with a suggested topic, see Appendix 2.)

HOW TO DEVELOP A GOOD CENTRAL THOUGHT

Next you will learn nine important skills to help you develop a good, purposeful central thought.

1. List all subjects relevant to your audience and your expertise
2. Choose the best subject
3. Develop suitable topics from your subject
4. Choose the best topic for your audience
5. Develop subtopics from your topic
6. Choose the best subtopic

When you have a good subtopic, you will learn how to

7. Choose a purpose to influence your audience positively
8. Phrase your central thought so that it indicates your subtopic and your purpose
9. Define any vague terms in your central thought.

⟦1⟧ List General Subjects

Keep your audience in mind as you list all the subjects you could speak about. Remember, subjects are very general. For example, sports, gardening, and cooking are all general subjects; baseball, bare-root trees, and crepes are specific topics.

1
List all the general subjects you could talk about:
_____
_____
_____

2. Choose the Best Subject

```
                    ┌─────────┐
                    │    2    │
┌───────────────────┴─────────┴──────────────────────┐
│ Consider both your audience and your own interests. Select │
│ the most suitable and interesting subject from those listed in box 1: │
│                                                     │
│              ──────────────────                     │
│                  Best Subject                       │
└─────────────────────────────────────────────────────┘
```

3. List Several Topics

Review your audience inventory (pp. 30–32) and decide upon a topic after you consider your audience's *interest, values, goals, language, sex, age,* and *racial-cultural orientation.*

For example, if you have a young audience of sports enthusiasts, sports is a likely subject, whereas baseball, football, or soccer would be timely *topics*.

```
                    ┌─────────┐
                    │    3    │
┌───────────────────┴─────────┴──────────────────────┐
│        List various topics that are related to the subject │
│        you chose in box 2:                          │
│ ─────────────────────────────────────────────────── │
│ ─────────────────────────────────────────────────── │
│ ─────────────────────────────────────────────────── │
│ ─────────────────────────────────────────────────── │
└─────────────────────────────────────────────────────┘
```

4. Choose the Best Topic

The best topic is the one that is most timely for your audience. Very often the topic that is most timely is the one that fulfills audience needs *and* fits the occasion.

```
                    ┌─────────┐
                    │    4    │
┌───────────────────┴─────────┴──────────────────────┐
│ Choose the best topic for you, your audience, and the occasion │
│ from those listed in box 3.                         │
│                                                     │
│              ──────────────────                     │
│                   Best Topic                        │
└─────────────────────────────────────────────────────┘
```

5. Narrow the Topic to Subtopics

Next, think about interesting aspects of your topic, called subtopics. For example, the subject of sports is narrowed to the topic of baseball, which can be narrowed to various subtopics. Study this table:

37

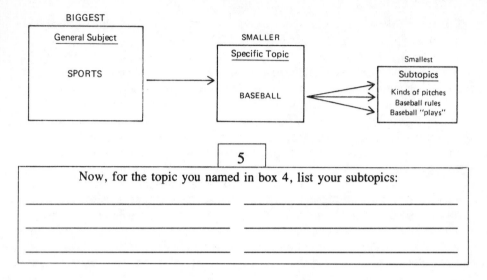

BIGGEST

General Subject

SPORTS

SMALLER

Specific Topic

BASEBALL

Smallest

Subtopics

Kinds of pitches
Baseball rules
Baseball "plays"

5

Now, for the topic you named in box 4, list your subtopics:

_____   _____

_____   _____

_____   _____

6. Choose the Best Subtopic

Next, from box 5 select the subtopic that best suits both the occasion and your time limit. For example, say that you and some young sports fans are experiencing "World Series fever" (the occasion). You will have your audience's attention for five minutes before a major-league game (time limit). You reason that if the youngsters know about the various kinds of pitches, the game will be more interesting, so you decide to talk about two or three "kinds of pitches" (subtopics) in five minutes. Many times all subtopics suit your audience interests and the occasion. Discover your *best* subtopic by asking yourself, "Which subtopic can I talk about in the *time* I have to talk about it?"

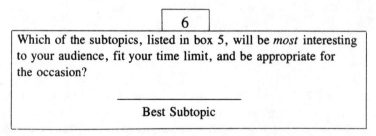

6

Which of the subtopics, listed in box 5, will be *most* interesting to your audience, fit your time limit, and be appropriate for the occasion?

_____

Best Subtopic

Having narrowed down a topic to one tiny aspect of the topic (subtopic), you are entering into the open stage of creativity. Now is the time to read and think and talk to others about your specific subtopic. This open, inquiring stage is usually chaotic. During this period many would-be speakers rationalize their bewildered feelings by complaining that they "don't have anything to say." In fact, they often have too much to say and feel overwhelmed by bits of information here, there, and everywhere. One way to get control of your fleeting thoughts is to jot them down on a big sheet of colored paper (colored so you won't lose it). When you are ready to organize, simply cut them apart and stack ''like'' information in ''like'' piles.

Individuals who have no plan for making some kind of sense and order out of these scattered pieces of information will often fall into pieces themselves, reporting unpleasant feelings and anxieties. Those who do not cope with anxious feelings (see Relaxation Exercise, pp. 202–204) procrastinate in an effort to avoid entirely the task of putting together the pieces of the speech puzzle. Yet, nearly everyone has known the agony and ecstasy of achieving a desired goal. And a good speech, one that meets audience needs by being clear and appropriate in purpose and organization, is just like any other goal—easier to formulate than to achieve, but you can master it.

In whittling down a broad subject to a specific subtopic, a speaker is like a sculptor. Both carve statements, the sculptor using wood or stone as raw material and the speaker using words. Both deal with their frantic, chaotic feelings until they bring forth some identifiable and unique work of art, which has both order and form: The sculptor displays the art object and the speaker delivers the speech. But before you can deliver a speech on your subtopic, you will be involved in some creative work requiring time, patience, and skill.

7. Choose a Purpose to Influence Your Audience Positively

Now that you have a subtopic, you need to gather information. But what information? Before you go poking around for bits and pieces of information, put yourself into your audience's shoes. If you were they, what would you want to know about your subject? If you analyze what they might be expecting, you can save yourself time, effort, and a bad case of nerves.

Why would people want to listen to you? Presumably, you have been asked to speak for some reason, some purpose. For example, your audience may want simple information; on the other hand, they may want your suggestions for solving a problem. In addition, they may want you to stimulate them with lofty ideals, or they may simply want you to entertain them. Most audiences want the speaker to do more than one thing, but *you* must decide your *primary purpose*. To decide that primary purpose, consider your audience's familiarity with your subject, your feelings about their involvement with it, the occasion, and the time limit. Once again, you must also keep in mind interests, goals, values, sex, age, and racial-cultural background. You may feel overwhelmed and in need of a computer, but press on. What feelings do you have about your audience? A good way to help you decide on a purpose for your speech is to ask yourself these questions:

□ What will my audience find interesting about my topic?
□ How much information do they already know about my topic?
□ What kind of new information would keep them interested?
□ Do they need to be

Informed about my subtopic?
Persuaded to my point of view?
Activated to do something, such as contribute time, effort, money?
Stimulated to contemplate lofty thoughts?
Entertained with light, amusing stories and banter?

In order to focus on a definite purpose for your speech, fill in this information:

				7	

Occasion?	Most Important Facts about Audience?	Your Subtopic?	Your Feeling about Needs of Audience	Time Limit?
_____	_____	_____	_____	_____
	_____		_____	

Next, you will use this information to decide how your audience would like you to present your information. To find the best purpose, finish the phrases below. Remember, the purpose determines how you develop your subtopic so that it suits your audience's interests and needs, the occasion, and the time limit. With my subtopic, I could

P ⎡ *Inform* them about _____
U |
R | *Persuade* them to _____
P | *Activate* (move) them to _____
O |
S | *Stimulate* them to _____
E ⎣ *Entertain* them with _____

Which of the above is the best *primary* purpose for your speech?_____

Which is the best *secondary* purpose? _____

Good! You are now well on your way to developing your train-of-thought.

8. Express the Topic and Your Purpose in the Central Thought

A good central thought relates your feelings about your topic to audience needs. You will accomplish this goal with one particular sentence, which names your subtopic (the subject of the sentence) and expresses a purpose (the verb of the sentence). That crucial sentence is called a *central thought* (sometimes called a *purpose statement*).

    How can you phrase a sentence that will indicate both the subtopic and the direction (the purpose)? To focus audience attention, the central thought should do two things:

    a. Name the subtopic as the *subject* of the sentence.

    b. Use a *verb* that states your purpose directly or implies it indirectly.

WAYS TO WORD A CENTRAL THOUGHT

You can work out a good central thought with very little effort. Here are some suggestions for writing a lively and interesting one. The five methods illustrate how you can word central thoughts in different ways, adding flair and interest to your main theme. You can phrase your central thought

    a. as a *question*
    b. as a *definition* of the topic
    c. as an *evaluation* of the topic
    d. as directly stating your *intention* as a speaker
    e. as revealing your *speaking techniques*

After working with the methods, you might notice that some techniques seem more neutral in style than others. For example, a central thought posed as a question generally gives the audience the *direct* impression that the speaker will give an informative talk. However, the question technique can also be effectively used as a low-key way to suggest a persuasive purpose, which is useful when you have to convince a hostile audience. Here are the ways you can put these methods to work for you.

    □ As a *question*

       Example: "How can you improve your speech?" (Informative or persuasive purpose is implied by *can improve)*

When the central thought is phrased as a question, an audience will often take notice and actively listen to an entire speech for the answer. The action words *can improve* tell an audience that the speaker will show them how they can prepare and improve their speeches. The use of examples and a demonstration would show the audience how they can improve.

8a

Write your central thought as a question:

_____

What purpose is stated or implied? _____ (purposes listed in box 7) _____

Does this central thought suggest the primary purpose of your speech? _____

◻ As a brief *definition* of the topic

Example: "A speech consists of three parts: an introduction, a discussion, and a conclusion."

After hearing this brief definition of a speech, you might expect the speaker to explain, or demonstrate, the three parts of a speech. The action word *consists* implies that the speaker's purpose is to inform the audience about the beginning, middle, and end of a speech. An audience would not expect to be persuaded that a speech has a beginning, middle, and end. Most things do.

8b

Write your central thought as a brief definition of the topic:

_____

_____

_____

What purpose is stated or implied? _____

Does this central thought suggest the primary purpose of your speech? _____

◻ As an *evaluation* of the topic

Example: "Practicing a speech in short time periods *is essential* for efficient learning."

Is essential tells an audience about the speaker's values, namely that short practice sessions are worthwhile; thus, the audience would expect the speaker to give some reasons why short practice periods help people learn faster than longer periods. The words *is essential* lead us to believe that the speaker's purpose is to persuade us.

8c

Write your central thought as an evaluation of your topic:

_____

What purpose is stated or implied? _____

Does this central thought suggest the primary purpose of your speech? _____

◻ As directly stating your *intention* as a speaker

Examples: "I'm going to *tell* you about the various parts of an informative talk—the introduction, discussion, and conclusion."

Here there is no implied meaning; the verb *tell* directly expresses the purpose. Expressing your exact purpose with a verb such as *tell* is clearly stating your intention to give a straightforward, informative talk. The direct-intention method can also be used when your purpose is to persuade, such as "I'm going to persuade you that . . . ," or when your purpose is to activate, such as "I'm going to urge you to . . ."

8d

Write your central thought by stating your intention as a speaker: _____
_____

What purpose is stated or implied?_____

Does this central thought suggest the primary purpose of your speech? _____

□ As revealing your *speaking technique*

Examples: "I'll *describe* three speaking styles." (You will describe the characteristics of three styles of speaking.)
"I'll *illustrate* three speaking styles." (You will use examples to point up differences in three speaking styles.)
"I'll *demonstrate* three speaking styles." (You will imitate three different vocal styles to demonstrate three speaking styles.)

Using words like *describe, illustrate,* and *demonstrate,* this method emphasizes the use of speaking techniques as a way of indicating purpose.

8e

Write your central thought so that it reveals your speaking technique:
_____

What purpose is stated or implied: _____

Does this central thought suggest the primary purpose of your speech? _____

Before choosing the central thought that best expresses your purpose, you may find it helpful to see the overall direction of the focusing skills you have learned so far. The table on page 44 helps you review the sequence of skills that can make your preparation easier. It shows how step 1 "Aim toward the audience" and step 2 "Get on track with a central thought" form a continuous chain of skills that help you write a strong, purposeful central thought.

STEP 1: AIM TOWARD YOUR AUDIENCE

HOW OCCASION AND AUDIENCE DETERMINE TOPIC

The Occasion	→	*Facts about Audience*	→	*Best Speech Topic*	→	*Best Subtopic*
Giving a talk before a major-league baseball game		Young sports enthusiasts, ages 8–10; level of information is above average but not sophisticated		Baseball		Kinds of pitches

STEP 2. GET ON TRACK WITH A CENTRAL THOUGHT

HOW FEELINGS AND TIME LIMIT DETERMINE PURPOSE AND CENTRAL THOUGHT

→ *Your Feelings about Needs of Audience*	→ *Time Limit*	→ *Main Purpose*	→ *Central Thought*
They should know what to look for to make the game more interesting	Ten minutes before a game	(choose one) to inform	"I *will tell* you about three kinds of throws pitchers make most often."
		to persuade (to move mentally) →	"Team A *will* beat Team B because . . ."
		to activate (to move physically) →	"*Look* for the three kinds of throws pitchers deliver."
		to stimulate (to move spiritually) →	"Playing baseball *means* more than playing a game!"
		to entertain →	"Baseball fans like to hear stories of their heroes . . ."

Can you understand how speakers frequently fail to reach their audience? They take off in the wrong direction with a purpose that does not fit the occasion, the audience, or the time allowed. To stay on the track, think of moving from left to right, answering questions systematically, and drawing conclusions, so that you can reach out to your audience with a strong, concise central thought. Without a relevant central thought, you will miss your audience and lose them in the first few minutes of your speech.

Which of the purposes do you think is most satisfactory for speaking ten minutes *before* a ballgame to a group of young sportsmen? (I would activate them (urge them to *look*) with the central thought: "Look for the three kinds of throws pitchers deliver.")

Step 2: Worksheet

- ☐ Now look over the five experimental ways you have written a central thought and choose the one that will tell your audience how you will develop your topic (your purpose). Which is best?
- ☐ Now write in your best central thought on your train-of-thought outline (pages 26–29) where step 2 appears in the introduction. It will be evidence of your first big focusing job.

---

9. Define Any Vague Terms in Your Central Thought

After you have written the central thought on your outline, read on to see how you can test your central thought for clarity. Emulate those good speakers who have a concise, clear central thought and are applauded by immensely grateful listeners. The audience must understand the words you use to express your central theme, and any other parts of your speech. If you use ambiguous words, the audience will simply wonder what you are talking about, and after a while they will even stop wondering. Instead they will become immersed in their own worries, and their eyes will look glazed. Take particular precautions to define vague words in your central thought so that you won't have to deal with a dazed audience. Ask friends and colleagues if any words seem vague to them. Here are some ways to define vague, ambiguous terms:[1]

1. *Explanation.* You can quote a dictionary definition or an authority, but make sure the authority is reputable and acceptable as an authority with your audience.
   Vague Central Thought: "Sometimes a person has to give a eulogy."
   Clarification of Central Thought Using Explanation: "A eulogy is a speech." (dictionary quote)
2. *Classification.* You can extend the explanation method by further description.
   Using Explanation and Classification: "A eulogy is a speech [*explanation*], but it is different from ordinary speeches because it is meant especially for paying tribute to the dead [*classification*]."
3. *Context.* You can put the ambiguous word in a clear setting. For example, you may want to put the word *get* into context. Does *get* in your central thought mean "get away" or "get to someone"? By using context, you can define the way your audience should understand *get*.
   Vague Central Thought: "Some speeches *get* to you, others *get* away from you."

Clarification of Central Thought Using Context: "Some speeches, such as eulogies, *get* to you emotionally, whereas boring ones *get away* from you."

4. **Synonym.** You can extend the meaning of a word, but you should combine this method of definition with other methods, because no two words have exactly the same meaning. For example, *to change* and *to alter* mean approximately the same thing, but *to change* suggests more of a difference.

Vague Central Thought: "Some speeches require reorganization."

Clarification of Central Thought Using Synonym: "Sometimes *reorganization* means *completely changing* the purpose of the speech, the central thought, the entire discussion; other times, *reorganization* means *slightly altering* the order in which you present discussion points."

5. **Etymology** (derivation of words). You can define a word and gain the interest of your audience by telling the story behind the word. For example, *salary* comes from the Latin word *salaria,* which originally meant "money paid to Roman soldiers for purchase of salt." From this ancient transaction comes the saying "not worth his salt," a common saying referring to someone not worth his or her salary.

Vague Central Thought: "Some speakers are not worth their salt."

Clarification of Central Thought Using Etymology: "Roman soldiers were paid *salaria* money for buying their salt. The men who were poor soldiers were said not to be worth their salt, their *salaria*. It means they weren't useful enough even for bare maintainence pay. If all speakers had to earn their salt, that is, their listener's attention, or be told to sit down, we might eventually hear better speakers."

6. **Purpose or Effect.** You simply define the purpose of the word or phrase such as "effective speaking."

Vague Central Thought: "There are many reasons for speaking effectively."

Clarification of Central Thought Using Purpose: "One reason for speaking effectively is to be understood by others."

7. **Negation.** You tell what the word *does not* mean. Essentially, you are saying, "I mean this, not that."

Vague Central Thought: "Good speakers have a good conscience."

Clarification of Central Thought Using Negation: "I do not mean conscience as it is often used in a negative sense today, implying guilt, but I mean it to be 'reflective mediation,' as Shakespeare used the word in the line, 'Thus conscience does make cowards of us all.' When I say, 'Good speakers have a good conscience,' I mean good speakers reflect and meditate over their material."

8. **Example:** You make use of detailed explanation.

Vague Central Thought: "Speeches can be analyzed. The good qualities stand out in the vital speeches, whereas they are missing in the poor ones."

Clarification of Central Thought Using Example: "One characteristic of a good speech is a sound attention getter. Here is an example of a famous opening, which evokes the past for a memorial speech: 'Four score and seven years ago our fathers brought forth on this continent a new nation . . .' "

9

- □ Define any vague terms in your central thought. Analyze your central thought carefully. Is it vague, colorless, or ambiguous? Does a friend or colleague question the meaning of any words in your central thought?
- □ If so, choose one of the methods just listed to define those ambiguous or vague words and bring your central thought into clearer focus.
- □ Write your definition of vague words where indicated on your outline (p. 27), immediately after the central thought.

Congratulations! With clear definitions you will help your audience to understand and appreciate your central thought as much as you do. You have just completed step 2, the one students find most challenging and difficult. Like the creative sculptor, you have carved out the main image of your speech. With a good topic, a clear purpose, and a concise central thought, you will more easily recognize relevant information. Gather information about your subject from direct observation or from other sources. Appendix 3 offers suggestions for finding additional information. As you gather information, remember your central thought exactly. It will limit and define your main discussion points and it will help you focus more quickly on information important for your speech.

Next you will learn how to complete step 3 and appeal to your audience's needs.

3

Speak to Your Audience's Needs

STEP 3: APPEAL TO THE NEEDS OF YOUR AUDIENCE

A good speaker told me, "Many speeches are six feet off the ground. I always find a concrete experience to ground the idea I'm talking about. I let them know I have their best interests at heart. For instance, I might say to a group of teachers, 'Have you wondered what to do with that hyperactive kid?' Then I let them know what my central thought is: 'My talk is about that kid.' " With this question, the speaker is appealing to the needs of the teachers, who must deal more effectively with the hyperactive child.

Audiences attend speeches with the hope that they'll hear about a topic of special interest to them. They go because they have certain needs, and they believe that the speaker has some answers that will meet these needs. Assess your audience's needs and ask yourself, "What do I know that people want?" Of course, what you "know" is your subject, but you must also be able to highlight special aspects of your subject to fill the needs of a particular audience.

It seems obvious that people do things, such as attend a lecture or a discussion, for particular reasons or with special motives. Always ask yourself, "How do an audience's particular needs affect me as a speaker?" "What is it that motivates my audience to leave their duties or their leisure activities to come and hear me?"

Essentially, you are asking yourself, "Why would anyone listen to me?" Answering that question can be a very sobering experience, but undoubtedly you can think of a couple of reasons for speaking. Probably more than one factor will motivate people to seek out you and your topic. Perhaps you are speaking to complete a classroom assignment or to volunteer your expert knowledge or to fulfill a job requirement by giving a committee report. If you speak out of choice, then it is likely that you believe you have a topic of interest to people. Whether your speech is an assignment or a volunteer task, remember that your audience is counting on the following:

1. That you will know what you're talking about
2. That your speech will help them solve a problem and therefore answer their needs
3. That you will talk in a lively, concise, easy-to-understand style

For example, suppose you are a local businessperson who owns a bowling alley. You are enthusiastic about bowling as a healthy, recreational, and social outlet. You search around for an audience who might be persuaded to buy your product, and you convince the recreational director of the adult community to give you ten minutes to speak at their next luncheon meeting. You decide to offer these people a free lesson on Saturday morning. By limiting your general subject of bowling to "sign up for a free lesson Saturday morning," you can meet the needs of those who are eager to try something new, as well as those who are curious about bowling but unlikely to sign up for a series of lessons. By narrowing your subject to a specific topic (free bowling lessons) and phrasing a good central thought, you can achieve at least two major purposes: You can urge the audience to bowl on Saturday (activating purpose) and you can tell them how their physical, recreational, and social needs can be met through bowling (persuasive purpose). You may also be informative, entertaining, and stimulating. If you want to drum up future business from this audience, then your best approach is to promise them a free opportunity to express their physical and social needs. With a free chance to try the sport, they might be convinced that bowling is good for them and sign up for regular bowling.

But how can you determine your audience's needs, that is, the motives or reasons why people would be interested in bowling? The motives (reasons) for taking your free offer will differ from person to person, but you must decide the most likely reasons for the majority of your audience. If you assess those unmet *needs* correctly, if you show the audience how your topic can speak to their interest, and if you motivate them to think, feel, and act, then you will establish rapport and relate to your audience. *Your appeal is made by saying specific sentences that tell your audience directly or indirectly how your topic is going to meet some of their needs.* Your speech will be considered relevant if you can deliver the product the audience wants, a product that will satisfy at least one of their needs. Many topics appeal to many needs in an audience. You may not want to cover every one but only touch on one or two.

KINDS OF NEEDS

The needs of audiences vary all over the world, but twentieth-century Western audiences are generally looking for fulfillment of these following needs:

- *Exploration needs:* to explore new ideas, cultures, places, objects
- *Economic needs:* to be secure financially; to possess material things
- *Psychological needs:* to be free of mental distress
- *Physical Comfort needs:* to be free of physical restraint and discomfort
- *Political Security needs:* to have political freedom, freedom of speech
- *Acceptance needs:* to be at ease socially; to make friends

Your appeal to an audience should satisfy one or more of the foregoing needs. In this example, the only need that is unrelated to the bowling topic is political security. Appeal sentences tell an audience "what's in it for them." Making an ethical appeal is the responsibility of the speaker; rejecting the unethical appeal is the responsibility of the listener. Notice that appeal material is specifically required in the introduction and the conclusion at step 3 on your outline (page 27). After you gain audience attention in your introduction, speak directly to your audience's needs with ethical "appeal" sentences. The appeal sentences will keep the attention of your audience only if they strongly suggest that you have information worth listening to. A startling statistic, a story, an anecdote, a series of questions can make your audience see how vitally important your topic is to them (you appeal to their needs).

For example if you were giving the bowling-speech, you could arouse the audience's needs in the appeal section of your introduction by saying:

Appeals

"Have you wanted the thrill of playing a competitive game?" *(exploration need)*

"Few sports are as inexpensive and fun—only two dollars for an hour's worth of fun and exercise." *(economic need)*

"Do you wish you could find something to do that would improve both your physical health and mental well-being?" *(physical-comfort and psychological needs)*

"Do you feel you do too many things alone and would like to join others in having fun?" *(acceptance needs)*

Exploration Needs

We are attracted to a speaker who can help us *explore* topics that appeal to our desire (motive) to know new things. Exploration needs can take many forms, such as wanting to know more about architecture, theater, music, art, anthropology, psychology, medicine, law, business, sports, and many more. There are adventures to be found in history and art, as well as in skiing or bird-watching. These topics may fascinate us, not because we think that such information will bring material profit, but simply because the new information is interesting in and of itself. We may have a need to explore new information for its own intrinsic worth and our own mental profit. The popularity of talk shows indicates our willingness to spend countless hours listening simply for the pleasure of knowing new things. The popularity of human-interest shows (such as *60 Minutes* and *The Undersea World of Jacques Cousteau)* and of travel series and adult-education courses, attest to our hunger for interesting facts about people and the universe.

HOW TO APPEAL TO EXPLORATION NEEDS
One student speaking on the subject of spelling captured the audience's curiosity by saying, ''Did you know that the word *circus* can be spelled forty thousand different ways?'' With this startling claim in the introduction, the speaker was appealing to our need to explore interesting facts and satisfy our curiosity.

Economic Needs

In our society the desire to acquire and own things has been largely shaped by an advertising industry that meets the needs of still other industries to sell their products. Whether or not we condone this acquisitiveness, most of us take great pleasure in owning things. The desire to possess material things has become a learned but powerful need for most people. If you talk about a topic that will help people get more for less, you will fulfill the need to acquire and you will draw appreciative audiences. If you can tell people how to get more for less money or effort, you are appealing to a desire to possess. Such topics as how to save on one's income tax, grocery bill, vacations, repairs, gas mileage, and many others will help people save money that they can spend elsewhere. One student referred to this need to possess as the ''greed'' need, but with the rising cost of living, to save is often a matter of survival. Will information about your subject help your audience acquire new things at low cost? What is your listeners' particular type of acquisitiveness? How strong are your listeners' needs to become financially secure? If they are very dominant, be sure to speak to these needs in your introduction.

HOW TO APPEAL TO ECONOMIC NEEDS
In a talk entitled ''How to Buy a Used Car'' a speaker appealed to our need to save money by saying, ''How many times have you had a big bargain turn into a lousy lemon?'' The implication was clear to all of us who are ignorant about cars but must depend on them. When they turn out to be ''lemons,'' we lose time and money. We even lose our lovable, patient selves. I could just see myself kicking my last ''lemon,'' and I was ready for that speaker's words of advice. She had appealed to my need to possess a reliable car, as well as my desire to be relieved of my mental distress.

Psychological Needs

Modern audiences are eager to hear speakers who promise to relieve them of mental distress or to be safe from physical harm. Topics related to earthquakes, floods, fire, disease, health, crime, and poverty hold the possibility that we will get new information about protecting ourselves and thereby reduce our fears. A speaker asking us to donate money to a charitable group, to join a worthwhile organization, or to subscribe to a worthwhile cause is often appealing to our desire to be relieved of a guilty conscience, a form of mental distress. Topics and occasions that provide opportunities for us to relieve our troubled minds are popular. In addition, funny after-dinner speeches can relieve mental distress by involving laughter, which is reputed to be good medicine for an ailing psyche.

HOW TO APPEAL TO PSYCHOLOGICAL NEEDS

Suppose you are a concerned parent who wishes to make a plea for more careful pickup of children from school. After a sentence to gain the attention of your audience, you could appeal to your audience's desire to be relieved of worrying about their children and uncontrolled traffic by quoting your own statistics: "Today I was stunned by the danger and confusion at the pickup curb. Fifteen car horns beeped for seventy-five children, who ran pell-mell between cars to get to their rides for the day. If just one thoughtless adult let a foot slip to the accelerator a second too soon or move to the brake a second too late, one of our children might have been injured today. Today was a miracle. Will we be so lucky tomorrow?" By using an eyewitness account, the speaker urges audiences to listen carefully to a serious subject. Here you would be appealing to your audience's need to solve a problem before it becomes mentally distressing. Of course, no audience consciously thinks, "Oh, with that story the speaker is appealing to my psychological need to be relieved of mental distress if such a tragedy should occur." Rather, the audience, feeling the emotional impact of the eyewitness story, is more likely to consider seriously the central thought that follows the appeal: "Let's agree on a plan for picking up our children safely." With the appeal of an eyewitness report, you are saying indirectly, "This is an important subject that you will want to do something about. Moreover, I'm appealing to your desire to avert tragedy and mental distress. Listen to me because I have a possible solution to the traffic problem."

Physical-Comfort Needs

When you appeal to the comfort needs of an audience, you are addressing their desire to be free from physical restraints, from the feeling of being closed in. These restraints may be other people (overcrowding, for example), or they may be physical factors that inhibit or limit our movement or concentration (poor highways, inadequate lighting, geographical limitations). Speeches that urge us to get away and see the world are appealing to our desire for physical freedom, as well as our desire to explore new territories. So are topics that spell out the overcrowded conditions of prisons, the ghettos, old people's homes, or schools for the mentally handicapped. All these topics remind us of our own physical freedom as compared with those people who suffer from some kind of confinement. An appeal to people's desire for physical freedom is inherent in topics such as "Learn to Dance," "Learn to Play Volleyball," "Climb a Mountain," "Write Your Congressman about Saving More Land for Recreation," "Let's Build Better Open-Air Zoos," or "Let's Send a Child to Summer Camp."

HOW TO APPEAL TO PHYSICAL-COMFORT NEEDS
A speaker urging us to vote for a tax bond for building another school could appeal to our desire for physical comfort by describing how fifty children sit elbow to elbow in rooms built to accommodate only thirty. Or suppose you are selling mobile homes and wish to persuade your audience about their roominess. In the introduction, you could say, "Do you think of a mobile home as a temporary trailer? If you do, you'll be surprised that the average mobile home has more room than the average house."

In your conclusion, you could again appeal to the audience's desire for physical freedom by saying, "With a mobile home, you have the world at your window. A couple happy with their mobile home said, 'You don't need to stay stuck in one place. After two or three months, you can pull up stakes and go on to the next 'window of the world.' '' We have all heard ourselves described as restless people. To relieve an audience of their "itchiness," you can use this appeal to people's desire for physical freedom with great effect.

Political-Security Needs

Closely related to our desire for physical freedom is our desire for political freedom. A free society is where people can move around without the barriers of red tape and governmental interference. As an American, if you had to report to authorities each time you moved or took a vacation, you would probably feel your muscles tighten; you would feel physically restrained (and mentally distressed). In essence, when people seek political freedom, they are asking for physical and mental freedom; they are asking for a voice in how they use their bodies and minds. Speech topics that appeal to our desire to be politically free include the following: "Strengthening America Will Strengthen Democracy Everywhere," "The American Civil Liberties Union Will Defend Your Freedom," and "Educational Television Is an Investment in Television Free Enough to Speak Out Honestly."

HOW TO APPEAL TO POLITICAL-SECURITY NEEDS
To arouse your audience's needs for political security, you might describe a problem and tell about the dangers it poses if it is not corrected. For example, if your central thought were "Watch out for political corruption," you might review briefly the history of reporter Bolles's exposé of political misuse of public lands in Arizona. That story illustrates how one man alerted millions to the misuse of political and financial power and of the terrible consequences for not staying alert to speculators. Another

technique would use a quotation warning us about the dangers of becoming lazy and taking our political freedom for granted: ''Vigilance is the price of freedom.''

Probably the most effective way to appeal to an audience's desire for political freedom is to pose the question ''What does political freedom mean to you?'' You might then go on, to answer that question, ''I'd like to tell you how we would live if our political freedom were limited even slightly. For instance, what would you read in the morning newspaper? What would you dare say to your fellow worker? How would you vote on a typical election day?'' The more real, objective, and lifelike you can make curtailment of political freedom, the more your audience will become involved in recognizing their need for political freedom and security. If politicians would do this more often, they might sense a new appreciation from skeptical audiences.

Acceptance Needs

To be socially accepted is a powerful drive in most modern audiences, especially those in large cities where anonymity and loneliness are more apparent. People wish to change their feelings of shyness and alienation and see themselves as capable of making friends and developing close relationships. Beginning with Dale Carnegie's *How to Win Friends and Influence People* published in 1926, the sale of self-help books aimed at helping people become socially confident has mushroomed into a multimillion-dollar business.

Many central themes for speeches relate directly to our need to feel accepted: ''Developing Intimate Relationships,'' ''Hosting the Perfect Party,'' ''Getting More Out of Life,'' ''Improving Your Self-esteem by Developing Social Skills,'' or ''Your Image and Your Rating.'' These topics aim to help people who feel socially awkward and inadequate gain self-confidence and poise.

HOW TO APPEAL TO ACCEPTANCE NEEDS

Suppose you wished to develop the following central thought: ''What does being intimate mean to you?'' In your introduction you could appeal to your audience's need to be socially accepted by asking a series of questions: ''Have you ever hesitated to strike up a conversation with a stranger, even though you wanted to? Have you told yourself it's not nice to ask personal questions about people's feelings?'' With vivid questions that address insecurities you will arouse audience interest and will appeal to their desire to be at ease socially. With these questions, you are asking the audience to remember how they behave in social situations. You are helping them relate to your topic.

Developing appropriate material for appealing to an audience's need for social acceptance may involve describing the distress of a person in an embarrassing or uncertain situation and asking questions that will encourage the audience to see themselves in such a situation. They will listen because they wish to overcome their inhibitions and fears in social interactions.

RING A BELL AND MAKE AN APPEAL

Speakers who appeal to an audience's needs ring a bell in the audience, so to speak. Isn't it pretty hard to consider speakers interesting or relevant if they don't touch base with your needs? Because audiences are often impatient and restless, you must relate to your audience's needs immediately. Assert that you have something they need and want. To do this, assess your listeners' needs and develop imaginative, exciting, "human appeal" material. In other words, tell them that you have a product (topic) that will relate to their interests and meet some of their needs.

Note where the appeal appears in the introduction of your outline (page 20). After the attention getter in your introduction, your audience must hear how their needs (the reasons for their coming to hear you) will be satisfied by you and your topic. You may appeal to audience needs several times in a speech, but definitely make an appeal in the introduction and repeat an appeal in the conclusion. The raw materials of the appeal are quotations, stories, slogans, statistics, questions, and direct statements. Often the attention-getter and appeal are one and the same thing. For example, a story can be attention-getting *and* suggest an appeal.

Extension Technique

There are some useful techniques for developing a unified style in the appeals of both the introduction and the conclusion. To make your talk "hang together," you can employ the extension technique by referring briefly to the *same* story, statistic, or quote in the conclusion that you presented in the introduction. For example, if your central thought is, "Vote Yes for rapid transit in October," you could use the "extension" technique in your introduction and conclusion in this way:

In the *introduction* make this appeal: "Most of us are exasperated by heavy, congested traffic, which shortens our day and causes us headaches, backaches, [*appeal to physical-comfort need*] and bad tempers [*appeal to psychological need to be freed from mental distress*]."
And again in the *conclusion*, appeal, "Remember, you can do something about the delays that cause you needless headaches and backaches [*appeal repeats need for physical comfort made in introduction*]. And you need never again end the day in a bad temper [*psychological appeal repeats need to be free from mental distress*]."

And here is how you can use the same appeal but different examples in each section:

In the *introduction*, make the appeal, "Why go horse-and-buggy when we could go jet?" (*physical-comfort need*)
And in the *conclusion*, appeal, "Our population will double in the next twenty-nine years, and so will our traffic congestion." (*physical-comfort need*)

Although it is not necessary to repeat an example in the conclusion, doing so will let an audience know you are winding up your speech, and they will appreciate that signal. A second advantage for extending the example to the conclusion is that the appeal is emphasized. A third advantage is that repeating an example supplies a terminal handle for you as a speaker. It will help *you* know that you are supposed to end the speech soon and sit down. There's always comfort in knowing you can be brief and concise at the end of a speech.

Combination Technique

Of course, an audience has more than one need. You aren't expected to fulfill every single one, but you should always ask yourself, "Which need does my topic fulfill best for this particular audience?" For example, suppose you believe that the vital interests of an audience are very much motivated by their desire to learn new things (exploration need). Or perhaps your audience wants to save money in order to buy other necessary commodities (economic need). To illustrate how you could appeal to *both* needs—exploration in the introduction and economic in the conclusion— examine the following appeals:

In the *introduction,* make this appeal: "Rapid Transit is telling us a new story that will affect our lives in positive ways. More time off the highways means more leisure for exploring your hobbies." *(exploration need)*
And in the *conclusion,* appeal, "Moreover, you will save eight dollars a week if you use Rapid Transit instead of your car." *(economic need)*

Step 3: Worksheet

□   Assess the needs of your audience now. Will your topic help your audience to:
    __   *Explore* new ideas? How? _____

    _____

    __   *Gain economic freedom? Possess material things?* How? _____

    _____

    __   Get relief from *psychological distress?* How? _____

    __   Be free *physically?* How? _____

    __   Gain *political* freedom? How? _____

    _____

    __   Become more *socially* acceptable? How? _____

    _____

- ☐   Which of the foregoing needs seem to stand out as a logical, dominant need that your topic can meet best? Which holds the strongest appeal for your audience?
- ☐   Next develop a real or hypothetical story, find a quote or statistic, or ask a series of questions to arouse your listeners' dominant need. Let there be no doubt that you will be talking about a topic that speaks to your audience's specific needs.
- ☐   When you have chosen relevant, interesting material, write in your appeal, sentences at step 3, on your train-of-thought outline (page 27).

To complete step 4, which discusses attention getters, move on to chapter 4.

4

Capture Your Audience's Attention

STEP 4: LIGHT UP YOUR SPEECH WITH ATTENTION GETTERS

A good introduction is like a handshake; it introduces you in a friendly way. However, to meet a group of strangers can be awkward even when you have a receptive audience delighted to be listening to you. Like seasoned speakers you may have nervous moments before your audience starts smiling or nodding their approval. Speakers agree that making an audience respond favorably in the first few minutes is downright hard work that must *not* look like hard work. Start easy and gently coax your listeners into a receptive mood. The skill for encouraging a receptive attitude in an audience requires careful preparation and precise timing. Fortunately, there are things you can do to warm audiences up.

It turns out that people relate, or are attracted to each other, by simple things, such as a common experience, a story (all the world loves a story), a familiar saying, or the stimulating words of a mutually admired person. Most audiences are eager for a speaker to help them enjoy themselves. As a speaker, you are the catalyst who brings together an audience and a subject. To do this, you can use fascinators—a startling statement, an object, a bit of color, or some startling movement, and many more. This chapter suggests several attention-getting ways that you can use to light up your audience and to overcome your initial anxiety when speaking before a group.

A good attention getter is an important technique for gaining your audience's acceptance, because it can help you calm your nerves and let your audience know you like them. A successful attention getter encourages your audience, thereby helping everyone get in the mood for listening. When you like your listeners and show it, and they like you and show it, you and your listeners will be warmly communicating. Both you and your audience will sense that you want to be together, with you eagerly sharing your message and with them enthusiastically receiving it. Communicating is a two-way process, and the sooner you set the stage for two-way acceptance, the better everyone will feel. You will be relating and extending yourself; your audience will be reaching out and enthusiastically welcoming you. A good attention getter, therefore, is a good antidote for overcoming your fear during those challenging minutes when you first face your audience.

TECHNIQUES FOR GAINING AUDIENCE ATTENTION

Audience Consideration

The speaker who wins the day with ideas must first win the audience. How can you do this? First, make sure you know who is in your audience (review the audience inventory, pages 30–31). Second, ask your host about the general mood of your audience. Frequently I have had my own fears and assumptions about an audience changed by my host's comments. Before one speech I inquired why my audience of Weight Watchers appeared tired and listless. I learned that my weight-conscious audience had been served a very caloric breakfast by the hotel caterers, and consequently no one had eaten a bite. No wonder they were feeling tired and looking hostile before a workshop in assertiveness training. I could then sympathize with their plight and gently encourage them to listen and participate.

Body Language

Another way to put your audience and yourself at ease is by walking to the podium with eagerness and assurance. Think of yourself walking tall and straight without faltering or looking down. Once you are there, take your time. Place your notes, look up with a friendly expression, meet the eyes of your audience, take a breath, and count four or five seconds before you begin.

Introductory Greetings

Keep your introduction short. No one wants to hear you say hello to seventeen different people. Simply say, "Hello, I'm glad to be here with distinguished colleagues, old friends, and relatives [or whomever]."

Establishing Who You Are
(and Who You Aren't)

The introduction is critical. You need to establish very quickly who you are, because the audience needs to put you into a category: "Is this going to be heavy? abstract? light? entertaining?" You must think about what pigeon holes you do *not* want to be put into, and use the audience's preconceived ideas about you creatively.

Phil Zimbardo of Stanford University admits that he sometimes creates a false expectation and then purposefully violates it to make a point. He asks himself, "Which pigeon holes do I want to violate? For instance, I might want the audience to perceive me as shy (I'm not) if I'm talking about shyness, and then I expose their stereotypical conceptions about shy people."[1]

Challenges

Sometimes you can begin a speech with a challenge: Zimbardo offers this example: "I say, 'Tonight I'm going to talk about madness. First, I'll cite four examples. I'd like you to discover what's common in these examples.' After I tell the stories, I'll ask: 'What is the common link in all these examples?'

"If anyone talks up, you can shape the reply toward the thesis of your talk: 'Yes, good, that sounds to me like you're saying . . .' If nobody speaks up, I use a 'we . . . us' technique: 'I'm sure it's obvious to you that any intelligent person would be thinking about . . .' (and once you say it, they *are* thinking about it.") *Caution:* Since an audience which doesn't answer will realize they failed your challenge, they are likely to feel put down if you tell them the answer.

Disclose Feelings About Your Subject

The dramatic pause can disclose your feelings very effectively if used judiciously. For example, after several false starts or hesitations, the lecturer confides: "You're probably wondering why I'm having difficulty starting. It's because today I'm going to talk about drug addiction and it's not a subject to be taken lightly, because all of you, like me, have probably known someone who died from overdose."

Acknowledge the Process

There are other times when acknowledging the process of what's going on as you are speaking is very important. For example, you might want to stop the ongoing lecture and explore why the audience is fidgeting or why you are not as coherent as you should be: "I'm having trouble because the character I'm telling you about is my mother . . ." The audience now gets new meaning as well as an understanding of my behavior. This technique should not be faked, but if you genuinely feel choked-up, embarrassed, or delighted, let the audience know the source of your feelings.

60

Stories

Stories can be about other people, real, or fictitious, or they can be personal experiences about you. The best stories are generally told in short, simple sentences that get to the point. Unless you are trying to create suspense, get on with the message. The delight of a story is knowing the punchline, so don't bury your audience in heaps of words while they wait for it. Using extra words when none are called for, either factually or stylistically, simply kills an audience's enthusiasm. A personal experience told as a story can create intimacy with your listeners, but it can also produce problems. Sometimes it is difficult to move from the personal to the abstract. Many speakers use an outline already prepared on a blackboard or transparency. Phil Zimbardo demonstrates this technique when he moves from a story involving a personal encounter with madness to introducing his first main point. As he points to his outline he says: ". . . and this story illustrates that discontinuity is a basis of madness." After the audience's attention is hooked with a lively, unique opener, such as a discursive tale, you can lay out the entire structure of what is to come by referring to your outline displayed on the board.

Personal experience is one of the best ways for people to retain information. Sometimes I say "A student of mine (or a friend, or I) once had the experience of deciding whether life was worth living. Perhaps some of you have felt a similar despair when . . ." This creates self-disclosure and closeness with an audience immediately, but it must be a story which is very appropriate for introducing your topic, and it must be practiced again and again, so that it will create exactly the right mood in your audience. A personal experience can be extremely powerful, but it should not be used without a lot of thought.

Humor

Use humor in your opening if it suits you, your subject, and the occasion. But a word of caution: don't strain at it. You don't need to be a leg-slapper. If you try to be funny by poking fun at minorities, ethnic groups, and women, you will most assuredly offend aware listeners. Modern audiences are very alert to slights because clichés and phrases that were considered complimentary ten years ago are blatantly unflattering today. For example, on one occasion I was introduced as my husband's "better half." My name is not "better half" and, in any case, I'm not a half (nor is my husband). The speaker used the cliché innocently, but he was made painfully aware of his mistake when a person called out, "What's better half's real name?" The moral of the story is: practice a speech with an alert, sensitive listener (a spouse, a teenager, a secretary, a colleague) who will catch oversights and save you grief.

Pauses

Make it easy for your audience to stay with you. Pause for a refresher; don't lead your listeners down a long, long trail without frequent stops. The speaker who uses judicious silence gives an audience a retreat, a place to rest and contemplate. It's not so easy to be silent. George Bernard Shaw noted that, like most speakers, he "believed in the discipline of silence and could talk for hours about it." Nevertheless, an audience appreciates the speaker who knows that "silence is golden" and who is disciplined to pause now and again.

Visual Aids, Movement, Dress, Color

The more I teach and speak the more I realize that people can process very little oral information. Particularly for a teacher, it's important to realize that others have come before you. That is, listeners have sometimes heard four or five teachers before you, so you must have props to carry the audience, such as handouts for notes, transparencies, slides, a blackboard, objects, costumes—anything to make the material come alive and stay alive for the audience.

A visual aid, unusual movement, dress, or color can all captivate an audience. Once I saw all four attention getters at work. Appearing on Halloween, a speaker used the eeriness of the occasion to put his audience in a receptive mood for his macabre topic. This speaker appeared in a black robe, and with exaggerated motions, he slowly pulled an unseemly object out of a brown paper bag as he asked, "Have you ever wondered how shrunken heads are made?" The awesome costume, the mysterious paper bag, and the ugly shrunken head, together with the suspenseful movement and the question, were all spellbinding attention getters for the special occasion of Halloween. Don't be satisfied with one device when two or more can work harmoniously.

COMMUNICATE CLEARLY

You can easily understand why short sentences are better than long ones—not only in the introduction, but in the entire speech. Long, complicated sentences are simply too difficult for a speaker to remember or, for that matter, for an audience to understand. While the eye can unscramble complex sentences and even return to sort out what is missed the first time around, the ear cannot easily rearrange words to make sense out of a poor sentence. Besides, while listeners are busy unpacking complicated grammar, they will not be listening to you. To keep an audience with you most of the time, use short sentences that are instantly meaningful.

For most listeners, to have more than ten words in a sentence makes quick comprehension difficult, so cut your long sentences to under twelve words if you possibly can. If you cannot cut, choose short, uncomplicated words. Another possibility is to make two short sentences out of one long sentence.

USE ACTIVE VERBS

It is not unusual for scientists (and other professionals) to use passive verbs for speeches, because in their writing of journal articles these professionals are instructed to write, "It was investigated" (passive verb), and so on. That may be standard form for writing scientific and business findings, but it is dull, boring, and difficult to understand ideas when speakers use the passive verb. Passive verbs seem to complicate an idea and we simply don't get the picture as fast as when speakers use active verbs. An example will show you the big difference the form of the verb makes in helping you understand an idea quickly.

> Weak, Passive:
>
> *"Trainer behaviors* were observed *[passive verb] during evaluation sessions, which consisted of the presentation of an instructional package and an instruction to train the confederate trainee."*

Isn't it difficult to form a picture of what is going on? Is it clear whether the trainer trained the confederate trainee or whether the trainer was to give the trainee only *one* instruction? Here is a clearer explanation (a clearer picture):

> Strong, Active:
>
> *We* evaluated *[active verb] the behaviors of trainees during special sessions. At these sessions the student-trainer* presented *[active] the instructional package to a confederate trainee. Next he* trained *[active] the confederate in each step of the program.*

To speak directly and sound livelier, make the simple adjustment to an active verb, so that information is easy to understand the very first time you say it. Direct statements, such as *"we evaluated,"* "trainers *presented,"* and *"he trained"* help listeners see people acting, thus the term *active verb* for such words. If people *(we, trainers, he)* are active *(evaluated, presented, trained)* then listeners can "get the picture" in their imaginations faster. In summary, *use active verbs that have people do things* ("she instructs"), and *avoid passive verbs, which have things being done to people* ("students were instructed").

DESCRIBE IN DETAIL

Search for vivid, unusually descriptive words that picture detailed information. Here are examples of such words.

> *"The weathered, grooved-face man"* instead of *"old man"*
> *"The tangy tinge of fresh lemon"* instead of *"the taste of lemon"*
> *"A heady, all-time high"* instead of *"a great experience"*

You can get the hang of it. First, observe carefully: Record what you see, hear, feel, and smell. Then search your vocabulary to find novel words to explain your experiences in vivid detail. A familiar word gains new meaning when it is explained in a new way; Lawrence Olivier adds to our meaning of *legend* when he tells two young people in *A Little Romance*, "What is a legend except the retelling of how ordinary people did extraordinary things?"

USE CONCRETE, DOWN-TO-EARTH WORDS AND
MINIMIZE ABSTRACT WORDS

For words to paint pictures in the minds of your audience, they not only should be unusual and colorful, they should be concrete. Try not to use long-winded, abstract sentences, which bore people and are difficult to understand.

Here are examples that demonstrate the contrast between abstract words and concrete ones.

Dull and Abstract	*Colorful and Concrete*
"We should realize that we often blame things and events, calling them the problem, when the problem is ourselves."	"D. H. Lawrence's character Richard Levitt did what most of us do: He wearied himself to death, struggling with the problem of himself, and called it Australia."
"When we have difficulty finding meaning in life, everything appears insignificant, even ourselves, and we must fight bravely to keep searching."	"A friend once wrote to Turgenev, 'It seems to me to put oneself in second place is the whole significance of life.' Turgenev replied, 'It seems to me to discover what to put before oneself, in the first place, is the problem.'"
"Most of us are pessimists who bewail our fate and never look for the silver lining."	"A pessimist recalls that Babe Ruth struck out 1,330 times, whereas an optimist remembers that he made 714 home runs."
"Most of us are unwilling to risk loss in order to win."	"Babe Ruth risked 1,330 strike-outs in order to make 714 home runs."

EXAMPLES OF ATTENTION-GETTING TECHNIQUES FOR "MY MOST ANXIOUS SPEAKING EXPERIENCE"

The more simply you present the attention getter, the easier it is for an audience to tune in to your subject. Long sentences, abstract ideas, ponderous thoughts are surefire audience killers. To understand attention-getting techniques, speakers like to take one speech topic and work out several opening attention-getting statements. Here are some examples of attention-getting materials suitable for an opening to a speech on stage fright. Which one would you use?

Story

"We all have different fears, and most of us keep our own all our lives. I once met that rare person who had disciplined herself to learn courage. She told me that she had overcome her fear of water by finishing a course in deep-sea diving successfully. Now she felt ready to defeat her fear of public speaking. Controlling one fear had given her the courage to control another.''

Startling Statement

''If you avoid public speaking because of your fear today, you will be even more afraid tomorrow. That's because running will be a relief for you, an escape from anxiety. Because relief from anxiety is naturally pleasurable, it is very likely that the next time you get stage fright, you'll run again. Each time you run away, it becomes harder and harder to defeat your fears.''

Statistics

''Authors of *The Book of Lists* asked 3,000 Americans, 'What is your greatest fear?' 41 percent answered: 'Speaking before a group.' ''[2]

Quotation

''William James, the famous psychologist, said, 'To feel brave, act as if you were brave . . . and a courage fit will very likely replace the fit of fear.' ''

Challenge

''Tonight I'm going to tell you about my three experiences with stage fright. I'm wondering if you can identify the common mistake I made in all three instances?''

Anecdote

''A friend insists she overcame her fear of public speaking the day she experienced the worst. That was the day she ran her only pair of nylons, had to change clothes so that she would match up with the remaining pair of nylons, discovered that the mike man had taken his phone off the hook and slept in, and faced the unhappy job of cooling off a hot audience in a small, stuffy room. Somehow she takes comfort in reliving that horror story. She figures that never again could so much go so wrong— and if it does, she has living proof that she'll live through it all again.''

Familiar Saying

''There is nothing like having done the thing before to give oneself courage.''

Reference to a Common Experience with Humor

''Most of you know what it feels like to be nervous, and since you out there have less than me right now, I'd like to share some of mine with you.''

Question

"Do you know what most Americans fear the most? According to *The Book of Lists* it is fear of speaking before a group."[2]

Limerick

"If you think you are beaten, you are. If you think you dare not, you don't. If you'd like to win, but think you can't, it's almost a cinch you won't."

Finding an Attention-Getter for Your Speech

Are you wondering what attention getter you should use for your speech? Why not stimulate your creativity by reading short human-interest stories that touch on your subject? The *Reader's Digest* is a good place to start, and *New Yorker* magazines are excellent for cartoons on current topics. *Bartlett's Quotations* can be a source for pithy statements. Often friends and relatives can help. You can get tips about articles, facts, quotes, all kinds of tidbits by simply asking your family and friends for ideas. Older children can often present the latest information and, if nothing else, a different point of view. Introduce your problem by saying something like this: "If you were giving a talk on overpopulation (or whatever), how would you get the attention of the audience?" or "What's the most unusual fact you ever heard about overpopulation?" You will be surprised how eager people are to help you as long as they don't need to give the speech. In fact, they often give a speech right on the spot!

Besides these colorful self-styled experts, serious research experts can help you gather information. I have never met a librarian who was not eager to help me find some suitable quote or story. And don't stop with librarians. One speaker went directly to the experts for information and stories on "The Virtues of Plumbing as a Trade." After interviewing several plumbers about their most unusual job, she had hilarious material for an informative and entertaining talk. Another ingenious speaker talking on "Unusual Traveling Jobs" sought out bizarre opportunities by placing an advertisement: "Have bag, will travel if trip is unusual. Write me about your job at Box 100, Small Town, U.S.A." Her "research" consisted of waiting for the mails that brought unusual job offers described in flourishing detail.

Finding the source material for unique attention getters can be adventuresome if you use your natural curiosity. If you simply sit and stare at your blank outline, thinking of an attention getter can be terribly tedious, but if you let your imagination help you seek out the source, you should have a great time. Human-interest stories come from being humanly interested in other people, other things. If you have yearned to be creative, then finding a great attention getter is your ticket to adventure and discovery.

Courage comes in knowing what you want to say. A friend told me about working out a detailed attention getter for his speech, in which he used a quote from

Alice in Wonderland. He ordinarily had a general idea how he would begin a speech, but he often experienced alarming nervousness for as long as five or ten minutes. He was determined to see if having a thoroughly prepared introduction, even to the point of memorizing the passage, would bring positive feelings at the podium. He was delighted with the results and amazed with his newfound confidence in those first crucial minutes. He claims he'll never speak again without preparing and practicing a specific introduction.

Likewise, a busy executive told me he needed help with a speech he had to deliver before his senior executives. He worked out a full-sentence outline and then came to me for a practice session. He needed to communicate immediately the confident style his company wanted in a chief executive but also wanted to strike just the right style—something that said, ''I have the right amount of confidence in myself to lead this company, but not so much that I won't listen to the rest of you who are equally confident and experienced.'' As he practiced the introduction aloud, he had difficulty remembering the long sentences, which were passive, impersonal, and dull! He shortened the long, complicated sentences, cut out fancy words, and achieved a direct conversational style that communicated personal confidence and interpersonal concern. He won the promotion.

It is not unusual for an audience to judge your style, wit, intelligence, compassion, and point of view by your first attention-getting words. It is your hallmark, as is your final statement, because it says so many things about you. It suggests to your audience your attitude toward them and your subject. Moreover, audiences tend to remember first and last statements. Do not leave such crucial lines to chance unless you like to live dangerously when you meet an audience.

Step 4: Worksheet

- □ Many speakers have decided that happiness is knowing exactly what they want to say in an introduction, so they are eager to say it.
- □ Eliminate indecision during the first few minutes by finding an attention getter that introduces both you and your subject in a style that you are proud to call your own. When you find it, express it in colorful, concrete words that paint pictures in simple, short sentences with direct-action verbs.
- □ Know precisely *what* you want to say to gain your audience's attention and exactly *how* you want to say it.
- □ Write out your attention getter at step 4 in the introduction on your outline (page 26) now.

To complete step 5 (''Choose your main-point boxcars''), move on to chapter 5.

5

Develop Your Central Thought

The main points make up the longest part of any speech, and most speakers spend at least three-fourths of their time talking about them. Sometimes these points are called the discussion, the body, the development, or the argument. These main points contain what Aristotle called "indispensable constituents" or "the statement of the case" or "the ensuing argument." They correspond to the boxcars in your train-of-thought.

ELEMENTS OF ORGANIZATION

The question for many students is, How will I know if my speech is well organized? It was Aristotle who first said that a good speech has main points which are unified, coherent, and emphasized. When you have these three characteristics in your speech, you'll know your ideas can make sense. Here's what these characteristics mean.

Unity

If you can fit your points together in a relationship of parts to whole, much the way pieces of a puzzle fit together to make the big picture, you will be unifying your main points.

To unify ideas you must have a master plan, a pattern, which both you and your audience can follow easily. If your speech is unified, you can be satisfied that you will be able to stay on track, because each point (boxcar) belongs there. Choose main points that are not only relevant but crucial to a sensible development of your central thought.

Coherence

You can help your audience understand how one idea relates to another by using connective sentences or phrases. Here are some examples of connective phrases:

> *"Before I go on, let me summarize the points made so far . . ."*
> *"Not only is that idea acceptable in principle, it is workable."*
> *"That is the first argument. Now, here is the second."*

These transitional phrases and sentences serve as connectors because they hook ideas together. They also provide solid links to help an audience understand the relationship between what you have just said and what you are going to say next. More than any other technique, connecting transitions help an audience follow your organizational pattern, your train-of-thought. They are pictured as connectors ⊐⊢⊏ between the introduction and the conclusion, and between main-point boxcars on your outline. As a speaker, you must also connect one example to another or a story to its punchline; however, only the transitional sentences connecting the large units of your speech need to be written out on your outline.

Emphasis

A third characteristic of a well-organized speech is that certain ideas will be emphasized more than others. Naturally, you will want to draw attention to your most important, strongest points. Your best points gain added emphasis if you do any or all of the following:

1. *Talk longer* about the important points. People will tend to remember those items you talk about longest.
2. *Repeat* important points. People will remember better if they are given a second or third chance to rehearse in their minds what you have said.
3. *Position important points first and last* unless another organizational pattern,

such as a spatial or chronological one, prevents it. People tend to remember the first and last items in a list—most often the last item—so end your discussion, of four topics or reasons, say, by talking about the most important one last. *Caution:* Be careful you don't run out of time and are forced to eliminate your last and most important point. Determine ahead which middle point you could eliminate or minimize if you begin to run short of time while speaking.

4. *Position the least complicated ideas first* if your subject is difficult to grasp, gradually developing the more complex ones. Move from what the audience knows to what they don't know. In that way you can lead your audience gradually through a complex process or line of reasoning.

5. *Position arguments* (points) that are *most acceptable* to your audience first, if you must convince an audience. If you come on with heavy arguments too soon, with more than they can swallow, you stand a good chance of turning off your audience. Research shows that audiences who do not like a speaker are less likely to accept that speaker's point of view.[1] Consequently, they will resist believing your ideas if they perceive you as an arrogant, aggressive, and offensive person.

6. *Vary* the normal organizational pattern to gain emphasis. In the reverse-order technique, you talk about the examples or story *before* you tell the audience the "moral of the story." (Usually examples follow the point.) By reversing the order you can use the story to emphasize the point. If you know that audiences notice and remember the unusual *exception* to the pattern, as well as the pattern, you can emphasize an idea with an unexpected pattern of organization.

In this chapter, you will learn to build the main points of your discussion. You will put boxcars on the tracks. Relevant main-point boxcars will add weight to the wheels of your central thought, but extraneous, senseless points, which do not add to your central thought, need to be removed from your train-of-thought. Just as overloaded boxcars can unbalance and derail a train, so can vague points simply overload your central thought. These extraneous, vague points will throw you and your train-of-thought off the track. If your train-of-thought falls off the track because of useless, ill-fitting discussion points, you will find it difficult to move forward. Make sure your main points develop your central thought, or you will confuse yourself and certainly baffle your audience; ideas that don't fit can derail an entire train-of-thought.

In order to eliminate unnecessary points so that you will not overload your train-of-thought, remind yourself of your purpose and your central thought: What is your purpose (step 1)? What is your central thought (step 2)?

Next write down any ideas that define, extend, or explain your central thought. Simply jot down any ideas that come to mind, and for now don't be concerned about the relevance of these ideas to your specific central thought. The important thing right now is to get *something* down on paper, any possible thought, in any order. Just let your ideas spill out on a big, clean piece of paper. Don't crowd your ideas; instead, leave space between phrases or sentences so that you can see them as separate points.

After jotting down ideas for a few minutes (or days!), set aside your points. You'll return to this list of ideas after reading about several patterns you can use to organize those ideas.

PATTERNS FOR ORGANIZING YOUR MAIN POINTS

Perhaps you are already familiar with some of the major ways you can organize ideas. These patterns of organizations are special guidelines useful for moving around ideas, and they are easy to understand, especially with the help of examples. Think of patterns as giant derricks; they help you to move around your main-point boxcars, so that your ideas are orderly and meaningful. Also, these patterns can help you identify points that don't belong to the same pattern (see page 76).

Knowing these simple patterns will not only help you organize a speech, they can also help you organize all kinds of information so that you can live with less worry and forgetfulness. Moreover, when ideas are patterned sensibly, you'll be able to remember a train-of-thought easier. People with good memories do not necessarily have bigger and better brains, but they most certainly have more efficient and effective ways to store information and to remember it easily when they need it. You can do the same thing. When you learn ways to organize points, you are also learning some quick and sensible ways to store ideas in your memory so that you can find those "storage areas" quickly. Therefore, a good memory can help you reduce the anxiety that forgetfulness produces.

As you read about these plans, decide on an organizational plan that will help you and your audience follow your train-of-thought easily. Organize *all* your main points according to the *same* pattern. Here are some common ways to arrange points in a speech:

Time Plan

This is the best plan when you are talking about a step-by-step process that takes place over a time period. For example, you may be describing how to bake a cake, construct a boat, take a picture, drive a car, shine a shoe, make a sale, or run a meeting. To show your audience how they can do these activities, you would naturally tell them what to do first, second, third, fourth, and so on, in recipe fashion. To help you locate these steps in your train-of-thought, simply associate each step with a separate boxcar:

- □ *Subject:* How to make a cake
- □ *Specific Purpose:* To inform the audience on how to make a chocolate cake from scratch ingredients, not a prepared mix

- □ *Time Plan:*   1. Read entire recipe
                    2. Assemble ingredients and utensils
                    3. Mix ingredients in the order named
                    4. Bake, cool, and frost cake

Besides the process speech, you can organize the "experience" speech by a time plan. For example, the history of a country, the life of a famous person, the development of a political movement—all these experiences can be organized and remembered by starting at some point in time and bringing us up to date.

- □ *Subject:* My life passages
- □ *Specific Purpose:* To inform the audience about my life history
- □ *Time Plan:*   1. Early childhood
                    2. Adolescence
                    3. Adulthood

Space Plan

Use this plan when each point talks about a particular location. For example, suppose you are describing a vacation spot or the design of a building. Include each part that your audience expects you to tell them about. For instance, if you are describing a building, talk about all the floors in order—1, 2, 3, 4—not 3, 2, 1, 4, because audiences become uncomfortable if you break their spatial "set." Here is an example of another spatial "set":

- □ *Subject:* Split-level homes in America
- □ *Specific Purpose:* To inform the audience about split-level homes in various parts of the country
- □ *Space Plan:*   1. Split-level homes in the North
                     2. Split-level homes in the East
                     3. Split-level homes in the South
                     4. Split-level homes in the West

Notice how the speaker talks about major geographical areas in a clockwise direction. If he spoke about those in the West, then South, North, East, he would distract the audience with an unfamiliar "set." With this plan, each direction would be a main point "located" as a separate boxcar in your train-of-thought.

Topic Plan

Perhaps your main points are separate topics, divisions, groups, or categories. Here is an example of a topic plan where each problem area is a separate but equally important topic:

□ *Subject:* Problems suitable for Assertiveness Training
□ *Specific Purpose:* To inform the audience about some problem areas requiring assertive behavior
□ *Topic Plan:* 1. Saying no to unreasonable demands
 2. Requesting information
 3. Protesting a rip-off
 4. Expressing anger with people close to us

In this example, each effect is a separate but equal topic:

□ *Subject:* Population growth
□ *Specific Purpose:* To inform the audience about the effects of population growth
□ *Topic Plan:* 1. Effects on the economy
 2. Effects on the environment
 3. Effects on political power

Causal Plan

When your audience wants you to talk about a problem in terms of its causes and its effects, use a causal plan. You have at least three choices.

First, you can organize your ideas from *problem to cause* if you want to emphasize the reasons (causes) for a problem. For example:

□ *Subject:* Devaluation of the dollar
□ *Specific Purpose:* To inform the audience about the reasons for the devaluation of the dollar
□ *Causal Plan 1 (problem/cause):* 1. The problems in devaluation of the dollar
 2. Causes of the devaluation of dollar

Second, if your major purpose is to give results or outcome (effects), organize your ideas from *problem to effect*. This would be an appropriate plan if, for example, you were telling an audience about the effects of a nuclear energy plant on their lives.

□ *Subject:* Nuclear energy plants
□ *Specific Purpose:* To inform the audience about the effects of nuclear energy plants
□ *Causal Plan 2 (problem/effect):* 1. The problem with nuclear energy plants
 2. Possible effects of mismanaged nuclear energy plants

Third, if you were planning to explain an entire problem, then you would organize your ideas from *problem to cause to effect*. You might use this plan if you want to talk about a total problem, such as vandalism or juvenile delinquency or divorce. For example, in the case of vandalism, you might first speak of vandalism in your school district; next, you would outline some probable causes for vandalism; and third, you would cite the effects of vandalism on the community. Your main points in the discussion would read

- □   *Causal Plan 3 (problem/cause/effect):*   1. *Problem* (extent of vandalism as it exists today)
  2. *Causes* of local vandalism
  3. *Effects* of local vandalism

The causal plan is more complicated than the time, space, or topic plans. Use it when your purpose is to persuade or activate an audience to do something. Also, it is effective for longer, informative speeches, when you have time to develop each of the three main points: problem-cause-effect. However, when you suggest that a problem exists, an audience often expects solutions, as well as proof of your assertions. In those situations, the problem/solution plan discussed later would be desirable.

Theory-Practice Plan (Principle-Application)

We live by many different principles. Because of our religious principles, we might try to imitate people who live by the Golden Rule. Our democratic principles shape our attitude toward universal suffrage, freedom of the press, and freedom of privacy. Certain legal principles determine people's guilt or innocence. Many new plans for action are proposed by citing theories or principles that experts tell us justify particular actions. It is not surprising that many speeches are organized around a pattern that consists of two leading ideas, the one outlining the theory or principle, the second developing the application of the theory to everyday living.

Some examples of this plan include the following: the principle of birth control followed by the description of various contraceptives; the theory of progressive relaxation followed by directions on how to relax muscles; the principle of reinforcement followed by ways to change behavior; the theory of law and demand and how it operates in a capitalistic economy. Preachers use the theory-practice plan when they quote a rule of conduct from the Bible and then suggest how we can live according to those principles in our daily lives. Here is an example of the theory-practice plan, sometimes called the principle-application plan:

- □   *Subject:* Equal Rights Amendment
- □   *Specific Purpose:* To inform an audience about ERA
- □   *Theory-Practice (principle-application):*   1. The principle of law (or principles behind ERA)
  2. How ERA would apply these principles to all women in every state

Problem-Solution Plan (Disease-Remedy Plan)

Problem solving is a major occupation for most of us. Not only in science, medicine, and technology but also in health care, the arts, and sports, we are continuously searching for new and better ways of doing things and improving the quality of life. Like the theory-practice plan, the problem-solution plan has only two leading ideas, one containing a description of the problem and the other explaining the solution. It is most often used when you want an audience to take some action to solve a problem (to activate).

Sometimes you may have to defend your solution against attack, as well as argue against other proposed solutions. For example, if you were *defending* a national health insurance plan in America, you would have to (a) defend that solution against the objection that it would create mediocrity in the practice of medicine, as well as (b) argue against the present system of voluntary health insurance, such as Blue Cross. Conversely, if you are opposed to national health care insurance, you could simply (a) deny that there is a problem; or (b) admit the problem but attack the proposed solution of nationalized health care insurance as being inadequate, impractical, or unworkable.

In the following examples, notice how one plan organizes main points and a second plan develops the subpoints in the discussion or argument part of the speech:[2]

□ *Subject:* Compulsory health insurance

□ *Specific Purpose:* To convince the audience that a program of compulsory health insurance should be adopted

□ *Problem/*
Solution
  1. The middle class gets inadequate medical care today.
     Situation/
     Effect
       a. Heavy expenses cannot be met.
       b. This leads to unfortunate postponement of this medical attention.
  2. Compulsory health insurance would extend adequate medical care to all.

Principle/
Application
  a. It is acceptable in principle.
     Related
     topics
       1. Everyone pays in proportion to his earning power.
       2. This plan is not socialistic.
  b. It can be made to work.

□ *Subject:* Compulsory health insurance

□ *Specific Purpose:* To convince the audience that a voluntary health insurance plan is more desirable than a compulsory plan

□ *Problem/*
  1. Compulsory health insurance is not desirable.
     Related
     topics
       a. It reduces medical efficiency.
       b. It increases medical costs.
       c. It encourages unethical practices.

Solution
2. Voluntary health insurance provides for all of the advantages and none of the disadvantages of compulsory insurance.

Related topics
a. It permits continuance of present satisfactory relations between doctor and patient.
b. It meets the average budget.
c. It is free from government red tape.

In the above examples all *main* ideas follow *one* plan, one pattern, that makes sense. Mixing your patterns of organization, as the next example does, will very likely mix up your audience, too:

▢ *Subject:* Rapid Transit
▢ *Specific Purpose:* To inform the audience about how Rapid Transit would operate
▢ *Mixing plans is confusing:* 1. Rapid Transit would cover sixty miles from San Francisco to San Jose. *(spatial)*

2. Rapid Transit would decrease commuter costs. *(causal)*

3. Rapid Transit would carry fifty thousand commuters. *(topic)*

Instead of many plans, choose your points so that they follow (relate to) one, unified plan which is easy to follow, as this example shows:

▢ *Subject:* Rapid Transit
▢ *Specific Purpose:* To inform the audience about how Rapid Transit would operate
▢ *Using one plan makes good sense:* 1. Rapid Transit will travel x number of miles in the Bay Area. *(topic is miles covered)*

2. Rapid Transit will run x number of hours per day. *(topic is hours in use)*

3. Rapid Transit will move x number of commuters each day. *(topic is commuters serviced)*

Step 5: Worksheet [1] [2] [ETC.]

You can put these plans to use right now.

- ☐ Read over the points that you wrote down on a separate sheet of paper earlier.
- ☐ Underline only the *main* points that develop your central thought.
- ☐ Arrange those main points (use separate cards if necessary) so that they fit one of the following patterns:
  time, space, topic, causal, theory-practice, problem-solution.
- ☐ Fill in *only* your main points at step 5 on your outline (pages 27–28).

You now have the main discussion points for your speech. These main-point boxcars must carry important information about your central thought. In the next chapter you will be filling up your main-point boxcars, making each one interesting and useful to your train-of-thought. Step 6, "Fill your Boxcars with Subpoint Cargo," will help you select interesting and useful subpoints. Read on!

6

Make Your Speech Meaningful

STEP 6. FILL YOUR BOXCARS WITH SUBPOINT CARGO

The main points of your speech outline are the boxcars in your train-of-thought. They provide the basic structure of your speech. Once you have the necessary boxcars, you add the subpoint cargo to each main-point boxcar. Just as cargo makes boxcars useful, subpoints make the main ideas workable, understandable, interesting, and memorable. Usually main points are abstract ideas, which only come alive when speakers show us what their ideas mean to us in our everyday living. If you stop short of telling us how or why a point is important, that is, how it relates to us, we'll be dissatisfied with your argument. Here is an example of stopping short. Notice how main points are not developed.

1. Causes of malnutrition
   a. The government is not doing enough.
   b. The government is not protecting us.
   c. We're conditioned to eat fast foods.
   d. We're hypnotized by attractive packaging.

Causes a, b, c, and d are not enough for a good speech; audiences want to know why or how the government is inadequate, how we are conditioned and hypnotized. Interesting quotes, statistics, stories, and examples would make those main points memorable. If an idea is worth including as a major point, talk about it, show why it's important and what it means, so that it can be justified and remembered in the lineup of other main-point boxcars.

It may be helpful to think of supporting materials the way you think of home furnishings. Furniture, decorations, and personalized mementos help define a house, make it different, and give it special meaning. So it is with subpoints: They define and give special meaning to the main points, making them understandable and memorable. Just as an empty boxcar, one without important cargo, would be discarded as useless, so should main points that have no supporting subpoints be eliminated from your train-of-thought.

It is not difficult to organize smaller ideas with unifying plans of their own under each main point. Simply determine which subideas should be included and how they are to be organized. To fill up those empty boxcars with cargo, develop undeveloped main points with smaller substructures. In the example that follows, various kinds of information develop the main points, giving us something more to think about.[1] The outline illustrates subpoint cargo.

- □ *Subject:* Malnutrition in the U.S.
- □ *Specific Purpose:* To inform a public-speaking class about the causes and effects of malnutrition in the U.S.
- □ *Organizational Pattern:* The overall pattern is cause-effect: Section I lists causes, and section II lists effects.

  A *topic* pattern organizes four causes (A, B, C, D) and three effects (A, B, C). Both the causes and the effects of malnutrition are arranged in order of importance; the first and last points are most important (A and D causes; A and C effects).

  I. *Causes* of malnutrition
  - A. The government is not educating us about nutrition. Why?
    - 1. Government budget is too tiny to meet public demand for information.
      - a. Compare budget *statistics* to estimated cost of proper publicity about malnutrition (on note card).
    - 2. Instead of teaching the poor about welfare, workers claim they spend time policing the poor so that the welfare laws are not violated.
      - a. Welfare workers' *quotes* (on note card).
      - b. *Quote* from *Shame of a Nation* (on note card).
  - B. The government is not adequately protecting us from harmful chemicals and food additives. Why?
    - 1. *Describe* a powerful, influential insecticide lobby.
    - 2. *Describe* how consumer is lost in confusion about what is happen-

ing and develops skeptical attitude toward all information, saying government cries wolf.
C. We are conditioned to eat fast foods on the run. How?
   1. *Story:* to illustrate that vending machines are used for quick, available breakfasts.
   2. *Slogans:* advertising slogans which make us think we'll feel good if we eat the fast foods (on note card).
D. We are hypnotized by attractive packaging.
   1. *Illustrations* (visual aids) to demonstrate how the public is fooled.
   a. Present real packages as evidence.
   2. Conclusion: Packages appeal to the senses, not to the search for good food.

II. *Effects* of malnutrition are long-lasting and irreversible because the undernourished are
A. Unable to think
   1. *Statistic:* relationship of retarded children born in the U.S. to malnutrition (statistics on note card).
   2. *Quote:* from victim of undernourishment (on note card).
B. Unable to do physical labor
   1. *Statistics:* to prove malnourished are accident-prone, slow workers, and absent more often than those who are adequately nourished (on note card).
C. Unable to cope psychologically
   1. *Quote:* from Minnesota study (on note card).

HOW TO CLARIFY AND AMPLIFY MAIN-POINT BOXCARS

Your supporting cargo should do one or more things for your main-point boxcars: It should clarify and sometimes prove your arguing point. Subpoints *clarify* main points by explaining, describing, or illustrating those points; they *prove* major points by making inferences and providing evidence.

It is crucial to clarify points in your discussion. Don't leave audiences dangling, wondering what you mean by a main point. Instead, clarify your ideas using any of the following techniques: description, illustration, explanation. Here are some examples of how you could use these techniques to clarify a main point such as "urban sprawl is hurting us."

Describe the Point: Paint a Word Picture to Clarify It

Twenty years ago, the corner of Alma and San Antonio was a rural oasis. Beyond a wooden lean-to a farmer could be seen pushing an old plow. Today busy shoppers and rows of cars have replaced the neat rows of vegetables, and the cement of a sprawling shopping center has replaced the lean-to shack of a small vegetable farmer.

Illustrate the Point: Narrate a Short Story to Clarify an Idea

When we first moved to California twenty years ago, I could look across the San Francisco Bay and see the magnificent hills of the East Bay every day of the year. Today, with a population that has doubled and has polluted its air, I am glad when I can see those hills one day a week. The rest of the days my eyes hurt as I look at the smog stretching endlessly to the East Bay hills.

Explain the Point: Present Examples to Clarify the Effects of Urban Sprawl

The effects of crowding can be seen on the pages of our local newspapers: outlandish crimes, unsolved social problems, high unemployment, and serious public health problems. What good can come from such crowding?

In order to develop clarifying material, such as descriptions, illustrations, and explanations, recall your experiences or ones that others have told you. In addition, find an appropriate story by referring, say, to "Urban Sprawl" or "Overpopulation" in the subject index at the library. Librarians are particularly helpful in making a point interesting, as are friends and relatives. Some of the best stories, descriptions, and explanations for speeches come from ordinary people who shy away from speaking. In this manner, you'll gather *several* stories, not all of them relevant to your current talk but nevertheless interesting and useful for some future speech or conversation.

Other techniques for clarifying an idea include *restating* an idea or recasting it in different words ("The quiet of the land gave way to the shrieks of the machines.") Also, use *quotations* that eloquently magnify an idea ("According to the governor of California, . . .") or a *rhetorical question* to involve an audience in your message ("Is concrete better than a lean-to?").

As you gather material for explanations, descriptions, and illustrations, keep a notebook or card file in which you systematically store supporting materials, such as quotations, examples, and statistics. Record useful supporting materials when you are waiting for doctors, dentists, friends, children, and spouses. Have appropriate magazines and books handy to skim through quickly whenever you have to wait for others. Keep 3 × 5 index cards in your pocket or purse so that you can file a quote or the gist of a story immediately. Use a rubber band or, better, punch holes and ring a few cards together. The cards should contain the following information:

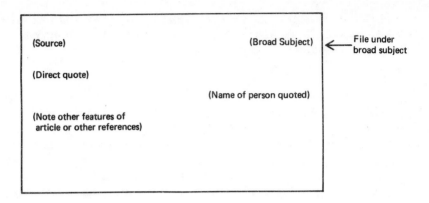

Here is an example of a quote that I store on a 3 × 5 card.

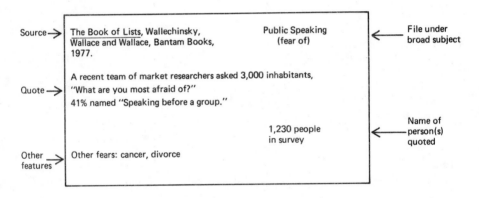

After entering information on the card, I put the card in an accordion file "Current Ideas" under "Public Speaking."

HOW TO PROVE YOUR MAIN-POINT BOXCARS

If you want to persuade an audience, it is important to know which forms of supporting materials work best. There are two kinds of proof used to validate a line of argument or the desirability of a particular solution or course of action: *facts* (evidence) and *inference* (reasoning).

In persuasive speeches we are asking the audience to agree with our points. Often, we are arguing for a particular perspective or interpretation of a problem. A persuasive speech depends upon the logical support offered for its main points as well as the dramatic flair with which they're presented. Here are a few ways to support the point you are urging. Since you have already learned most of these in your lifetime from listening to, or being caught up in, many arguments, the following methods should appear familiar to you despite the fancy words.

Factual Evidence

When you cite authorities, statistics, and examples, you are using facts to prove your point. Suppose you are trying to persuade your audience to adopt some policy, to abolish the death penalty or to eliminate salt in foods, for example. The following are common methods to support one's recommendation:

1. *Cite authorities.* We refer to a prestigious authority who recommends our policy. This may be a scientist, a governmental agency, a celebrity—anyone the audience is likely to consider trustworthy on the issue. Often in technical matters all of us must rely on expert authorities.
2. *Cite statistics.* Statistics are summaries of many cases. Thus, we may compare homicide statistics in a state which has the death penalty to a state which does not; or compare homicide rates in a state during years before death-penalty adoption to the years after its adoption.
3. *Cite examples.* We refer to one or more specific cases which demonstrate the wisdom or need for our policy. Thus, we cite the case of John Doe who murdered his wife in a fit of passion and who claimed he would have been undeterred by the death penalty. Or we may cite the instance of an acquaintance who ate lots of salty food and had high-blood pressure.

Let us go over the pitfalls of these methods. First, in citing an authority, you should check out the source. Ask yourself these questions:

1. Is this person an *unbiased observer* or does he or she "have a bill of goods to sell"? For example, U.S. presidents are not unbiased observers of the achievements of their administration.
2. Has the person you quoted had *ample time to observe?* Under what conditions and how long ago did he or she do the observing?
3. Are the findings of your authority supported by the *observations of others?* If you find that many people in a field are skeptical about the "evidence," beware.
4. Is the authority *recognized by his or her colleagues?* Those who are respected because they do sound, careful work are known to other professionals in the field as leaders. Be sure to check more than one source in order to get a reliable estimation of your authority. Warning: Just because a person is an authority in one field, such as baseball, does not mean that he or she is an authority in another field, such as nutrition.

Second, while statistics are a popular form of proof, they can be misleading or just plain baffling. A speaker can make data sound impressive with exaggerated claims such as "More doctors recommend Brand X more than any other pain reliever." What might such a claim really mean? Suppose that "evidence" is based on a skimpy, unrepresentative sampling? Perhaps only three doctors were asked which pain reliever they would recommend from a list of three brands, and the "others" consisted of two very inferior products.

Speakers who do not have a good understanding of statistics can unwittingly mislead themselves and their audience. Know the meaning of your statistics. Ask an expert, such as a scientist or math teacher, to help you interpret the significance of a statistic.

For a speech, follow these guidelines in presenting statistics:

1. *Round off numbers* so that people can remember them. Instead of saying 1,512,329 say, "approximately one and a half million."
2. *Make numbers meaningful.* For example, instead of saying, "*x* billion tons," say, "the weight of a 17-story skyscraper that covers 4 square blocks."
3. *Use only a few statistics at one time.* Break up the monotony of listing statistic after statistic by interspersing an anecdote or using a visual aid. Or change your body position or rate of speaking.
4. *Present meaningful measurements.* Don't speak in feet, miles, or pounds if your audience knows only how to calculate in meters, kilometers, or stones.
5. *Use lots of visual aids to present statistics.* Almost all of us have trouble holding numbers in our head. Simplify the memory task by writing your statistics in big numbers on the blackboard or write with thick, hard felt pens on flip charts or overhead projector plastic. If you use slides, present only a *few readable numbers per slide.* Do not crowd.
6. *Dramatize the statistic.* If a statistic is worth mentioning, it is worth making it stand out in a meaningful way. Use pictures and symbols to stand for words. For example, two money bags, one large and one small, can graphically demonstrate what money was needed to retire comfortably twenty years ago and what is needed today.

Third, while examples are an excellent way to get the attention and interest of the audience, you must choose relevant ones which will help prove your point. Here are two important guidelines for choosing a good example that will work to prove your point:

1. The example should be *typical* and not the exceptional or unusual case or example.
2. Use *enough examples* to constitute a fair sample. (Usually, you will need to present additional statistical information to support the conclusions you draw from one example.)

Authorities, statistics, and examples are subpoint cargo. They will help make your discussion points memorable and believable.

Deductive Reasoning

Examples and statistics by themselves do not make an argument. An argument is a combination of facts or principles that leads to some conclusion. Thus, statistics showing that women are paid less than men for the same work does not *per se* argue for anything. That fact must be combined with something else, such as a moral principle of "Equal pay for equal work," in order for you to deduce a conclusion, namely, that wage-earning women are being unjustly discriminated against. In combining facts and principles to argue for a given conclusion, you are using *logical deduction*.

In this practice, you support a policy by arguing that it "follows logically" from other principles that people accept. Thus, if I can get you to accept the principle that no human life should ever be taken, then it follows that you should support abolition of the death penalty. There are many forms of logical deduction; only a few will be noted here.

1. *Hypothetical*. These are of the form: "If X, then Y", and "If X is true, therefore Y is true." An example is "If we want to maintain our liberty, then we must fight to defend it." Often the "X is true" part of the argument is unspoken since the speaker assumes the audience already believes that part.
2. *Specific case*. A general principle or rule, such as "All policemen support the death penalty," is applied to a specific case, "John Doe is a policeman," to obtain the inference, "John Doe supports the death penalty."
3. *Eliminate alternatives*. To argue for policy A, you first convince your audience that the only possible policies are A or B; then you argue that B can't work; therefore, A wins by a process of elimination. The problem here is convincing your audience that only A or B are possible.

Deductive reasoning is limited in so far as it can only bring out the logical consequences contained in the "first principles" or premises of such arguments. Therefore, much of your argument and persuasion goes into convincing your audience that your principles or premises are reasonable or acceptable. Where do those premises come from? Many are moral rules such as "Human life is inviolable," "A long healthy life is a great good," or "Everyone should be treated equally before the law." The problem with moral principles is that they often conflict with one another in specific cases, so each person has to argue for the relative importance or "dominance" of one principle over an opposing one.

Causal Relations

The major source of premises in arguments are guesses about causal relations. Thus, I guess that high salt-intake causes high blood pressure; I guess that the death penalty will (or will not) deter prospective murderers. We refer to causal relations in practically all of our everyday conversation and arguments. We use them in several ways.

1. *From cause to effect:* Striking a match against an emery board causes the heat of friction which causes the match to burst into flames. This reasoning moves forward in time. We use it when we recommend that taking some action today will lead to certain consequences tomorrow.

2. *From effect to cause:* This is the style of the troubleshooter or diagnostician. Your car's engine won't turn over (effect). That's probably due to a dead battery (cause). Water won't drain out of your bathtub (effect). That's probably due to debris clogging the drain pipe. We use this to explain how a present condition arose from a past condition or event. Detectives use this method all the time.

3. *Effect to effect.* One event or condition can cause several outcomes. If we observe A, it's a good bet that B will be there also. Car engine won't turn over? Bet that your headlights also won't work. Both are effects caused by a dead battery.

COMMON FALLACIES

I have mentioned several ways to support your thesis or point of view. People also make many errors of thinking or go astray in arguments. Here are a few of the common mistakes or fallacies of thinking you should try to avoid. See whether you can catch other speakers using these mistaken methods.[2]

1. *Mistaking evaluations for observations:* People often confuse what exactly are the facts with their opinion or evaluation of the facts. They then argue from their opinion rather than the facts themselves. Thus, they argue "Kids today watch far too much violent television" rather than "Kids today see an average of nearly 10 acts of violence per day during their television viewing." This distinction between reality versus evaluation is often hard to follow in describing human behavior but nonetheless very important.

2. *Hasty overgeneralization:* Too few cases are examined before you "jump to a conclusion" or make a "snap judgment." If you hear of one crooked woman banker, you shouldn't suppose that all women bankers are crooked. Overgeneralization from insufficient evidence forms the basis of stereotyping and prejudice.

3. *Unrepresentative examples:* You cannot logically argue for a general point about a group of people by pointing to an extreme or unrepresentative case. You cannot argue against scholarships for college athletes by pointing to one extreme case of excessive payoffs and cheating on grades—it is atypical.

4. *Inappropriate comparisons:* The mistake here is to assume that because two objects or conditions are alike in a few respects they will therefore be alike in other significant respects. An example is, "This diet worked for me, so it'll work for you too," which assumes the similarity of your weight problem to mine. Another example is "You are supporting political objectives A, B, C, and so does the Communist Party; so you must be a Communist." That line of mistaken analogy contributed to the Communist witch hunts of the early 1950s.

5. *False alternatives:* This uses the "either/or" argument but there are other alternatives besides those listed. "Either you're with us or against us" is a familiar example. But one may be neither for nor against; or you may be partly for and partly against the several goals of the speaker. When either/or alternatives are presented, ask yourself whether you really must choose just one, or if there are other alternatives or combinations. The nation's energy supply of the future need not be solely oil or solely nuclear power; some of each will be used as well as other sources like solar energy.

6. *Ducking the issue:* In this condition the speaker ignores or ducks the central issue, or argues it on irrelevant grounds. This has several vicious forms:

   Ad hominem attacks on the personality of the person proposing a policy rather than arguing the merits of the policy itself.

   Overwhelming gobbledegook floods the audience with technical details of which they're ignorant; these complex details are then claimed to support the policy recommended. Another form of this is use of privileged "inside information" from a secret or anonymous informant. The audience cannot question the source.

   Appeal to prejudice is a vicious form of argument. The speaker refers to occupational, religious, racial or national stereotypes to "prove" his point; a policy may be attacked simply by labeling it as un-American, racist or sexist, without defining the necessary terms or proving the charge.

   False authorities are used in advertising but are logically indefensible. Popular athletes probably aren't experts on cars, clothing, beer, after-shave lotions, or coffee makers. The expertise of the testifier regarding the topic he or she is recommending should be made clear.

7. *Question-begging:* "When did you stop beating your wife?" "How long have you been overweight?" The belief to be proved is presupposed in the question. A speaker may try to prove his point by simply asserting it or talking as though it were self-evident. "I'm here to argue that we shouldn't draft members of the weaker sex [meaning women] into the armed services." If you accept that characterization of women, you've conceded half the speaker's argument. Related to question-begging is circular reasoning: I assume belief A and use it to prove belief B; when asked to justify A, I say it is supported by B. "God exists. It says so in the Bible. The Bible must be true. Why? Because it's the word of God." Question-begging and circular reasoning are often hard to detect. But stripped to barest essentials, they are saying "Believe this because I say so."

8. *False causal inferences*. It is often difficult to prove that event A caused event B, and there are many pitfalls in causal inferences. Ideally, when A occurs, B always follows. But causal relations affecting humans are usually chancy, so we say A is *usually* followed by B. Overeating doesn't always cause overweight: it depends on other things like metabolic rate, work, and exercise habits. A common error is to assume that correlation of two events in time proves that one causes the other. During a lengthy national doctor's strike in Great Britain several years ago, it was found that many *fewer* people died. Are we to infer that the doctors had been causing those excess deaths? Hardly. The mystery disappeared when someone noted a "third event" related to the other two. During the strike, all non-emergency surgery for repair of longstanding medical problems (e.g., coronary bypass) was stopped, so the occasional fatalities from major surgery were thus temporarily avoided (really postponed).

Whether people believe a time association of two events implies causality seems to depend on their implicit theories of how the world works. For example, we know that despite their close association in time the appearance of autumn leaves does not cause weekend football games, because the two events aren't the "right type." In contrast, long ago people believed that walking outside in the damp evening air caused malaria, because that fit their theory about vapors causing disease. We know now that walking outdoors at night probably led to bites from anopheles mosquitos and that caused malaria. Thus, correlation of events in time is not enough to establish causation. One also needs a sort of "theory" of how one event gives rise to the other. Of course, speakers, as well as professional scientists, argue over the reasonableness of particular causal theories. The goal of supporting your thesis or point of view is to argue that it rests on solid ground and reasonable assumptions.

SUMMARY

In this chapter, you have learned that the main point boxcars of an informative talk often need to be clarified by vivid language which uses descriptions, illustrations, and explanations. Very likely you will also use facts, such as testimony, statistics, and examples (subpoint cargo) to develop your discussion in a meaningful way. However, if you wish to persuade your audience to your point of view, then you must also prove your thesis. The examples, statistics, and facts must be soundly combined with other principles to argue your point. Review the several fallacies of reasoning and make sure that your argument avoids these fallacies and relies instead on sound reasoning.

Interesting supporting material can make the simplest, most ordinary topic novel and inspiring. Speakers who present captivating supporting material to clarify and prove their main ideas sound more authentic and lively, whereas speakers with no supporting material to back up their assertions sound opinionated and smug. And even if we agree with the opinions of the latter speakers, their speeches are boring and uninteresting. Your speech will be as interesting as its supporting material, so search until you find some fantastic material that excites you and others.

Remember, now is the time to get down to facts—cases, examples, stories, statistics, surveys, reports, authorities, illustrations and analogies. Use them to clarify or, with the help of reasoning, prove your points.

Step 6: Worksheet ▢ ⌂ △

Make sure that your main point boxcars have subpoint cargo:

- ▢ Look at all the main-point boxcars on your outline. Are some points undeveloped? First, fill in with subpoints that clarify your main points: use descriptions, illustrations, examples.
- ▢ If you want to persuade your audience, you will also need proof to support your main ideas: Use facts and reasoning.
- ▢ What kind of proof are you using? Testimony? Statistics? Examples?
- ▢ Are you using these forms of proof ethically?
- ▢ What kinds of reasoning are you using? Generalization from examples? Deduction? Causal reasoning?
- ▢ Are you making a sound argument or are there fallacies in your reasoning?
- ▢ Include important subpoints on your outline wherever step 6 appears.

In the next chapter, step 7 helps you connect your ideas. Steps 8 and 9 help you work out a conclusion to your train-of-thought. These last important steps, 7, 8, and 9 can be completed quickly as you read chapter 7. After you complete outlining your conclusion, the next chapter will help you revise your initial outline and plan visual aids which help dramatize your most important ideas.

7

Connect, Conclude, Revise, and Dramatize Your Train-of-Thought

STEP 7. CONNECT YOUR BOXCARS WITH TRANSITIONS

Transitions connect the basic parts of your speech, providing both you and your audience with essential memory links. Connecting words or phrases allow you to move smoothly from one point to another; and, in giving your speech, help you associate one point with the next one. By connecting ideas one to another you are giving your audience the necessary cues that help them to understand the relationship between one idea and the next, thereby avoiding being thought of as a speaker who is hard to follow.

To make it easier for you and your audience to remember the ideas you want to convey, use verbal, visual, or vocal transitions. While you should use verbal transitions (and sometimes visual and vocal ones) whenever you want to connect ideas, your train-of-thought outline calls for verbal connectors at three specific places:

1. Between the introduction and the discussion (connect the engine to boxcar 1)
2. Between each main point of the discussion (connect each boxcar)
3. Between the discussion and the conclusion (connect the last boxcar to the caboose)

Coherence of your speech often depends upon your skill and care in applying connectors at these strategic places.

Verbal Transitions

Verbal transitions emphasize a transition in thought and provide coherence. Basically, you can use six different kinds of verbal transitions, each one corresponding to a different purpose:[1]

- ☐ *Addition*—used when you want simply to add a point
- ☐ *Contrast*—used when you want to contrast one point with another
- ☐ *Result*—used when you want to show that the next point shows a result
- ☐ *Alternation*—used when you want to link two different points of view
- ☐ *Cause*—used when your point presents a reason
- ☐ *Repetition*—used when you want to emphasize a point
- ☐ *Signpost*—used when you want to call attention to the *sequence* of your next points.

The following outline will help you understand these seven types of transitions when they are placed in the most strategic locations: between the introduction and the discussion; between each main point in the discussion; between the discussion and conclusion. The connectors (transitions) are designated as ⊐⊏ . In the following example sometimes two or more connectors are illustrated. Choose the transitional sentence you think is best. Notice that the signpost transition is very effective as a connector between your introduction and first main point of the discussion.

Train-of-Thought Outline Demonstrating Seven Transitions

Introduction (Engine)

 "I think that I shall never see a poem as lovely as a tree."

 Trees provide beauty, shade, utility for your garden.

 Consider carefully the best tree for your garden.
(Choose one):

Because trees are a big investment, both of time and money, be sure you consider the soil and the climate. (cause)

⊐⊏ → In other words, choosing the best tree for you makes sense in terms of pleasure, time, and money. (repetition)

Soil and climate and two important considerations. (signpost)

91

Discussion (Boxcars)

Consider the soil

    Its mineral content

    Its density

(Choose any one of these):

Besides the soil, consider the climate when you plant a tree. (addition)

→ But the soil is not the only consideration. Climate counts, too. (contrast)

Not only should you consider the soil, you should also consider the climate. (alternation)

Consider the climate

    Its growing season

    Its temperature extremes

Therefore, in considering both soil and climate, you can be more confident that . . . (result)

Conclusion (Caboose)

Your tree will be at least as satisfying as a poem,

and will give you the shade and beauty you want in a pleasant and useful garden.

Make sure you consider only the best trees for your garden by looking at

    1. the soil

    2. the climate

Then, as the happy gardener, you can sit under your tree and read poetry, the sports page, the funnies—anything that adds to your satisfaction.

At first, it may seem artificial and difficult to choose a transition, but after deliberately connecting a few ideas, you will soon learn to do it easily and automatically. Here is a chart listing transition words for the six major types of transitions. To use it, simply decide which purpose will help define the interrelationships between your ideas, and then choose the best transitional word listed under your purpose. For example, if your purpose is to add a point, you would choose the best word in the Addition column to accomplish your purpose.

TRANSITION WORDS CHART[2]

Addition (to add a point)

And there is another point:
Further, . . .
Furthermore, . . .
Besides, . . .
Also, . . .
Moreover, . . .
Likewise, . . .
Again, . . .
Finally,
And then, . . .
In addition, . . .

Contrast (to contrast one point with another)

However, . . .
But . . .
And yet, . . .
Still, . . .
Nevertheless, . . .
Despite . . .
On the contrary, . . .
On the other hand, . . .
In spite of, . . .

Result (to show that the second point is a result of the first)

Therefore, the upshot of this matter is . . .
Hence, . . .
Consequently, . . .
Accordingly, . . .
Thus, . . .

Alternation (to link two different viewpoints)

In a different manner, I would say it this way:
Otherwise, we can consider . . .
In other ways . . .
Either . . . or
Both . . . and . . .
Not only . . . but also . . .
On the other hand, . . .
In other respects, . . .

Cause (to show that the second point is the cause of the first)

When . . . , then . . .
Inasmuch as . . . , then . . .

Repetition (to emphasize a point)

In fact, I can't say too many times,
Namely, . . .
Indeed, . . .
In reality, . . .
In other words,
In truth, . . .
To be sure, . . .
That is to say, . . .

Signpost (to list the sequence of points)

First, I'll talk about . . .
then I'll . . .
. . . and . . . follow . . .
. . . and . . . will answer my question.
My points are . . .

Visual and Vocal Transitions

Use all the cues you can to help everyone, including yourself, remember your speech. For example, if you take a couple of steps when you move from one idea to another, you can help an audience to hear—and see—a connection between ideas. A straight-forward, meaningful walk from one side of the podium to the other while you are saying a transitional sentence ''carries'' the audience from one place to another both verbally and visually. The new physical place helps them "place" a new idea in memory.

Rehearsed movements can help you remember ideas better. Actors can relate many stories in which they suddenly remembered a line because a learned gesture or movement cued the line for them. Also, moving will often release tension so that you can momentarily relax and remember.

Transitions also provide a natural time for you to take a good look at your note cards. You can slow down and catch your breath when you pause before and after the transition. The pause alerts your listeners to a change of pace—and a change of ideas. Any vocal change in rate or force will tell an audience to stay alert because you are changing pace and moving to a new idea with your train-of-thought. And don't be afraid of silence. It can help your audience catch up with your train-of-thought before moving on to the next idea.

Don't be surprised if you feel corny practicing the transitional sentences while you take a step or two and alter your vocal force or speaking rate. To change position is not natural at first, but sufficient practice will make you look and feel naturally confident. Simply walk and talk at the same time until it feels easy and natural to do so. This may take seven or eight practice walk-throughs, but with persistence, you will feel better as you move more naturally out of habit.

Step 7: Worksheet ⊐⊏

- ☐ Find each step 7 ⊐⊏ on your outline, pages 27 and 28.
- ☐ Look at the point *before* and *after* each of these transitional places and decide what relationships exist between these points.
- ☐ Which *purpose* should each transition serve? Addition? Contrast? Results? Alternation? Cause? Repetition? Signpost?
- ☐ Use the word chart on page 93 to assist you in choosing the best connector for your purposes.
- ☐ Write in the exact transitional sentence you intend to say at each step 7 on your outline.
- ☐ Will you emphasize any of these verbal transitions with visual techniques, such as movement, gestures, and vocal changes? Which ones? During practice, speakers often mark their note cards wherever they plan to connect ideas with a change of voice or body.

STEP 8. CONCLUDE YOUR TRAIN-OF-THOUGHT WITH A CABOOSE

A good conclusion can unify your speech and give the important ideas added emphasis through repetition. You will need to do four things before you jump off your train-of-thought and sit down:

1. Signal with another *attention getter* that you are concluding.
2. Remind your audience of how your subject has *appealed* (has related) to their needs.
3. Repeat the *central thought*.
4. Repeat important *main-point* boxcars.

First, gain audience attention for your concluding remarks by either repeating the same attention getter from your introduction or creating a new one.

Second, appeal either to the same needs made in your introduction or appeal to new ones. For example, in the introduction of a speech titled "Conserve Energy," you could appeal to the economic needs of your audience with, "For every gallon you save, you save twenty cents." Then, late in your talk, suppose you assert that "conserving energy is a way to gain freedom from outside dependency." Your conclusion, then, could appeal to needs for economic and political security: "Will we allow ourselves to be controlled economically and politically by OPEC nations?" Using different appeals in the introduction and conclusion is the "combination technique" (page 56). By appealing to needs again in your conclusion, the relevance of your ideas is strengthened.

The third requirement in your conclusion is: Repeat your central thought. Express the central thought with the same words you used in the introduction. If you change the wording, you may alter the meaning and confuse your listeners just as you are finishing your talk.

Fourth, repeat your main points (only the boxcars, not the cargo) in your conclusion. If you can, express them in the same words you used in your discussion; however, if you change the wording, be sure you do *not* change the meaning. By repeating the same words you help an audience identify and remember those ideas. This final summary of main points provides your listeners with the good news that you are winding up your talk. No matter how exciting and interesting a speaker has been, a concluding sign is generally welcomed. Because listeners are eager to get up and move on, take only a minute or two to restate your main points in a concise and lively manner.

Step 8: Worksheet

▫ Find step 8, the conclusion of your outline, pages 28–29.

▫ Will you use the same attention getter you used in your introduction? Would a

different one work better? Write it in your conclusion.

▫ Will you repeat the same appeal you used in the introduction? Did you suggest any new appeals in your discussion? If so, could you add them to the appeal made earlier? Write it in your conclusion.

□   Write your central thought *exactly* as in your introduction.

□   Write in your main-point boxcars (but *not* the subpoint cargo).

Now you have most of your conclusion finalized. Only one more step remains—deciding on a final statement.

STEP 9. JUMP OFF YOUR TRAIN-OF-THOUGHT WITH A FINAL STATEMENT

The happy character jumping off the train represents you making a memorable final statement. The first thing to remember about a final statement is to have one. Because these are the last words you will say, audiences will remember them whether or not they are provocative and stimulating. If you disappoint them by being too vague or wishy-washy—"That's about all I have to say . . ." or "I've run out of time, so I'll sit down"—you'll leave the audience with a poor image of yourself. They will conclude that you have rambled on aimlessly and have carelessly run out of ideas and time. Your final statement is your last chance to influence your audience, so choose those words carefully and leave your audience stimulated and satisfied. Ideally, your finale should be so memorable that it reverberates in their minds for hours—even weeks and years from now! Listeners forget long, colorless, and complicated endings. One short, exciting, simple sentence, delivered enthusiastically and unhurriedly, may be all an audience will remember from an entire speech; therefore, make sure it is as easy to remember as a familiar tune.

Final-Statement Techniques

Several techniques can be used to make a good final statement. One way to compose a memorable final statement is to take George M. Cohan's advice and "always leave them laughing when you say good-bye." This is fine, but if you use humor, make sure it is appropriate to your subject and the occasion.

Another way to be effective is to close with a poem or a quotation. It should be short—four lines seems maximum—and it must definitely fit the subject, the time, the place, and the audience. If you choose a familiar poem that people know and love, they will associate pleasant thoughts with you. Your librarian can help you locate many suitable poems which will emphasize and dramatize the central thought of your speech. Similarly, a minister can help you find an appropriate biblical quotation. Occasionally, a quote used as an attention getter in the introduction can be worked into the final statement. Using the same quotation can be effective if it is personalized in the final statement. For example:

Introduction (Engine)

"Eleanor Roosevelt said, 'No one can make you feel inferior without your consent.' "

Conclusion (Caboose)

"I hope my message today has helped you gain some will power and skill power, so that no one can make you feel inferior without your consent."

Sincerely complimenting your audience can be an effective final statement if it, too, is made in a personal way. You'll probably agree that ending a speech by saying, "Thank you for your patience . . . or your time . . . or your attention" is boring and puts you in an unflattering light. Rather say, "It has been a pleasure for me to speak to you today—thank you." or "You have been an exciting and interesting audience—thank you."

Another possibility for a final statement is to combine a quote and a compliment: "It has been said that happiness is doing one's utmost under good conditions. You have provided me with the good conditions where I felt I wanted to do my utmost for you. Thank you."

In summary a final statement should be short and sweet: short to listen to and sweet to remember. If you refer to an earlier statement and apply it to your audience you can strike a satisfying note with your audience. Also, it lends a quality of well-roundedness and unity to your speech. Memorable final statements should leave the audience in a reflective mood with a definite positive feeling that you were worth listening to.

Step 9: Worksheet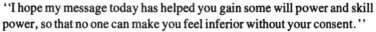

- ☐ Should your final statement tie in with remarks made in your introduction, or should it be a brand-new statement?
- ☐ Will you use a quotation, poem, familiar saying, question, or your own personal words as your final statement?
- ☐ Write it in your conclusion (page 29) at the sign of the happy speaker.

Congratulations. You have prepared an outline using the nine train-of-thought steps. Relax and reward yourself. Then go to the following section, which will help you to revise your train-of-thought outline carefully yet quickly.

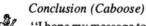

REVISING YOUR TRAIN-OF-THOUGHT OUTLINE

Now that you have worked out your outline, it is time to read through it two or three times. Test your train-of-thought by asking yourself these questions:

1. *Does each step contain sentences, not just single words or short phrases?* Instead of using cryptic words scattered here and there, develop sentences to express a whole idea. Single words and phrases are often too brief and they can be misleading because they suggest that an idea has been formulated when often only parts of the idea have been sketched.

2. *Do you like each part of your outline?* If something feels wrong, continue to search for the right angle, the exact information to satisfy yourself. If something looks dull on paper it is almost guaranteed to get duller as you practice it aloud. Why bore yourself? If you can't remedy the weak spot immediately, be patient as you search for relevant and lively anecdotes, stories, and facts. Ask friendly critics. Get help!

3. *Do your ideas fit together* in a way that allows your audience to follow your train-of-thought easily?

4. *Is your outline unified?* Do main-point boxcars fit together logically in an obvious organizational pattern? Does each boxcar add significantly to the train-of-thought, or is it excess baggage? If it could be eliminated without harming your central thought, you might consider discarding it.

5. *Is your outline coherent?* Are your connectors strong? Do they use the right words to show the proper relationships between your points? Make sure that each transition accomplishes the purpose you want it to.

6. *Does your outline have the emphasis in the right place?* Do you have one main-point boxcar overloaded with subpoint cargo while others are nearly empty? Balance your points by making sure you talk about important ideas longest and, unless an organizational pattern dictates otherwise, that your strongest points are both first and last in your discussion.

7. *Can you identify memorable parts of your speech?* Read your outline aloud several times. If possible, record your outline on a tape recorder and listen to the playback. It gives you an opportunity to discover the rough spots, to eliminate the irrelevant words, the meaningless facts, and false reasoning, as well as to note the memorable parts.

8. *Is your outline a mess?* Don't crowd. See good example pages 213–214.

A good way to test the logical progression of your train-of-thought is to answer each point in your outline by pretending that *you* are the audience. Your ''dialogue'' with your outline might go something like this for an introduction (engine):

□ *Attention-Getter:* "Eleanor Roosevelt said, 'No one can make you feel inferior without your consent.' "

   You, answering as your audience might say: "Sounds good, but I'm not sure—how do I give people my consent?"

□ *Appeal:* "So you remain silent and resentful when someone calls you 'too sensitive' or 'too pushy' or 'too insecure'? Or does your silence turn to aggressive name-calling: 'How can you be such a male chauvinist bully?' "

   You, answering as your audience might: "Yes! What can assertiveness training do for me? How can I change?"

□ *Central Thought:* "The whole purpose of assertiveness training is to help you gain the willpower and the skill-power so that you neither put down yourself nor put down others."

Continue responding to the key points on your outline as you think your audience would. Imagine your audience's response to your ideas.

At this point you must decide whether you will use your newly revised outline as a springboard for practicing your speech, or whether you will delay practicing until you have written a full draft of your speech and outlined the draft, and use that as your springboard for practicing. Decide how to proceed: should you take the route for easy speeches or the longer route for harder speeches? An explanation of these two routes on page 4 will help you decide wisely. After deciding your route from here on, return to the following discussion of visual aids. Because visuals often take time to produce, it is important to arrange for them early and avoid a last minute rush that will upset both you and your graphic artist.

DRAMATIZING YOUR TRAIN-OF-THOUGHT

Decide on Visual Aids Soon

Whichever preparation route you take from here on, now is the time to start thinking about visual aids. If some need to be made, get the process started now so you have them for your practice sessions. Visuals can add interest and vitality to your talk, but unless they are thoroughly professional and gracefully handled, you are better off without them. Do not rely on them as a crutch to communicate your message. That's *your* job and there isn't a visual aid in the world that can replace a clear, concise message from you.

Importance of Visual Aids

We have a brain that can absorb more information by sight than it can by hearing. Although in America we speak about 125 words per minute conversationally and 100 words per minute before an audience, it is known that audiences can think at a rate of four or five hundred words a minute. The difference between speech speed and thought speed presents a problem, namely how to keep an audience interested. A good, attractive visual aid will help the audience stay with you. Because a good visual aid will help listeners focus on something relevant while your words catch up with their thinking, they will have less opportunity to daydream.

Kinds of Visual Aids

Briefly, visual aids can be classified as

- □ *Diagrams:* bar charts, organizational charts, pie charts, maps, outlines, and schematics, which you can put on posterboard flip charts or handouts, draw on the blackboard, or project via a slide or overhead projector.
- □ *Illustrations:* photographs, drawings, graphics, which you can also present via posterboard, flip charts, handouts, blackboard, or slide or overhead projector.
- □ *Three-dimensionals:* objects, models (a skeleton, molecular model, etc.).
- □ *Audio aids:* tape recordings, records.

A Caution about Visual Aids

In order for these visuals to work well, they must help *illustrate* your point. They should never be used to make the point alone. A friend told me about his football coach, who wanted to prove to the team that alcohol was harmful. He took two worms and dropped one in a bottle of water and the other into a bottle of beer. The watered worm just swam lazily, apparently having a great time. The other worm dropped into the beer bottle, writhed in pain, and dropped dead quickly. "You see," said the coach, "actions speak louder than my words." "I see what you mean," offered the biggest guzzler on the team. "If we drink beer, we won't get worms!"

The story illustrates important advice: Don't take for granted that your visual aid says exactly what you want it to. Sometimes your audience will draw its own false conclusions about a visual aid's message. Actions do not always speak louder than words; you still must emphasize the point a visual illustrates.

Presenting Your Visual Aids

The best way to present yourself and your own visual aids is to clean up the debris of the last speaker. Clutter distracts an audience. Erase blackboards, discard old coffee cups and used water glasses, empty dirtied ashtrays, and rearrange chairs. Adjust backdrops and draw shades so that glare does not blind your audience.

Secondly, remember that visual aids are tricky, and beginners should never use them without practicing with them several times. Although you may have scribbled on a blackboard in your youth, shown home slides and films, and created school posters with felt pens, you will discover that "going public" with your homey skills presents some new challenges.

OBJECTS OR MODELS

Particularly if you are demonstrating the use of an object, you should practice with that object several times. Even though you have used a camera a thousand times, you will need to display it, which means holding it up and away from your body. Be careful not to cover the whole object with your hands. Also, do not use objects unless they are big enough for the entire audience to see. It helps if the object can be passed around in a small audience.

SLIDES AND TRANSPARENCIES

These visual aids are very useful if you are describing the way something functions, such as a form of government, an industrial plant, or a university. Complicated processes that require a long series of actions, such as a scientific experiment or the workings of a computer, can be clarified with simple, darkly drawn or printed slides or transparencies. So, the best use for slides are cartoons, scenery, scientific objects, or works of art. Make sure that slides and transparencies *are* simple: few words, large diagrams, dark lines, lots of white space. Spend money for the work of professional graphic artists (consult the Yellow Pages). Big audiences cannot see typed slides easily, and they are boring; instead of helping you, they become irritants for your audience.

If you do use slides, make sure you have practiced with them. Know what button does what. Mark your notes "Slide on" and "Slide off." It's exacting work. Sometimes you need blank cardboards between slides so that the old slide isn't on while you go on to another point. If an assistant will be changing slides, provide the person with a copy of your text with indications for on and off, or agree on a verbal signal. Stay calm if the slide gets jammed. Ask for help. "Please unjam the slide," not "Oh, dear, I knew I shouldn't have relied on mechanical machines!"

Transparencies can be very useful in presenting organizational hierarchies, pie drawings, charts, and maps. Like slides, they can be professionally done to include several colors. An overhead projector that uses "transparencies" (clear plastic sheets) has a few advantages over slides: (1) the new machines are silent; (2) they don't get jammed; (3) transparencies are generally cheaper to have made; (4) they are flexible; either prepare them before your lecture or write on them as you lecture; (5) you can make them yourself; and (6) you have direct control when showing them and don't need to rely on an assistant.

FILMS

Films can be helpful if they present useful and appropriate information in a unique way. The film should enhance or help prove your main point, or it should stimulate questions. Never use a film without viewing it and timing it. The hassle of ordering the film, worrying about its arriving on time, and securing a workable projector and competent assistant has to be worth your bother and the money.

HANDOUTS

The fact of the matter is that handouts can help your communication—or they can hinder it. Are they vital for helping your audience understand your presentation? If they are necessary, work them out carefully. Use few words and plenty of white space, so that ideas stand out vividly.

Handouts are often useful in the following situations:

□ Workshops when you want people to use the handouts as a workbook
□ Lectures when you need to diagram a complicated process or present formulas and want students to listen without constant note taking
□ Times when no slide projector, Viewmaster, flip chart, or blackboard is available.

Follow some simple rules with handouts. For instance, if you are giving a workshop, then a booklet can be very useful, but keep it simple. Five or six pages will not overwhelm an audience meeting all day, but several pages can confuse an audience listening to you for only a half-hour presentation. To refer to it easily, print the booklet pages on different colored papers. Audiences can flip to the yellow page a lot faster than they can find page 4.

An outline helps an audience follow a complicated lecture more easily. Also, the handout will allow students to look at you most of the time instead of frantically taking notes. Believe it or not, it is far less distracting to have people look at you than it is to have people staring at their notes, but proof-read your handouts accurately or you'll have distracting explanations to make.

Finally, you may want to prepare handouts if you can't be sure of the equipment. For instance, some places, such as summer camps, winter retreats, churches, and conventions are notorious for their broken-down slide projectors and burnt-out bulbs. On the other hand, industries and schools are generally reliable. The rule of thumb is: If a handout is crucial to understanding, make it available. Don't rely solely on equipment for presenting the same critical material. If you do rely on equipment and it fails, you have set yourself up for a colossal case of nerves.

Besides deciding what should go on a handout (less is more—don't crowd information), decide exactly when a handout should be introduced: before, during, or after a speech? Timing depends on two things: (1) when is it going to be needed? and (2) When will its distribution be least distracting? Obviously, workshop booklets and lecture outlines should be passed out as people come in the door, or else they can be placed on seats before the audience arrives (this is the least distracting). On the other hand, when your handout contains information you do not want your audience to see before you come to it in your speech, you must delay distribution. During a break is a good time to distribute handouts that aren't necessary until the second half of your presentation. That way the audience won't be peeking through the handout while you are speaking about different points.

Handout information is not that surprising or earthshaking that you will want to disrupt the flow of your speech with assistants distributing them. There may be a few exceptions: when you are asking people to donate money, give blood, sign petitions, or the like. In these cases, it is better to provide the necessary handout after you have persuaded them—at the end of your speech or as people leave the room. Also, handouts containing bibliographies or addresses, that is, information that is not critical to the understanding of the speech itself but is useful supplemental information, should be given people as they leave.

Handouts are expensive, usually from three to ten cents per page. Ask yourself, Does my audience absolutely need the information in handout form? Why? When?

BLACKBOARDS OR FLIP CHARTS
These tools are good, but you shouldn't rely on them either. Check on their availability, and if you decide to use them, come prepared with your own chalk, eraser, and felt pens. Blackboards and flip charts are best when you want to:

□ Illustrate ideas with cartoons
□ List audience responses
□ Write one-word reminders
□ Work out mathematical or chemical formulas and technical terms
□ Make a pie drawing with slices indicating the percentage of the whole

In other words, use blackboards and flip charts for emphasis, not for developing complicated ideas (even mathematical equations and scientific formulas should be stated in a more permanent fashion in a book or on a handout). Blackboards and flip charts are effective for small conference groups, not in auditoriums.

Checklist for Visual Aids

□ On your outline, indicate now which visual you will use and when you will use it. (On your final note, mark "Slide 1 on" and "Slide 1 off," and so forth, in the margins.
□ Clean up your predecessor's visual aids before you put up your own.
□ Use one if (a) it is necessary in order to clarify an idea; (b) it is not distracting to your audience; and (c) you also state the point the visual is making.
□ Diagrams and illustrations must be simple, big, and bold so that everyone can see them easily.
□ Draw all but the very simplest diagrams and illustrations on the blackboard or flip chart *before* your speech.

- ☐ Invest in your own chalk, eraser, or felt pens as emergency backups.

- ☐ Show the visual aid *only* when you are making the same point it does. (Keep blackboards and flip charts covered when not in use.)

- ☐ Point with the hand that is *closest* to the blackboard, flip chart, or screen. Use a pointer so that you won't hide information.

- ☐ Stand to the side of the screen as you refer to it with your hand or pointer.

- ☐ Look at the visual aid only when you first refer to it. Don't keep staring at the screen or object and don't keep an arm rigidly pointing.

- ☐ Turn off the visual when it is not needed (use blank cards between slides if you wish to keep the machine on without a picture).

- ☐ Practice several times with your visual aids. (Practice Session 4 in chapter 11 suggests when to practice with visual aids.)

- ☐ Double-check with your host about all equipment, and arrive thirty minutes early to check out its working condition.

SUMMARY

When you are satisfied with your final outline and your choice and placement of visual aids, you will be finished with Part I of this book, ''Get Your Speech on Track: Prepare Your Topic.'' You will be ready to start Part II, ''Get Yourself on Track: Prepare Your Delivery.'' You will soon start a practical desensitization technique for reducing your anxiety. Then, as soon as you can, put into practice some of the useful memory techniques explained in chapter 9. In order to look forward to speaking with ease, take a couple of days (or whatever time schedule fits your needs) to read chapters 8 and 9, and put those practical suggestions to work for you before you start practicing your train-of-thought. In chapters 10 and 11 you will learn how to develop your confidence and polish your style through a systematic practice program. In chapter 12 you'll learn how to bolster your confidence during the last week before you speak.

GET
YOURSELF
ON TRACK:
PREPARE
YOUR DELIVERY

8

Imagine
Speaking
With Ease

HOW YOU CAN DESENSITIZE YOURSELF TO ANXIETY

By now you have prepared your final outline and decided on visual aids, and yet you may be overwhelmed with the thought of having to deliver it. You are sure that your mouth will go dry and your stomach will flutter with butterflies. Your situation is much like that of inexperienced actors who, although they have their lines memorized, still have opening-night jitters. What can be done to control the anxiety you might expect as you speak to an audience? In *Asserting Yourself* I present techniques useful in helping people speak up for their rights.[1] One of these techniques, systematic desensitization,[2] can be used to relieve anxiety before, during, and after a stressful situation, whether it is speaking up assertively, giving a speech, or making a point in a meeting.

You can understand the desensitization procedure by comparing it to the way you get used to hot water in a shower or bathtub. Few people can tolerate jumping into an extremely hot shower. Rather, they enter a warm shower, then make it progressively hotter. Just think of an intensely stressful situation as though it were analogous to extremely hot water. To learn to tolerate intense stress, you begin by exposing yourself to a very mild stress; then once you are accustomed to that, you move up to a slightly greater stress, much as you would increase the hotness of your shower; and then you keep repeating this cycle of habituate-then-advance up the scale.

In using systematic desensitization, you carry out this exposure to stress through *imagining* a series of mildly stressful scenes while relaxing your muscles. First, you make up an "anxiety hierarchy," a series of scenes that progressively resemble or that come progressively closer to the fearful situation in which you're giving your speech. To construct an anxiety hierarchy for your problem scene (the one in which you are to give a speech), consider that situation as the highest point on a "fear thermometer." Label the fear it arouses as 100 degrees. Then, starting from that 100-degree fear situation, alter or remove various elements from the imaginary fear situation in order to create scenes that produce progressively less fear—one scene that registers 90 on your fear thermometer, one that registers 80, and so on down the scale to zero. The low-scoring scenes should be ones that are remote in time from the speaking event.

To illustrate a fear hierarchy, the following scenes are used in a course I developed on control of speaking anxiety. This series of scenes is used by students in desensitizing themselves to their first class speech, which is videotaped. They start by visualizing the least frightening scene first—the 0 degree scene—which is sitting at home reading a book. Read *up* the thermometer.

These steps represent events that cause most speech-anxious students to become progressively more nervous just thinking about them. Students are encouraged to practice the Progressive Relaxation Exercise (see pp. 202–204) five or six times before they begin to desensitize themselves to one scene after another in this

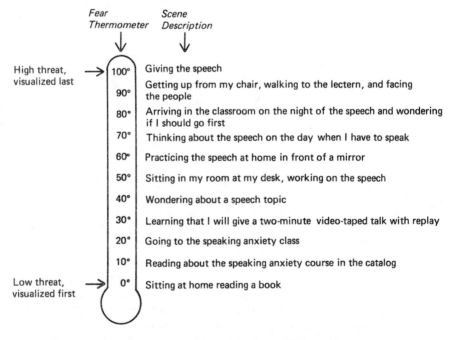

Example of a scene hierarchy for public speaking.

speech-fear hierarchy. You can use the hierarchy to try out the desensitization procedure. Briefly, you would use it this way:

- First, relax thoroughly.
- Next, close your eyes and imagine for ten to twenty seconds the *lowest*-threat scene (relaxing at home).
- Stop imagining that scene, relax for fifteen seconds or more and allow your muscles to let go.
- Next, move up to imagining the next scene in the hierarchy, seeing and feeling yourself in it for ten to twenty seconds.

If you experience much tension with any image as you visualize a scene, then practice seeing your *last* scene again. Advance to the next scene only after you have eliminated *all* tension provoked by the current scene. Work on only two or three scenes of the hierarchy each day if they are causing tension, repeating steps each day as you move up the complete hierarchy while remaining relaxed. Eventually, you should be able to imagine yourself in what was formerly your most terrifying scene (100 degree scene) while remaining relaxed, without fear. By that time, your fear when thinking of those scenes will have been overlaid and replaced by deep relaxation. That is what systematic desensitization is all about.

Build a Hierarchy for Your Own Speaking Situation

It is easy and fun to work out your own fear hierarchy, which should briefly describe the scenes you will live through before you give your speech. Keep in mind some suggestions for making your own hierarchy.

- First, improve your memory for details in a scene. Practice noticing and remembering the shapes and colors of things: the weight, texture, sound, taste, and smell of things. Attending to details will help you sharpen your senses by observing a scene, closing your eyes, recalling details, checking out missing parts, then closing your eyes a second time to retest your memory of details. Such exercises teach you to concentrate and to discriminate features of your world. These abilities are useful in describing and picturing vivid scenes for your hierarchy.
- Avoid vague memories of a setting, such as: "The room is large and dark. It probably seats many people." Instead, attend to detail for the development of strong, impression-making scenes: "The room is an auditorium painted medium gray. It has high windows draped in black. The podium is set on a sixty-by-twenty-foot stage elevated six feet above the audience. The curtain in back of the podium is black velvet. The audience sits in folding chairs that

accommodate 150 to 200 people. Lights are bright on the stage but dim on the audience.''

☐ Choose scenes that allow you to take on small degrees of fear, say 10 degrees, not 20 or 30 degrees. In the earlier ''thermometer'' example, if the scene where you are sitting at a desk preparing a speech had been eliminated, it would be necessary to make a grand leap in imagination from wondering about a topic to practicing a speech. Most people would get too nervous imagining themselves practicing a speech before they had seen themselves prepare it. If you get very nervous when visualizing a particular scene, develop an additional scene with fewer degrees of fear to help you move easily from one scene to a more anxious one.

☐ Make the scenes realistic; that is, they should be similar to or, better yet, represent actual experiences you have had or threatening speaking situations you can imagine you might have to face in the future.

☐ Insert a lot of concrete detail so that you can easily picture the mildly anxiety-producing scenes. For instance, it is important to be able to picture yourself wondering about your speech in a particular place, such as at the breakfast table. This makes it easier for you to see yourself doing those tasks in your imagination.

☐ Try to include a broad sample from an array of situations in which the fear might operate. Usually eight to fifteen items are adequate for most people who are nervous about their performance.

☐ See yourself performing successfully in each scene.

Systematically planning how you will approach a threatening situation is a useful skill, whether you are dreading the thought of ten guests for your first big dinner party, nervously anticipating the arrival of a new baby, or reluctantly thinking about the introduction you have to make at your club next week. Did you know that people who systematically think about their successful approach to a performance are more likely to perform effectively than those who do not imagine themselves succeeding? So, you should look forward to speaking with ease by planning and rehearsing the scenes that will help you attain your goal successfully, and see how it bolsters your courage!

Try your hand at preparing scenes that can help you cope imaginatively. Plan a hierarchy of scenes for your very next speech. Use this worksheet to help you develop a hierarchy right now, when the idea is fresh in your mind. Use page 108 as a guiding example.

Use Your Hierarchy to Reduce Anxiety

After you've constructed your hierarchy, memorize the sequence of scenes. One way to remember the sequence is to name the scenes on a tape recorder. Some people report difficulty imagining vividly because their mind wanders and fills with intrud-

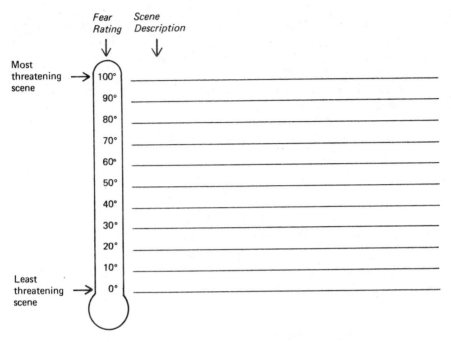

	Fear Rating ↓	Scene Description ↓

Most threatening scene → 100°

90°

80°

70°

60°

50°

40°

30°

20°

10°

Least threatening scene → 0°

Constructing your own scene hierarchy for public speaking.

ing thoughts. If this is a problem for you, you can focus attention on a scene and increase its vividness by forcing yourself to describe aloud and tape-record the scene as it unfolds in your imagination in all its concrete particulars.[3] If you do not use a tape recorder, simply picture your scenes one by one. Some people find it helps their concentration to describe each scene silently as they are picturing it in their imaginations.

The next task is to choose a "comfort zone," a scene or place where you can go in your imagination and that is free of stress and anxiety for you. You could choose a beach, a quiet forest, a flower garden, or an easy chair. Make it relaxing. Put yourself there in your imagination. Decide on your own personal comfort zone. You'll use the comfort zone when you practice the desensitization procedure.

It is usually worthwhile to practice the progressive relaxation exercise in Appendix 1 before each desensitization session. If you're already had some relaxation training, you can dispense with the full 30 minutes of relaxation and begin imagining your first scene after only a few minutes of relaxing; however, beginners do the entire relaxation exercise before they practice desensitization, so they can imagine themselves speaking with ease more easily than they might if they were physically tense to begin with.

The objective during the desensitization process is to remain relaxed while visualizing, one by one, the increasingly threatening scenes in your hierarchy. The remarkable fact is that desensitizing yourself to a threatening speaking scene in your imagination carries over and allows you to remain calmer when you enter the real-life scene. Take only two or three scenes in any one session. Here is how your first session would go. When you are relaxed with your eyes closed, proceed as follows:

1. Picture scene 1 for ten to twenty seconds while remaining relaxed. Vividly see yourself in the scene and transport yourself into the scene by responding to the sights, sounds, odors, and touches of a scene. Don't worry if you can't feel yourself into the part the first few times you try it. The more you visualize the detail, the more you will achieve the feeling of actually being there and living the scene actively. Remain deeply relaxed as you visualize the scene for about ten to twenty seconds.

2. Now stop visualizing scene 1 and immediately place yourself into your "comfort zone," retreat into the familiar, relaxing, and comfortable place in your imagination that means security and peace for you. Return to this pleasantly relaxing scene after each visualization of a scene in your hierarchy. The objective at this step is to allow your muscles to relax and recuperate after imagining the previous scary scene. Take your time relaxing in your comfort zone; you can go on for as long as a minute.

3. Then picture scene 2 for ten to twenty seconds while remaining relaxed. If you feel any tension at scene 2 (or any other scene), stop the scene. Return to your comfort zone for a minute and then see the difficult scene again. Only when you feel no tension should you proceed to the next scene.

4. Now turn off scene 2 and return to your comfort zone in your imagination. Continue the procedure with successive scenes, always relaxing during the visualization when you are picturing your comfort zone. The first time practice seeing *only two or three scenes* and work for no more than about ten minutes. Always stop before you are tired, bored, or feeling tense. The next time start visualizing again your 0 degree scene and picture each scene in succession, adding a few scenes each session.

Desensitization requires that you be more than a spectator of your pictures; rather you should pour yourself into your role, feel yourself moving and speaking as though you were living the real scene. Close your eyes and visualize each specific scene in as vivid detail as possible. If you have difficulty visualizing details, check out the real scene. For instance, if you want to improve your ability to visualize your kitchen, go there and examine it carefully—see the clock on the wall, the stove, the cupboards, and so forth. Notice the lights, the smells, the textures, the sounds around you. Now close your eyes and see and sense the details of that scene in memory. Open your eyes and check your memory for what you missed. Close your eyes again and include the missed items in your altered image. The more detail you can see, the more vivid will be your memory of the scene and the more easily you can experience and feel the scene in your imagination. A good memory that is rich in detail is useful in the desensitization procedure.

As you see these scenes in your imagination, identify which muscles become tense; learn to relax them as you imagine a stressful scene. You will know you have achieved success when you can think about a former scene without feeling anxious and upset. Because you cannot be nervous and relaxed at the same time, you will be replacing nervousness with relaxation. If you can rehearse your imaginal hierarchy several times while remaining relaxed and fearless, you will be ready to speak to your audience with greater confidence.

Use the Desensitization Technique for Other Speaking Situations

You can also use desensitization to reduce upsets from a variety of everyday speaking situations. Instead of building toward a single performance, you can list a number of speaking situations that threaten or frighten you. Rank these items by the degree of discomfort they cause you. For example, how do you rank the following eleven scenes? (Use 1 for most scary, down to 11 for least.)

Rank Order
___ Talking to a close friend about my vacation
___ Introducing one person to another
___ Making a toast at Thanksgiving dinner
___ Telling two or more friends about a vacation
___ Explaining a job to two or more friends
___ Giving directions to a stranger
___ Introducing a guest speaker at a club
___ Explaining a job to a new employee
___ Presenting a description of our division's work and defending our progress record at monthly staff meetings
___ Leading a meeting
___ Being interviewed for a job

On a separate page, list several different situations that evoke a range of anxious speaking scenes for you. Assign to each one a fear rating from 0 to 100 degrees and arrange the scenes in order. Next carry out the desensitization procedure with your hierarchy, starting with the low-fear scenes. Start easy—with one toe in the warm water, so to speak—and work your way up in relaxed fashion to more anxious scenes. The idea here is to use desensitization to reduce the fear you might experience in a variety of settings requiring you to speak. That is, you imagine yourself acting and reacting positively in various speaking situations, confident that you will have less fear when you actually speak in those situations.

Psychologists believe that people's performance depends in part on their conviction that they can perform the action successfully.[4] That is, a firm expectation that you can carry off some task masterfully is a major determinant of whether you will start it or persist at it. Many experiences influence our expectations of being able to do something, such as seeing others perform successfully or actually having performed successfully ourselves before. In summary, the desensitization procedure suggests that we imagine ourselves performing the target behaviors successfully a number of times; the net result of those mental rehearsals of mastery is to build up expectations of mastery at the actual performances.

USE POSITIVE THOUGHTS TO HELP YOU SUCCEED

Desensitization is a procedure to prepare yourself for a stress situation when you know in advance that it's coming up. However, most everyone wants a second "crutch," in order to allay any fears that might arise when they actually confront the stressful situation. They want to know if there is some antifear, coping strategy to use when the unexpected happens as they are speaking. The best thing to do is to learn how to control your thoughts so that they don't stampede your emotions into an exaggerated anxiety attack.

But how can you control your irrational thoughts? Let's equate your thoughts with the sentences you silently say to yourself. Emotions are partly controlled by a conscious interpretation of what is happening around us or to us (see figure, page 7). You can feed new information into the interpretive process by the sentences you say to yourself. Thus you can control your fearful thoughts when you are speaking to others by silently saying to yourself a stream of fear-reducing statements. Some silent statements might be: "Relax; take several deep breaths; keep calm; this is really a minor matter in the grand design of the universe; this will pass; keep cool; this audience can't hurt you; relax, it'll be over soon." The method requires that you make up your own stress-coping remarks, memorize them, and recite them feelingly as an internal monologue whenever you enter any stressful situation. Time spent tuning in to your coping thoughts will pay off with less fear and better performance.

Remember, what you say about a situation determines how you feel about yourself. If you feel a little tense, tell yourself it's okay because you know that you are coming alive, feeling energetic and eager to speak. This is how you can use your new arousal sensations for your benefit. Compare the following maladaptive self-statements on the left with the positive substitutes on the right. Learn to fight your negative thoughts with honest, positive substitutes!

Self-Defeating Negative Thoughts	*Encouraging Positive Thoughts*
While Preparing a Speech	
"I've got too many bits and pieces of information that will never make sense."	"If I proceed slowly and pile 'like information in like piles,' I'll start to see a pattern."

Self-Defeating Negative Thoughts	*Encouraging Positive Thoughts*
"I should have all the answers but I don't."	"No audience is that unreasonable. I'm well-prepared and I'll give them what I have."
"I have to prepare the perfect speech."	"There is no perfect speech. Even excellent speeches can be improved."
"If my ideas don't convince everyone, then that proves I have a bad speech."	"It is likely that some people hold very different beliefs, and it is unreasonable to think that one speech can change their minds. I will simply present my point of view calmly."

While Approaching the Day of Speech

"I can't make a mistake because it'll spoil my speech."	"Everyone makes mistakes. Admit it, and go on. One mistake cannot spoil an entire speech."
"If I forget, I'll fall apart and be humiliated."	"It is in the nature of people to forget. Ask for help and get on with it. Treat it as a human error, not some catastrophic unnatural happening."

While Practicing the Speech

"What if my listeners are bored with my topic and fall asleep?"	"Some listeners may not be as interested as others, but I'll do my best. Some people are just plain tired."
"My speech isn't 'meaty' enough."	"They want clarity and brevity. I can go into detail if necessary."
"I'll never be able to speak from notes."	"Practice one chunk at a time. Repeat it in slightly different language. Have fun."

While Speaking to the Audience

"I'm not sure what to say next. Where am I? Help!"	"Stay with the present. A few seconds of silence is okay. Look at your notes."
"I'm nervous."	"I'm prepared. Just keep going with one idea at a time and the edginess will pass."
"I don't think they are responding. They don't like me."	"Some people have behavioral listening deficits. I can't be loved by everyone. People have different tastes."
"Why is that person leaving? He must think I'm a bore."	"He may have another appointment; too bad. He'll miss a good speech."

After Speaking

"People didn't clap enough. They didn't like me."	"Different audiences have different habits. Some clap louder than others."

Self-Defeating Negative Thoughts	*Encouraging Positive Thoughts*
''Maybe they identify me with the bad news I presented. Maybe thay blame me for it.''	''Maybe, but they're grown people and they will recognize my role.''
''It didn't turn out as well as it should have.''	''I did as well as I could under the circumstances. It turned out better than it might have.''
''It wasn't worth it. It took too much out of me.''	''Every experience puts something *into* me. The next speech will be easier.''
''I could have done it better if my boss (husband, wife, coach, etc.) hadn't been there evaluating every word I said.''	''Maybe, but I'm learning better how to come through under pressure and next time I'll be better.''
''I didn't give the speech I prepared.''	''Speeches rarely turn out exactly as planned, but the one I prepared helped me with the one I gave.''

Experiments show that coping self-statements like the following lists can be used as a general stress immunization. Thus one advantage of self-control statements over desensitization is their generality. Whereas you might use a particular scene hierarchy to help you approach a specific speech, you can use your coping statements for a range of stressful situations. In particular, you can use self-calming remarks when you encounter unexpected or novel stresses.

Examine the four classes of self-statements that follow. The first class, preparing for a stressful situation, contains statements said to yourself (with meaningful emphasis and genuine feeling) as you anticipate a stressful confrontation. (Of course, some stresses, such as accidents, fires, or attacks, arise unexpectedly and you don't have time to prepare.) The second class of self-statements, confronting and handling the stressful situation, contains statements to be used when the situation actually arises. These keep you oriented to the task at hand, concentrating on the problem to be solved rather than on your inadequacies. The third class contains self-statements to help you cope with the feeling of being overwhelmed. Saying these statements silently helps you control anxiety during the confrontation. Reinforcing statements, the fourth class, are used to reward yourself for coping successfully just *after* a stressful confrontation. It is important that you deliberately reward yourself for coping with situations where formerly you went to pieces. Chances are that you will be less likely to fall apart in the future if you reward yourself for present successes.

EXAMPLES OF COPING SELF-STATEMENTS[5]

Category 1. Preparing for a Stressful Situation

- ☐ What is it I have to do?
- ☐ I can develop a plan to deal with it.
- ☐ Just think about what I can do about it. That's better than getting anxious.

- □ No negative self-statements, just think rationally.
- □ Don't worry. Worry won't help anything.
- □ Maybe what I think is anxiety is eagerness to confront it.

Category 2. Confronting and Handling a Stressful Situation

- □ I can meet this challenge.
- □ One step at a time; I can handle the situation.
- □ Don't think about fear—just about what I have to do. Stay relevant.
- □ This anxiety is what they said I would feel. It's a reminder to use my coping exercises.
- □ This tenseness can be an ally, a cue to cope.
- □ Relax; I'm in control. Take a slow, deep breath. Ah, good.

Category 3. Coping with the Feeling of Being Overwhelmed

- □ When fear comes, just pause.
- □ Keep my focus on the present; what is it I have to do?
- □ Let me label my fear from 0 to 10 and watch it change.
- □ I was supposed to expect my fear to rise.
- □ Don't try to eliminate fear totally; just keep it manageable.
- □ I can convince myself to do it. I can reason my fear away.
- □ It will be over shortly.
- □ It's not the worst thing that can happen.
- □ Just think about something else.
- □ Do something that will prevent me from thinking about fear.
- □ Just describe what is around me. That way I won't think about worrying.

Category 4. Reinforcing Self-statements

- □ It worked; I was able to do it.
- □ Wait until I tell my buddy about this.
- □ It wasn't as bad as I expected.
- □ I made more out of the fear than it was worth.
- □ My damn ideas—that's the problem. When I control them, I control my fear.
- □ It's getting better each time I use the procedures.
- □ I'm really pleased with the progress I'm making.
- □ I did it!

The preceding self-statements are simply suggestions as to how you can make up your own positive list. I suggest that you try this as an exercise right now. You know better than anyone else what calming self-statements will help you when you are feeling anxious. Change the self-statements to suit your speaking situation and reword them in meaningful personal phrases. As you write your positive self-statements, group them into the four categories shown below. Aim for at least four statements in each category.

MY COPING SENTENCES TO REDUCE STRESS IN SPEAKING SITUATIONS

Category 1. *Preparing for a stressful speech situation*

_____

_____

_____

_____

_____

_____

_____

Category 2. *Confronting and handling a stressful speech situation*

_____

_____

_____

_____

_____

_____

Category 3. *Coping with the feeling of being overwhelmed as I am speaking.*

_____

_____

_____

_____

_____

_____

_____

Category 4. *Reinforcing self-statements when I'm finished speaking.*

_____

_____

_____

_____

_____

_____

_____

Fine. Now study this list until you can smoothly recite each category of self-statements. Put each category on separate note cards and repeat them with conviction several times. Your aim is to become so proficient at reciting these that, as you prepare and give a speech, you can silently and swiftly run over them with only 40 percent of your attention.

Once you memorize and rehearse these self-statements, you can more easily use them automatically in any stressful situation. When rehearsing your speech, use category 1 self-statements (preparing). As you approach the actual speaking performance, repeat the silent monologue using the self-statements in category 2 (confronting). Use category 3 statements (coping) immediately before and during delivery of your message. When the speech is over, use the self-reward statements from category 4 (reinforcing).

It is a good idea to refresh your coping-statement list periodically, deleting old or adding new statements. Keep them available on small cards in your purse or billfold. Use your list flexibly, dropping out whatever statements don't fit the occasion. As you say your silent statements, remember to invest them with emotional significance; don't let the monologue become a superficial recital without emphasis or meaning. Like a good actor or actress, try to sustain a deep emotional impact in your monologue, despite reciting the lines hundreds of times.

SUMMARY

Giving yourself positive information is one of the most valuable ways to control your speaking anxiety. This chapter has introduced you to three practical skills: progressive relaxation, desensitization, and positive self-talk. Moreover, the skills can be used in many different contexts—in studying, in thinking creatively, in negotiating a contract, in a musical performance, in interviewing for a job, in carrying out some complex procedure (learning to drive), and in asserting yourself in conflictive situations. Your relaxed body, positive mental pictures, and silent sentences can tell you what to do and how to feel in such situations. They represent a simple but powerful way to deal more effectively with stress.

9

Remember
Your
Train-of-Thought

Many people believe that if they are just interested enough in their subject, they will remember automatically what they want to say and can deliver it with punch and flair. Alas, this is simply false, and there are no such simple panaceas for success in public speaking. While interest in your topic helps you convey enthusiasm, that intensity will be off target unless you harness it to two skills—skill in *remembering* your speech and skill in *communicating* your ideas in an intelligent and winning way. Happily, these two skills are learnable. This chapter will work on the first skill, suggesting ways to remember your ideas. The next chapter gives pointers on communicating these ideas effectively by carefully practicing.

How can you remember your speech? A lot depends on the way you've composed the speech. The speeches easiest to remember are those that are composed of your own experiences or arguments, developed in a logical sequence familiar to you. The inner logic and familiar direction of our experiences causes the speech to flow along effortlessly. However, few speeches we deliver concern such familiar, personal material. Rather, we must think of a number of unfamiliar points and arrange them into some organization, each point supported with facts, statistics, examples, and other supporting material. The idea is to develop your points logically, so that the end of one point flows into the beginning of the next by a coherent transition. But even the most organized and logically coherent speech is still hard to remember, since so much supporting material must be recalled. Some basic principles of memory will help you learn your speech more quickly.

PRINCIPLES OF MEMORY

You can remember three main principles of memory by associating them with OAR, a tool to help you steer your learning:

Observe accurately to impress it on your memory in the first place.

Associate the impression with a known observation.

Repeat the impression in a sensible manner.

Programmed practice sessions (chapters 10 and 11) put the powerful OAR memory principles to work for you, so that you learn your train-of-thought easier and better. Here's what the OAR principles mean:

Observe!

First, you must observe accurately, concentrating on your outline and notes with intense attention. When you practice your speech, be sure that you re-create the meaning of the words rather than just idly glancing over your outline without deep thought. One way some people force attention to the words is to underline key words on their outline.

Associate!

People remember a new fact most easily by associating it with another, familiar one. Try to connect the new fact to things you already know. See if it reminds you of something; if so, use those connections to memorize the new fact. Thus, you remember a person's name by thinking of other people you know with that same name and associating those known people in your mind with the new person. Moreover, to remember a fact more easily, think about that fact in many different ways many times. People with good memories have thought over their facts and experiences many times and woven them into meaningful relationships with facts and experiences they already know. In this chapter you will be introduced to techniques for associating one idea with another systematically, so that each fact or idea in your speech reminds you of the next idea. In chapter 9, you will learn how to associate pictures with ideas in order to remember faster and better.

Repeat!

Third, repetition helps us remember if it is done sensibly. First, concentrate upon the meaning of the words by repeating them aloud rather than silently. Abraham Lincoln had the habit of reading the newspaper aloud; when asked why, he explained: "When I read aloud, two senses catch the idea: first, I see what I read; second, I hear it, and therefore can remember it better.'' Take Lincoln's advice: Express your ideas aloud several times to help impress it on your memory.

Many memory experiments have found that deliberate repetition distributed over many sessions leads to better memory than one long, tiring session. The practice sessions are designed to pace your learning by suggesting that you start practice early and spread it out over several sessions. So lesson two is: don't postpone practicing until the last moment, since learning a speech is too hard to do so fast.

Third, experimental findings indicate that learning is optimized by gradually increasing the spacing between practice sessions. Initial practice sessions should occur at short intervals, then sessions should be spaced at progressively longer intervals between practice sessions. This does not mean you should not practice the last two days before a speech! On the contrary, you *should* practice several times during the last days before your public talk but you should space out the practice. For example, do three ''run-throughs'' spaced out over six hours, not three in one hour.

Fourth, going over notes, charts, statistics, and reviewing the organizational flow of your talk immediately before a speech will definitely help make the material ''on the tip of your tongue'' when you need it during your talk. Last-minute reviewing of *practiced* material not only makes repetition effective, but it will discourage anxiety, since you won't have time to conjure up pictures of personal failure. If you review material, you can prevent negative thoughts from turning you into a nervous wreck.

Instead of reading (or practicing) a whole speech again and again in a futile attempt to remember it all, your programmed practice sessions suggest that you practice small ''chunks'' of your speech. For example, first you will practice the introduction, then the second big chunk—the first main point and subpoints of your discussion section—and so on.

How Train-of-Thought Practice Sessions Use OAR Memory Principles

O- You will isolate key words on your outline to help you focus and *observe* important details.

A- You will use key words, pictures, stories, pegwords, and loci methods to help you *associate* the to-be-learned information with things you already know.

R- You will *repeat* your speech in ways that will enhance your memory, enliven your practice, and improve your delivery.

METHODS FOR REMEMBERING

What kind of observation, association, and repetition can help you link your facts together systematically and improve your memory? While there are many techniques which can help you remember better, these five methods are most adaptable to remembering your train-of-thought in your speech: *Keyword, Picture, Chained Associations, Pegword, Place.* Read about all five methods and decide which ones are most appealing to you. The point is to settle on one or two techniques, practice them with a small chunk of your speech (say, only the introduction), and see which method works best for you.

Keyword Associations

One way to link ideas is to select the key words, generally the subject, noun and verb of the sentence. If you can remember the significant words, they will prompt the words necessary to communicate the idea extemporaneously.

PRACTICE THE KEYWORD METHOD

- The underlined words express the key ideas in this attention-getting sentence: "Two great *talkers won't walk* far *together.*"
- Repeat the sentence aloud several times.
- On your note card, you would simply write the key words. For example:

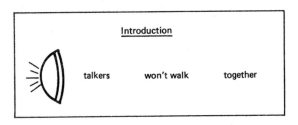

- Next, repeat only the key words aloud four or five times.
- Picture the key words and associate the modifying words, such as *two* and *great* talkers with the key words: Say the sentence silently.
- Repeat the entire sentence aloud several times, emphasizing the key words with your voice.

In Practice Session 2 you will put the keyword method to practical use as a first step in learning your speech. Remember, the key word is *the* key to using the other methods effectively. The idea is to know the sequence of key words which make up your train-of-thought. The following methods use key words in novel ways to impress the ideas into your memory.

Picture Associations

An important technique for memorizing new material is to convert it into visual images. Psychological research has repeatedly shown that memory is greatly facilitated when people construct mental pictures or draw actual pictures to symbolize their main ideas.[1] Our memories deal best with concrete objects, and pictures are a good way to make real our abstract ideas. Your pictures may be somewhat crude, even silly, but so long as they are meaningful to you, they will improve your memory. Although people differ in their ability to visualize key ideas, I've never had a student who couldn't use the stick-picture memory method after a few trials. Here is how it works:

PRACTICE THE PICTURE METHOD

- □ Underline the "highlights," or key words, that communicate the message. For example, "Do you sometimes feel *light-headed, giddy,* and *confused:* Are you speechless? Do you feel *unreal* to yourself and fear you may appear so to *others?*"
- □ Familiarize yourself with the flow of several ideas by reading those sentences aloud several times, saying the key words louder than the other words.
- □ Draw a stick picture of those key words *interacting*. In this picture the words in parentheses are the key words represented in the picture.

- □ Close your eyes, concentrate on those parts of the figure that show the characteristics of light-headedness, confused thoughts, and so on.
- □ Repeat the sentences of the text *as you visualize the details of the picture*.
- □ Repeat this process with the key words in your speech and transfer your stick figures (but not the key words) to a note card.

By drawing pictures about key words, you ignore superfluous words, which interfere with your remembering the main idea. You are literally cutting away the little words, the function words, such as *of* and *the*, because these will come automatically as you talk about the main features of the picture. The motto here is "Less is more." Cluttered notes make for confused speakers.

You can represent an entire chunk of your speech—say, the introduction—as a series of pictures. Aim for the simplest picture that will evoke many aspects of your key words, because a picture containing too many features is difficult to remember.

Here is an example of how three pairs of stick figures represent a series of ideas for me:

Notecard	Text of Speech Outline

"Two great <u>talkers won't walk</u> far together."

When you are doing all the talking. "Do you sometimes feel <u>lightheaded</u>, <u>giddy</u>, <u>dizzy</u>, and <u>confused</u>? Does your mind sometimes go <u>blank</u>? Do you feel <u>unreal to yourself</u> and afraid you may appear so to <u>others</u>?"

"Good conversations are <u>shared</u>: a <u>talker pauses to listen</u>; a <u>listener starts to talk</u>. That way, you can <u>walk far together</u>."

Chained Associations

What if your facts are a potpourri of unassociated ideas? If you want to remember a list of unrelated key words (such as a key word for each fact), then you will need to relate those facts or points to each other. You can do this by chaining each idea to the next one that follows it using imaginary associations. It is important to symbolize each abstract idea by a concrete object or picture before beginning. Suppose you wanted to tie together four key words or phrases, such as *television, children, books, publishers*. To learn these, you would first link yourself to *television* (see yourself walking into a gigantic TV set); then link *television* to *children* (see many kids watching TV); then link *children* to *books* (throwing books at the TV) and *books* to *publishers* (printing press churning out books). The links of pictured associations form a chain, starting with yourself and television and going through to the end. As you construct each linking picture, visualize it for five seconds or so to fix it firmly in mind. You then use the linked associations to recall, asking yourself, "Where was I going?" To the television. "Who did I picture with the TV?" The children. "What did I picture the children doing?'' Throwing books. ''Where do books come from?'' Publishers.

This chained association method is helpful when you have a very long list of key words to be memorized, say at least ten. Most people's rote memory will fail for that length, so some aids are needed. The paired chains of associations come in handy then.

Another interesting way to remember points is to weave the linking associations into a story, with the key words serving as major points of the story. Almost any ridiculous story will make it easier for you to remember the order of your key ideas. A logical story ''connects up'' unrelated words, so that each idea becomes associated with the one before it and the one after it in the series. The story method is an easy way to tie together separate items, such as causes or effects, reasons, steps of a process, or a series of events. You should practice using it with any unrelated set of concrete words.

PRACTICE THE CHAINED ASSOCIATIONS METHOD

◻ Suppose the key words for each main point in your speech are *elephant, table, coffee, incense*.

◻ Now look away from the book and try to remember all four points.

◻ Now tie those four words together by linking them into an absurd story, with a picture for each scene. For example: ''The *elephant table* held a cup of *coffee,* which smelled like *incense.''*

◻ Now recall the four points. Does the story work as a memory aid?

◻ To use this method, follow this process with key words for each main point in your speech and link them together in some absurd story.

Pegword Associations

A quick way to memorize the exact sequence of points in a speech is to associate the numbers of the points with pictures whose names rhyme with the numbers. The pictures for the first ten numbers are suggested below. These pictures will be used as ''pegs'' to associate with the successive points of your speech. You visualize some bizarre interaction between a *bun* (one is a bun) and a concrete image representing the *first* point of your speech, between a *shoe* (two is a shoe) and an image representing your second point, and so on. Here are the details:

PRACTICE THE PEGWORD METHOD

◻ First you should learn a word that rhymes with each number. Take a few minutes to memorize these picture words and their corresponding number. You can make up rhymes for numbers above ten.

1 → bun	Visualize a hamburger bun.
2 → shoe	Visualize an old shoe.

3 → tree   Visualize a tree without its leaves.
4 → door   Visualize a sturdy wooden door.
5 → (bee) hive   Visualize only the hive, no bees.
6 → sticks   Visualize a bundle of sticks.
7 → heaven   Visualize the stereotypical "Pearly Gates in the clouds."
8 → gate   Visualize an old-fashioned gate to a yard.
9 → wine   Visualize a bottle of wine.
10 → hen   Visualize a red hen.

- □ After association the picture with the number, you will have a pegword (example: *one-bun*) on which you can "hang" another picture, namely your point.
- □ Now hang a point on the pegword. Suppose your first point is, "When you are *physically relaxed,* you cannot feel *tense.*"
- □ To memorize this first point, you associate relaxation and tension with point 1 (the bun). For example, you could visualize a bun squeezing out tension (T) and, quite appropriately, out pops a relaxed figure.
- □ Next, draw every bit of information into one picture. The picture of the opening bun, the large T (tension), and the relaxed figure help you remember the first point, namely, that when you are relaxed, you cannot feel tense. The picture will stand out in your memory and could look something like this:

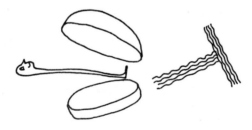

- □ To use this method, you would link the key words of, say, your introduction and associate them with various parts of a picture that you create.

The pegword technique is an easy and absorbing way to remember the sequence of main points in your discussion. Trust your humor and ingenuity to provide you with ideas for objects to picture.

Place (or "Loci") Associations

The method of place or "loci" is similar to the pegword and picture methods except that it uses mental images of familiar locations in place of peg images such as those of a bun or a shoe. You should choose a number of locations along a familiar route, such as a route through your house, a route to your job, a route through the building where you work. Make up ten to twenty distinct mental snapshots of locations ordered along that familiar route. You are then to use these locations as imaginary pigeonholes, to which the key words of your main points or a listing of facts can be connected by imaginative associations. It is the method Mark Twain used. He could entertain audiences for hours at a time without a single note. Before speaking in a new town, he'd take a walk through the town park. There he'd attach ideas for his speech to the water fountain, a park bench, the biggest tree, the most beautiful flowerbed. When he gave his speech, he would simply walk through his mental park, sipping an idea from the water fountain, picking up a second idea from a park bench, another off the trunk of a tree, and so on, until he had walked through his mental park, picked up all his ideas, and delighted his audience with his humorous stories and easygoing style.

PRACTICE THE PLACE (OR "LOCI") METHOD

- ☐ Pigeonhole your main points (or subpoints) in those places you associate with getting up in the morning and going to work or school. Also, choose a specific object in each location to serve as a memory peg for each point in your discussions. For point 1, use the bed in your bedroom. For point 2, use the washbasin in your bathroom, the table in your kitchen, the seat of your car, the entrance of your parking lot, the desk of your office (school, store, and so forth) for other points.

- ☐ Use the key words from your first point and picture those key words doing something unusual on the bed in your bedroom. For example, suppose point 1 is, *"Audience laughter* is a great healer of *stage fright."* Using the place method, you could picture a stage-frightened speaker on a bed being healed by a laughing audience.

- ☐ If your second point contained the key words *looking* and *rapport,* you would place them in the washbasin of the bathroom. Your memory picture could have faces with big, friendly eyes and extended hands, symbolizing *looking* and *rapport.* You would draw friendly faces looking up from the washbasin in your bathroom.

- ☐ To use this method you would continue down your list of main points, underlining key words, making a vivid picture for each, *and associating them to your successive memory rooms.* Finally, you would draw the picture for each point on your note card as a reminder of the point to be made. The speaker then practices aloud, using the pictures to prompt his or her memory.

The "place" or "loci" method is very effective for remembering a long list of items. Use just one route for any given speech, whether it is through your house or along a well-marked path. When you wish to recall your points, simply take a mental walk along that well-memorized route, letting each location suggest the image and the point you've stored there. Of all the methods for remembering points, many speakers find that this one is the easiest to use and has the best results.

USEFUL MEMORY HINTS FOR SPEAKERS

When You Are Preparing and Practicing

Here are some important suggestions to help you develop a train-of-thought that will be easy to remember:

- ☐ Organize the ideas in order so that one flows easily into the next.
- ☐ Emphasize coherent transition sentences to connect one idea to the next.
- ☐ Use some memory technique to learn the order of your ideas easily.
- ☐ Practice saying the main ideas aloud several times in their proper sequence (see chapters 10 and 11).
- ☐ Convince yourself that you will remember your ideas when you come to them one after the other as you speak in public.

When You Are Waiting Your Turn

Just before you get up to speak, there are a few do's and don'ts to follow. One important "do" is to calm yourself just before you speak. You can do this by talking silently to yourself, pumping up your courage and confidence with positive self-statements. A typical monologue would be, "I can do this speech. I am calm and collected. This audience is friendly, and they really want to hear what I have to say. I'll be just fine." Make up your own positive monologue to say to yourself. If you fill your mind with this positive monologue, you'll be unable to think of negative, frightening thoughts. Review chapter 8, pages 116–117, which explained how to make up your own positive, coping sentences.

An important "don't" is this: During the last minutes before you stand up to speak, don't try to review your *entire* speech all at once. It simply is too big a task and you may get discouraged and start to lose confidence. Avoid that. Instead, repeat to yourself only the first few lines of your introduction as you walk to the podium.

When You Are Speaking

Suppose you are well started into your speech and you do momentarily forget what your next point is. The main point is not to panic; seasoned speakers know they will forget something, so they plan ways to keep calm themselves during their lapses until the thread of their speech comes back to them. Here are a few suggestions:

▫ Admit that you are momentarily distracted and ask the audience to help you remember by saying, "Where was I?" Obviously this technique is best for small groups.

▫ Buy thinking time by taking a couple of steps. This technique often relieves tension and helps you free the mind to remember the errant thought.

▫ Say something like, "Wait a second. I want to refer to my notes to see if I have covered everything I wanted to."

▫ Ask the audience, "Am I speaking loudly enough?" or "Can you hear me in the back of the room?" Of course, you are not seeking information. You are seeking precious time to grasp the forgotten idea.

SUMMARY OF MEMORY METHODS

Memory is a precious thing for anyone at any time. As a public speaker, even momentary lapses of memory can be frightening. While it is possible to recall a speech without any undue effort, you probably shouldn't expect miracles when you are under stress. Most speakers want the security of knowing that if they are distracted while speaking, they will still be able to recall their next idea without discomfort and embarrassment. How easily an idea comes to mind depends on how well you have learned it during practice.

This chapter urged you to use three powerful learning principles (the OAR): **O**bservation- **A**ssociation- **R**epetition. Using these principles, you can plan efficient and effective ways to learn your speech. Whether you choose the keyword method, or the picture, chained associations, pegword, or the place method, you can be assured that your practice time will be well spent. Each method involves picturing ideas, which helps you to concentrate on what you must know to remember a train-of-thought easily. I urge you to experiment with the various methods, perhaps using different lists of ten unrelated words, or a small portion of your speech, such as the introduction. Find out which method works best for your memory and put it to use. In addition, this chapter has encouraged you to

▫ repeat aloud manageable chunks of your speech several times before going on to the next section

▫ space out your rehearsals over progressively longer intervals

- ☐ go over your statistics, charts, and main ideas repeatedly up until the last five minutes or so
- ☐ repeat your positive self-statements and your introduction during the last five minutes

Finally, once you are sure that you are prepared, stop worrying and relax. Worrying only distracts people; it is not task-oriented. Besides, you can be confident that an idea ''lost'' while speaking will reemerge in a few seconds, because ideas given so much tender loving care won't be out of mind for long. The next two chapters will help you practice saying your ideas in a winning and compelling way.

10

Develop Your Confidence: Practice Sessions 1–3

Like thousands before you, you may try to ignore practicing your speech by distracting yourself with activities. You might seek escape by mowing the lawn, going to a movie, washing your underwear, writing next year's holiday cards.

Or perhaps you procrastinate by putting off the starting time; you tell yourself that you'll practice your talk at some unspecified future time. Do you tell yourself, "I'm not ready to practice, I still need more ideas"? If you are a compulsive, gather-more-material nut, you probably find yourself overwhelmed with several books, magazine articles, clippings, and half-baked ideas scattered here, there, and everywhere the day before your speech. By having to make sense out of so much stuff the last minute you can work up to a first-rate case of stage fright.

Or perhaps you defeat yourself by cramming your practice into one fitful session. All over the world scatterbrained speakers squeeze practice into the last fitful hour or two, or else they don't even practice at all. It is a surefire way of rushing yourself into hysterics.

We all know these escape routes, but they do not develop courage or boost confidence. Often these irrelevant tasks don't get our minds off ourselves at all, and we wind up running around doing silly jobs, knowing full well we are procrastinating.

Since there is no permanent way to stop thinking about an upcoming speech, you may as well get to it. Think about it *constructively;* don't allow your imagination to control you *destructively*. Henry David Thoreau said, "As long as a man stands in his own way, everything seems to be in his way.'' Get out of your own way now. Determine now to practice for a few hours in order to foster your own personal self-improvement program as a public speaker. All accomplished performers spend hours practicing: dancers practice their steps; artists constantly make sketches; actors repeat their lines; musicians practice their scales; athletes work out their movements. These determined people have dragged themselves to the studio or the theater, to the auditorium or the playing field, to work out. And a good public speaker, like a good athlete or artist, is not just born, but develops over many hours of practice and performance.

However, practice does not make perfect, it makes permanent; therefore, it is vitally important to practice in ways that will enhance your memory and develop your confidence. By doing one preparatory task after another you will be using your nervous energy constructively. When you focus your efforts, you will stop anxiety from misusing you. Your obsessive thoughts about "the speech" as well as your persistent procrastinations will end. By practicing sensibly, you will begin to feel that *you* are in control—a crucial first step in mastering your anxiety about speaking before a group.

Perhaps setting specific goals and following a practice schedule is a new idea, but consider some benefits from programmed sessions. First, you can determine where you are going (goals); second, you can decide how you can meet those goals (tasks); and third, you can determine how long your practice will take (time management)

Think about it. Don't you do a job best when you know what you have to do to complete a task? Don't you feel more like doing it if you decide *when* you will do it and *how long* it will take? That's what the practice sessions in chapters 10 and 11 will help you do. For example, for a five-minute speech, you are advised to schedule your practice sessions over three or four days, practicing one or more hours per day.

If you are determined to practice until you are fluent, a good rule of thumb is to spend at least one *hour* of practice for each *minute* of performance; thus, the ideal amount of preparation time (including researching, organizing, and practicing) for a novice speaker delivering a five-minute speech is approximately five hours or longer. Obviously, many people can't meet the ideal, but think of practicing for hours, not minutes.

To help speakers approach performance confidently, I have developed six practice sessions that make practice time a more positive and creative experience. I have also urged structured practice of an assertive message in *Asserting Yourself*.[1] The aim of the six practice phases is to help you make the most of your speaking style. Each session is designed to help you meet certain specific goals and to master certain skills that should help you communicate more effectively. These practical techniques can help you translate a good speech into meaningful communication with dramatic emphasis. Speakers who practice all six sessions report exciting changes in their speaking *and* in their attitudes toward speaking. Here are the phases of practice that will help you deliver your train-of-thought in an intelligent and lively manner.

Chapter 10

- □ *Session 1:* Prepare for Practice Sessions. This session helps you set realistic practice goals. How long will you practice? Where? When?
- □ *Session 2:* Remember Your Speech. This session helps you learn your train-of-thought.
- □ *Session 3:* Develop Your Spontaneity. This session helps you move and gesture as you rehearse. These special exercises will help you deal with distraction, the enemy of a good memory.

Chapter 11

- □ *Session 4:* Practice Your Delivery. This session suggests ways to practice with visual aids, using a "mock-up" audience.
- □ *Session 5:* Develop Your Style. This session suggests exercises for helping you adjust gradually to a real audience.
- □ *Session 6:* Critique Your Speech. This session helps you put your critic's suggestions to good use.

When will you start? If you promise yourself to begin soon, you are strengthening your willpower and getting in shape for performance. Plan to succeed by practicing carefully, systematically, and deliberately. Each session helps you plan for success by suggesting a flexible practice program, which you can adapt to meet your own schedule and level of speaking expertise. An introduction to each session describes the activities for that session. Following each introduction are step-by-step practice directions. Read to understand the method; practice to perfect your delivery. Remember, people who have definite, realistic ways to succeed usually make it!

INTRODUCTION TO SESSION 1: PREPARE FOR PRACTICE SESSIONS

How Long Will You Practice?

Session 1 introduces a plan for taking the frenzy out of your speech practice. You will estimate the difficulty of each session for you. Notice that sessions 2 and 3 are more demanding and generally require more time than later ones, because you will be learning the sequence of your ideas and developing spontaneity.

When Will You Practice?

For example, if you have five days to practice, you might schedule:

- □ Practice Sessions 1, 2, and 3 over a period of one or two days
- □ Session 4 for the third day

- ☐ Session 5 on the fourth day
- ☐ Session 6 on the fifth day

Or if you have only two days to practice, you might schedule:

- ☐ Session 1 in the morning
- ☐ Session 2 in the afternoon
- ☐ Session 3 in the evening
- ☐ Sessions 4, 5, and 6 the second day

The ideal way to proceed is to *plan* your practice time and to space it out, so that you won't be exhausted trying to do all six sessions in a couple of hours on one day. There is no better way to give yourself a good case of speech fright than to pressure yourself into mastering in one hour what you should practice during four or five hours over a couple of days.

In this session you should decide how to "chunk" your practice sessions. Decide how many sessions you can work efficiently in one day. For example, could you schedule sessions 2 and 3 on the same day? It is better to "mass" sessions, that is, do not skip a practice day, because we remember better when we aren't interrupted a long time between sessions. Also, it takes a little time to get into the swing of your practicing, and you will want the excitement and spirit of your speaking to carry over to the next practice session. To prevent mood slippage, mass as many sessions as you can tolerate without feeling exhausted. It is demanding to work yourself into the speaker's part after skipping a day; it is easier to pick up the mood after an hour's break or on the next day than after two days. For this reason I encourage speakers to

- ☐ practice during a weekend when they have a block of time free from other worries
- ☐ schedule more time than they think necessary for preparation and practice

A sensible practice schedule is one of the best guarantees against nervousness. Do yourself a favor: Think of practice as a way to make permanent your most winning ways.

Where Will You Practice?

Next plan *where* you will work. Don't scatter yourself all over the premises. Session 1, 2, and 3 can be done in your office or in your bedroom. Clear your desk of all busywork. Session 4, which designates furniture as a mock audience, and session 5, which requires a mirror and suggests a tape recorder, are done best in the privacy of a bedroom or bathroom. When you invite a listener for your sixth practice session, you might return to your furniture scene or speak at your listener's home or at a more public place, such as a schoolroom, boardroom, or meeting hall. You should review the activity of each session and decide where you will practice each session.

What Are Practice Props?

Next gather note cards, felt pens, tennis balls, and all the materials you will need for each practice session. Get organized for each session, and you will be putting yourself in control.

What Clothes Will You Practice In?

Also, arrange to practice in a bright, comfortable place in cheerful clothes. Make practice sessions a good time for yourself and you will be more likely to practice. Decide to be physically comfortable by practicing your early sessions (2 and 3) in the most comfortable clothes you own. It's no use putting on a sackcloth and feeling miserable. A friend once gave me a Japanese silk "happy coat" which for years has robed me in luxury and comfort when I practice a new speech. Wear your most comfortable clothes, whatever that means for you. In session 4, wear your actual speaking clothes in order to get accustomed to speaking in them. In session 5, look your best, because nothing is so discouraging as seeing yourself look worn out and bedraggled.

How Can You Encourage Yourself?

Finally, during this first session, as you get yourself organized, decide how you will reward yourself for completing each session. People generally learn fastest when they are rewarded. You may say that just practicing and completing something for once in your life is enough reward. That kind of acknowledgment is important, but why count on your own private gratitude as your reward? It's not always that exciting to shake hands with oneself. Moreover, we are not accustomed to complimenting ourselves for doing things we think we ought to do. Instead, design your reinforcement by planning to give yourself something nice. "Nice" might mean a positive self-statement such as "I'm really improving" or "I can speak better with practice," but plan for more tangible rewards for completing each practice session, too. For example, treat yourself to dinner out, a special book, an exciting film, or a new outfit.

The idea is to plan rewards that are big enough to encourage you to finish each session, so that you motivate and encourage yourself to practice. Promise yourself the biggest reward after the most difficult session. For example, although the last session will have built-in rewards, such as compliments from a sympathetic listener, you could also phone your best friend or favorite relative as an additional reward. These calls give you a chance to say that you are done practicing a speech and you are ready to present it. If you know that your relatives and friends are sympathetic with your self-improvement program and will praise your efforts, they will provide a long-distance cheering section.

Another form of encouragement is to take a break between sessions—relax and rest—and return to practicing after a brief respite of minutes or a few hours, not days. Research on learning tells us that we can learn faster if we take short periods of relaxation with rewards after short work sessions, and sometimes within a session if it is a long workout.

Make a Promise to Practice

One way to overcome your own resistance is to go easy on yourself. Right now make a contract with yourself. Tell yourself you can stop practicing after x number of minutes if you want. Say, "I will practice for ten minutes." By the end of ten minutes, you can contract with yourself "for ten more." If you are not doing well by ten minutes, stop, but not before you promise to return at a specific time after you've rested.

Session 1: Prepare for Practice Sessions

Goal:
- To make practicing an easy and enjoyable task by organizing your time and making arrangements for a practice room, props, clothes, and rewards.

Tasks:
- Review chapter 9, "Remember Your Train-of-Thought," for ideas on how to learn fast.
- Prepare your outline in final form, typed or clearly written. Leave lots of white space for additional writing. For example, put the introduction on one full page, main point 1 on the next page, main point 2 on the next page, and so on, and the conclusion on the final page.
- Read over the description for sessions 2–6 and decide when, where, and approximately how long you intend to practice for each session, as well as the reward you will give yourself for completing each practice session.
- Choose blocks of time when you won't be interrupted: Take the phone off the hook; lock the door to your practice room; tell people not to disturb you. Eliminate all possible distractions now.
- Arrange for whatever materials and props you will need: clock, 3 x 5 note cards, fine-point felt pens or pencils, tennis ball, table and cardboard box, podium, tape recorder, mirror, your visual aids.
- Decide which clothes and shoes will make you feel good as you practice.
- Make your note cards look like the following examples.
- Prepare your 3 x 5 note cards by following the directions below:

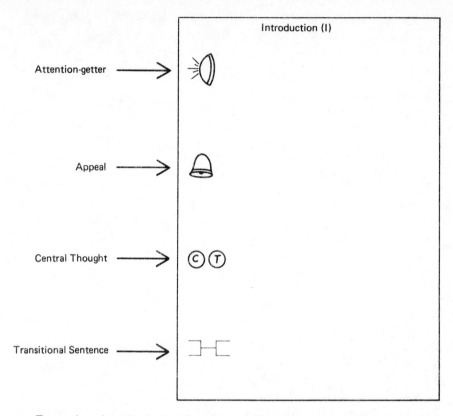

□ For each main point in the discussion, make a separate card. Here are three main points on three separate cards. Card numbers correspond to main-point numbers.

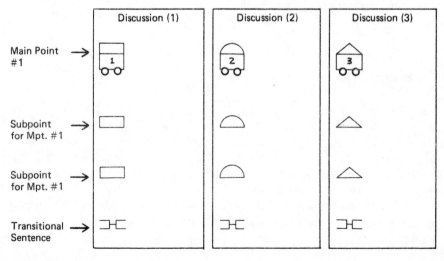

❑   On the card for your conclusion, make symbols for its various parts like this:

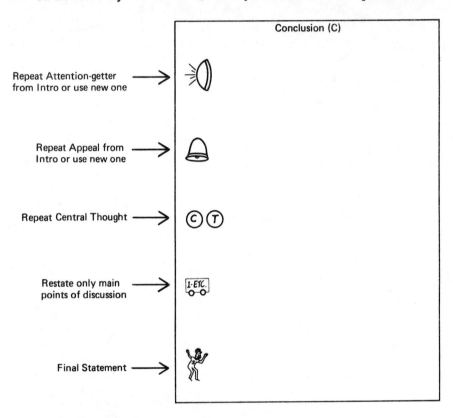

❑   Decide now when you will begin session 2.

❑   REWARD YOURSELF.

INTRODUCTION TO SESSION 2: REMEMBER YOUR SPEECH

Most speakers wonder how they can stop worrying about making a mistake or forgetting a point. The answer may lie in the practice sessions, where you can deliver your speech and correct mistakes privately without the censure of an audience. By carefully learning how to remember in a safe and private atmosphere, you can develop the confidence you will need in public. It's not easy, but you can do it with some old-fashioned push and perseverance.

In this session you will make use of three powerful learning principles to perfect your memory. These methods, described in chapter 9, are contained in three specific steps called OAR, which stand for:

- ☐ OBSERVE and read aloud the sentences that belong to a small chunk of your outline and underline key words. (*Observe* carefully.)
- ☐ ASSOCIATE the key words and/or pictures with the ideas they represent. Enter them into your memory by seeing them in your imagination. (*Associate* ideas with key words and pictures.)
- ☐ REPEAT the idea aloud, using only the key words and pictures to prompt your memory. (*Repeat* ideas *aloud*.)

Now, just go through the following steps for session 2 one by one.

Session 2: Remember Your Speech

Goals:

- ☐ To associate key words and pictures with big ideas; to make readable note cards.

WHEN will you practice? _____

WHERE will you practice? _____

HOW long will you practice? _____

HOW will you reward yourself? _____

Tasks:

- ☐ Review chapter 9 for memory, especially "picture memory," on page 125.
- ☐ In the following example, notice how key words are translated into pictures. On the right is a speech outline with main idea words (key words) underlined. On the left is the picture note card for the introduction to a speech entitled "Forty-five Years to Catch Up."
- ☐ Now refer to your outline. Use the following three steps (OAR) with each part of your introduction:
- ☐ OBSERVE by underlining the key words on your *final outline*.
- ☐ ASSOCIATE those key words with pictures, which in turn will cue your memory. Squeeze an idea (which may take four or five sentences to communicate) into a single symbol or key word on your introduction card. Don't crowd. Write out only direct quotes.
- ☐ REPEAT each chunk of your introduction, using only the note cards with key words and pictures as prompters. If you have difficulty remembering your key words and pictures, check your note cards. Are they too cluttered, too confusing? Eliminate excess words and symbols and print a new card. A few words and vivid symbols will help you focus clearly and remember. Your goal is to talk about the pictures one after the other. Experiment with communicating the key word pictures with slightly different wording.

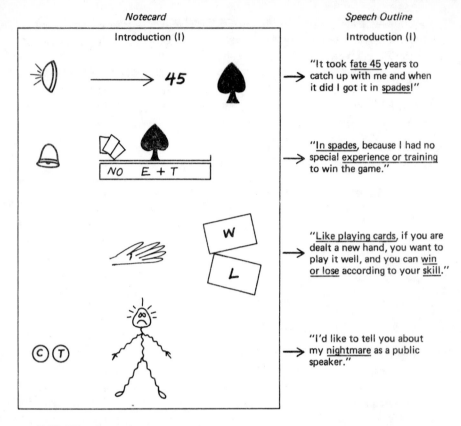

Notecard	*Speech Outline*
Introduction (I)	Introduction (I)

"It took <u>fate 45</u> years to catch up with me and when it did I got it in <u>spades</u>!"

"<u>In spades</u>, because I had no special <u>experience or training</u> to win the game."

"<u>Like playing cards</u>, if you are dealt a new hand, you want to play it well, and you can <u>win or lose</u> according to your <u>skill</u>."

"I'd like to tell you about my <u>nightmare</u> as a public speaker."

□ RELAX a few minutes.

□ Repeat the OAR steps for the first main point of your discussion and its subpoints. Take your time. This task takes thinking.

□ RELAX.

□ Repeat OAR steps for each of your other discussion points and their subpoints.

□ RELAX.

□ Repeat OAR steps for chunks of your conclusion.

□ Decide now when you will practice session 3.

□ **REWARD YOURSELF.**

INTRODUCTION TO SESSION 3:
DEVELOP YOUR SPONTANEITY

Another effective way to remember important points (which I also used in *Asserting Yourself*[1]) is to use oratorical emphasis. The problem is how do you emphasize important ideas? You may think you're a "ham" when you first try a dramatic pause or changes in volume, inflection, movement, and gestures, but these techniques can actually help you remember your speech if you have experimented with gesturing and moving *before* you meet the audience.

This means that you need to practice increasingly difficult movements as you proceed in Practice Session 3. Challenge yourself as you practice. By now you should be able to speak fairly well from your note cards. The next task is to wean yourself from the notes. During the first run-through in session 3, put the notes on your bed or desk, where you can glance at them when necessary. Think of your train-of-thought.

What's first? The light, of course! Rehearse aloud the attention getter as you walk around the room.

When you feel good about talking and walking, try something more complicated—a small, routine activity that is not associated with giving a speech. As you repeat the attention-getting sentences aloud, tie a shoe, button and unbutton a jacket, erase a blackboard—anything you can do automatically without giving the activity your full concentration. After you master the entire introduction fluently under such bizarre conditions, do the same activities as you practice the discussion and conclusion. Remember to practice *small* chunks of your speech as you repeat these activities.

Next move on to bigger and more complicated movements, such as vacuuming, clipping the hedge, or washing windows as you practice the introduction once again. Notice that when you practice your speech with a new activity, you sometimes forget it momentarily. That's because the new activity momentarily occupies your mind and distracts you from your speech. Distraction is exactly what happens when we speak—and forget—in public; therefore, as you practice, you must teach yourself to remember in spite of distractions. You can accomplish this feat if you simulate a distracting environment as you practice. For example, you will learn to communicate ideas while you walk about, gesture, turn note cards, use visual aids, and so on.

Next I suggest that you bounce a tennis ball as you practice your lines! As you talk about your ideas, you naturally will have to keep your eye on the ball in order to catch it. By speaking and moving *at the same time,* you will be teaching yourself to talk in spite of the distracting ball. By training yourself to do both tasks simultaneously, you will be teaching yourself to focus on two things at once. This skill comes in handy when you are communicating your ideas *and* watching for audience reactions at the same time.

Of course, you will not deliver a speech bouncing an imaginary ball, but this exercise will help you feel freer to move, to gesture, to let go and speak easily. Moreover, your movements and gestures, which will emphasize significant key words, will help you remember main ideas more easily. This "muscle memory," as actors call it, seems to come automatically, cueing the memory for the word.

Finally, bouncing a ball with energetic arm movements will help you develop a more forceful delivery. For example, if you bounce a ball *hard* as you say an important word, you will automatically say that word louder and with forceful emphasis. By moving the ball around you, high and low, outlining different patterns with the ball as if you were fingerpainting, you will free up your spontaneous spirit, as well as your voice, and you will speak with a more lively expression. Try it and you'll see. The voice will follow the body. Observe someone with an expressive voice and you will very likely see a person who moves more freely and with greater variety and emphasis than does someone with a dull voice. Simply follow the steps suggested.

Session 3: Develop Your Spontaneity

Goals:

□ To train yourself to deal with distractions; to heighten your vocal expression and bodily movement; to develop a spontaneous style.

WHEN will you practice? _____

WHERE will you practice? _____

HOW long will you practice? _____

HOW will you reward yourself? _____

Props needed for this session: *your note cards, tennis ball.*

Tasks:

□ WALK around the room as you rehearse one chunk at a time the introduction, say, until you are satisfied. Then walk around as you practice the discussion separately and, finally, the conclusion. Then practice your entire speech beginning to end—during a walk around the premises. Let yourself go: add sentences which will expand your outline and develop your extemporaneous style.

□ RELAX.

□ TIE your shoe as you practice each chunk of your speech. Repeat small chunks, such as the introduction, until you can speak your ideas smoothly as you tie your shoe. Then rehearse the entire speech as you tie and untie your shoe. Again, don't be afraid to say your ideas in different ways.

□ RELAX.

□ POLISH your desk (or make a bed or scrub a floor) as you practice each chunk of your speech. Rehearse the whole speech as you do a chore. Each time experiment with a slightly new way to say your ideas.

□ RELAX.

□ BOUNCE a tennis ball as you practice extemporaneously. Have fun!

□ Decide now when you will practice session 4.

□ REWARD YOURSELF.

This completes your first three practice sessions. The emphasis of these three sessions has been on training you to remember your ideas in increasingly distracting situations and to expand and elaborate on your train-of-thought with slightly different words as you steadily communicate more fluently and extemporaneously. The next three sessions will help you to develop your own individual style of speaking with the emphasis on your delivery.

11

Polish Your Speaking Style: Practice Sessions 4–6

The practice sessions in chapter 10 offered specific suggestions for helping you remember your speech and develop a spontaneous spirit. By now you should be familiar enough with your note cards so that you will feel comfortable looking away from them during these next practice sessions.

The next three sessions will help you put the final polish on your delivery. Your goal now is to express a natural look that is both compelling and fascinating. In session 4 you should practice before a pretend audience. In session 5 you will speak into a tape recorder (if you have one) and observe yourself in a mirror as you practice talking about your train-of-thought. Finally, in session 6 you will be speaking to one or more critics, who will identify your speech mannerisms with the help of the Train-of-Thought Critique. Special exercises designed to eliminate your distracting mannerisms are explained at the end of this chapter.[1]

INTRODUCTION TO SESSION 4: PRACTICE YOUR DELIVERY

This practice session is fun. Simply pretend that a sofa, a rocking chair, plants, and pillows are your audience. Set up a card table with a cardboard box to serve as your podium. Look over your familiar surroundings. Before you begin your introduction, look at the most pleasing item in your room. Take your time. Take a breath and begin speaking. This is the session to help you look at specific places in your audience and to gain confidence standing and moving around a podium.

Session 4: Practice Your Delivery

Goal:

☐ To develop good eye contact and physical composure when using your props and note cards.

WHEN will you practice? _____

WHERE will you practice? _____

HOW long will you practice? _____

HOW will you reward yourself? _____

Tasks:

☐ Set up a mock audience of furniture, pillows, grandfather clocks, pictures, and so forth to serve as your make believe audience.

☐ Set up a podium by putting a cardboard box on a table.

☐ Practice with visual aids, such as slides, overhead transparencies, objects, flip charts, note cards. If things don't work or slides are unclear, now is the time to make corrections and additions before the next session (see pp. 103–104).

☐ Practice the introduction several times until you feel confident. Look at various "pieces" of your audience; practice moving and gesturing. Use your note cards only when necessary.

☐ Practice chunks of the discussion several times. Mark your notes where you repeatedly forget. Practice transitional sentences carefully so that you can move smoothly from one idea to another. Repeat aloud until you are satisfied.

☐ RELAX.

☐ Practice the entire speech two or three times or until you are satisfied. Time your speech now, and cut or expand it to fit your time limit.

☐ Decide now when you will return for session 5.

☐ REWARD YOURSELF.

INTRODUCTION TO SESSION 5: DEVELOP YOUR STYLE

Probably the most important thing to say about speaking style is that you should have one. Secondly, you should have one that enhances your message and does not distract from it. You have noticed some people in a crowd standing out from the others because of their unusual coloring or size or manner of speaking. If you take your outstanding features, which already make you different, and accentuate those features with clothes that heighten your hair color, accentuate your height, and compliment your eyes, you can help define your unique and personal style.

But physical features are only a part of your style as a speaker. Just as important as your physical appearance are your walk and your gestures, your facial expression and the sound of your voice—in other words, your speaking personality. Although you may not want your appearance to be absolutely perfect, it is necessary to eliminate those habits that are grossly distracting.

One way to modify an undesirable speaking habit is to become aware of your everyday speaking style. Tell a sympathetic friend about your desire to improve your speaking style. What does he or she consider your *best* features? Your worst? What movements and expressions make for your individuality? Some of your personal expressions will be useful to emphasize a point. However, if the same gesture is used to emphasize every point, the gesture will distract the audience and they will not hear your message. The point to be made here (without the benefit of a gesture) is that, when speakers get tense, they often have too many or too few of their natural, everyday gestures. The way to enhance your best behaviors, to accentuate them but not overdo them, is to know what is appealing about your everyday speaking style and then to amplify those positive behaviors when you speak before a group. However, your style should be so natural that an audience never gets so enraptured with your melodious voice or the winning tilt of your head that they fail to catch the meaning of your speech. Practice your best style until it is comfortable for you and for your audience.

As you work with the tape recorder and see your reflection in the mirror, you will notice that some of your speech mannerisms should be modified or eliminated. It is best to correct bad mannerisms by practicing a *very small* part of your speech in order to see and hear improvement. If you concentrate on improving a specific behavior while delivering only the introduction again and again, you'll notice that your entire speech improves in later practices. Work on improving one or two of your speaking behaviors during session 5. Look for specific exercises at the end of this chapter to help you eliminate distracting and unattractive mannerisms. Also, listen to the comments of your friend and practice projecting your attractive characteristics. Very often projecting our most positive attributes goes a long way towards eliminating our unattractive ones.

During this session develop a sense of continuity. Time your speech one last time. If it is a minute too long, cut it. Take a black felt pen and scratch a section off your cards. If you run overtime you stand a good chance of alienating your audience and undoing all your best efforts to be a painless public speaker.

Session 5: Develop Your Style

Goal:

☐ To make the most of your best speech characteristics and the least of your worse habits.

WHEN will you practice? _____

WHERE will you practice? _____

HOW long will you practice? _____

HOW will you reward yourself? _____

Tasks:

☐ Read the Train-of-Thought Critique (pp. 152–153). (Pay special attention to behaviors in item 8.)

☐ Speak to a mirror. Make movement and expression look natural. Chunk material. Take it easy. Say the introduction, repeat it until you feel confident enough to tape-record it.

☐ Tape-record your introduction. Play back. Compliment yourself on your good points and improve the rough spots. Use appropriate exercises from pp. 154–160 to correct distracting mannerisms or an unpleasant voice.

☐ After you correct the most glaring mannerisms in your introduction, rehearse chunk-style portions of the discussion and conclusion.

☐ RELAX.

☐ Practice the entire speech once or twice *without stopping*. Time your speech!

☐ Decide now when you will return for session 6.

☐ REWARD YOURSELF.

INTRODUCTION TO SESSION 6: CRITIQUE YOUR SPEECH

Arrange a Dress Rehearsal

You have been practicing to communicate energy and intelligence in a winning way. By now you should have the good feeling that you can remember and communicate your train-of-thought not just with one set of words but with several extemporaneous versions, so it is time to test yourself with a friend, colleague, or relative. Choose an honest, intelligent, and tactful person to help you practice confidently. Speak in a familiar setting with your homemade podium. When you first speak to a critic, you may be disconcerted, but you will soon forget about your nervousness as you feel yourself speaking and moving easily. After all, you have a whole train of good ideas to deliver!

How to Use the Train-of-Thought Critique

Right now familiarize yourself with the Train-of-Thought Critique (pp. 152–153) so that you can explain it to your friendly critic(s), who should use it to evaluate your performance in this session.

Notice that there are two columns with identical listings, one for checking off your *best* speaking behaviors and one for indicating behaviors that *need improvement*. Suppose your listener in this session gives specific, positive, feedback such as, "You hesitate with too many *ahs*." If you decide to correct this disfluency, you should fill out the Self-Improvement Contract (pp. 153–154). Perhaps you will agree to eliminate all *ah's* from the attention-getting part of your speech. (You would remember to be silent, rather than use a filler like *ah*. Then you would deliver a *small* chunk of your speech to your critic, and repeat it until you both are satisfied with your performance.) It's good to remind yourself that it takes as much discipline to be a good speaker as it does to be a good athlete, musician, dancer, carpenter, executive, or any skilled worker, for that matter.

How to Get Positive Feedback
from a Vague Critic

Work toward changing only one or two behaviors that your friend calls distracting. While some people give specific criticisms, most will make judgments about your speaking style instead of making criticisms of specific behaviors. For example, your listener might say that you should "be more friendly" (vague suggestion). It then becomes very important to ask, "What could I *do* to *look* more friendly?" That is, you ask for specific directions. Perhaps you need to look at the audience more often—or smile at least 50 percent more. Always clarify well-meaning but vague criticism so that you know exactly which behaviors work well and which ones need improvement. For example:

Vague Criticisms from Your Critic	*Ask for Specific Clarification*
"You really established a rapport."	"Thanks! What did I do or say that gave you that feeling of rapport?"
"You need more expression."	"Do you mean I should show more life, and should it be in my face or in my voice? In what ways can I show more expression?"
"You really caught my interest!"	"When did I catch your interest? Was it with my material or with my delivery?"

How to Use the Self-Improvement Contract

It is very important to know *exactly* which behaviors to change and how much to change them. For example, on the Self-Improvement Contract, you will notice the words *I agree to* and *Under the following circumstances*. This is where you will indicate which *behavior* you agree to change and *how much* you intend to change it; thus this contract becomes your criterion for a successful practice. Be sure that it *is* exacting and specific. For example, if you agree to ''improve my eye contact with the audience,'' you still have not specified the change *exactly*. Rather, specifically decide what percentage of time you want to look at your audience (for example, 75 percent of the time instead of 20 percent). This part of your Self-Improvement Contract would look like this:

> I agree to: *increase the amount of time I look at the audience.*
> Under the following circumstances: *from 20 percent to 75 percent of the time.*

The Self-Improvement Contract also encourages you to set up a reward system when you do improve and to decide on a new course of action if you do not meet your goal. Try the reward system if you have trouble motivating yourself.

Experts agree that to be good in anything requires sheer desire and drive, time, skill, and careful, planned practice. Sometimes fear can prompt us to run away from ourselves. However, some will practice for a friend in spite of the awkward and anxious feelings they may feel at first. They know that if they run away from constructive criticism they may never cage their anxious feelings and that they will continue to be misused by their awful feelings. William James, a famous psychologist, said, ''To feel brave, act as if you were brave . . . and a courage fit will very likely replace the fit of fear.'' To feel confident that you can improve, you have been urged to correct a poor speech habit by repeating one small chunk of your speech several times. Now is your opportunity to replace old feelings of inadequacy with new feelings of mastery.

Session 6: Critique Your Speech

Goal:
□ To have a friend critique your speech and point out your effective speech behaviors, as well as those you need to improve.

WHEN will you practice? _____

WHERE will you practice? _____

HOW long will you practice? _____

HOW will you reward yourself? _____

Tasks:

□ Arrange for a friend, colleague, or relative to hear your speech in your home or office. Ask for an hour's time.

□ Brief your audience on item 8 of the following Train-of-Thought Critique before you deliver the introduction *only*. (You'll deliver entire speech later).

□ Get feedback on item 8. Agree on a behavior to change, and fill out the Self-Improvement Contract following with your friend.

□ Repeat the introduction as you correct one bad habit. Get feedback.

□ Agree on a second behavior to change. Deliver a small part of your speech—say, the conclusion only. Get feedback.

□ Deliver the entire speech without stopping. Pretend it is the real performance. Time the speech and get final feedback from your friendly critic.

□ For any persistent behaviors that you find difficult to correct, look to the body-language and vocal-expression exercises for help (pages 154–159).

□ Practice the exercises and repeat parts of your speech in front of a mirror after this session. Meet your own standards for looking and sounding good!

□ REWARD YOURSELF.

CONGRATULATIONS. You have completed six programmed practice sessions and will be "filled with your speech." To reduce your speaking anxiety between now and when you give your speech, turn to chapter 12 for some helpful hints.

Train-of-Thought Critique

Assume that you are one of the members of my audience. Please answer the following questions about my speaking.

1. Did I get your attention in the very beginning? _____ Yes _____ No _____ Partly

   How could I improve? _____

2. Do you think I related my subject to your interests and needs?   _____ Yes

   _____ No _____ Partly

   How could I improve? _____

3. What did you hear as my central thought? _____

   _____

4. What do you think my major purpose was?
   ___ to inform (give you the facts) ___ to stimulate (help you to
   ___ to persuade (get mental   think lofty thoughts)
       agreement)   ___ to entertain (get you to laugh)

___ to activate (show you how to
do something)

5. What were my main points?

1. _____

2. _____

3. _____

6. Do you think I talked about my main points long enough to make them clear?

and interesting? ___ Yes ___ No ___ Partly

How could I improve? _____

7. Do you think I made transitions from one idea to another smoothly? ___ Yes

___ No ___ Partly

8. Please critique my delivery

Check (✓) *which were best:*	Check (✓) *which need improvement:*
___ Eye contact	___ Eye contact
___ Facial expression	___ Facial expression
___ Gesturing	___ Gesturing
___ Posture	___ Posture
___ Body movement	___ Body movement
___ Volume	___ Volume
___ Vocal force and emphasis	___ Vocal force and emphasis
___ Articulation	___ Articulation
___ Pitch expression	___ Pitch expression
___ Rhythm of speaking	___ Rhythm of speaking
___ Rate of speaking	___ Rate of speaking
___ No disfluencies	___ Disfluencies
___ Use of visual aids	___ Use of visual aids

9. Which behavior do you think I should improve first? _____

10. What kind of change would you suggest? _____

Self-Improvement Contract

Goal: To change a distracting behavior.

I agree to: _____
                        (specify behavior)

Under the following circumstances: ————————————————————

(Specify how much you will change)

——

——

Rewarding Myself

If I achieve my goal in fewer than three run-throughs, I will ————————————

If it takes me more than three trials to achieve my goal, I will:

(1) rest ——— (2) reduce the size of the goal ——— (3) decide on another goal and

return to achieve this goal later today ———

Work on those distracting behaviors that you wish to eliminate by following the suggestions for improvement in the next section, "Exercises for Polishing Your Speaking Style." Look for the exercise that will help you with your specific problem, and do it now for best results.

EXERCISES FOR POLISHING YOUR SPEAKING STYLE

First, review the *distracting* messages your body sends (see p. 153). Read over the following list of speech mannerisms from *Asserting Yourself*[1] and get them clearly in mind. One way to do this is to observe yourself in a mirror as you practice your speech. Which mannerism would you like to change? Find your distracting behaviors and follow the directions for eliminating them. Practice these exercises in front of a mirror as you say short chunks of your speech. Then practice to improve your everyday expressiveness. Here are some suggestions for changing behaviors that are distracting and annoying to audiences.

Body-Language Exercises

EYE CONTACT
The eyes are powerful communicators. Use them by looking at people, making contact. Our eyes, more than any other part of our body, lift us over the void that can stand between us and our audience.

Not looking? If you are not seeing yourself in the mirror, focus your look by selecting a spot on your face in the mirror. Each time you look away from your face in the mirror, focus back on your face.

Shifting your head and eyes excessively? Be careful not to look as if you are watching a tennis match. Determine to focus on one part of your face for at least five seconds before shifting your head or eyes. If your head constantly moves, stop your speech and begin again.

FACIAL EXPRESSION

Our faces can tell an audience immediately whether we are strained or relaxed, eager or bored. They mirror our inner feelings to an audience, and certain expressions can be very distracting.

Clearing your throat excessively? Frequent clearing of the throat signals nervousness. Clearing the throat actually tightens muscles, however, so practice relaxing it before the day of the speech. Drink oodles of water for days before speaking so that your body won't run dry. Notice the wave of relaxation that ripples down your throat as you swallow. Exaggerate the feeling of the open throat.

Swallowing repeatedly? Drink *lots* of water for days before speaking, and take a sip of water before speaking. Each time you swallow, feel the deep throat relaxation. Memorize that good feeling of an open, relaxed throat. Practice relaxing your throat by *recalling* that feeling in your throat several times a day. Right before speaking recall the feeling of an open throat. Just let your throat muscles do nothing. Yawning helps, too.

Wetting your lips? You may express fear and tension by getting dry lips. To relieve tense lips during practice, purse them into an extreme kiss position. Hold for ten seconds, then let go. Feel them relax. Repeat this several times throughout the day and before you speak. (Using a lip balm can help, too.)

Wrinkling your forehead? Ask someone close to you to call attention to your "worry wrinkles." Stroke away those lines by running your fingertips gently over your forehead. It is difficult to get rid of wrinkling, so you may need to go to extreme measures: Stretch out your wrinkles with tape, or put on an egg yolk mask, which will solidify and give you instant feedback by cracking each time you begin to wrinkle.

A prissy, tight-lipped, mouth? Do you keep your mouth rigid, hardly opening it? If so, your volume will be poor and your words mushed together. To correct this, pucker lips very hard, then let your jaw hang loose and relax your tongue. Practice letting go of the muscular-tension in your tongue throughout the day.

GESTURES

Hands can describe ideas and emphasize important words. They help mold your ideas and add expressiveness. But they can become distracting if they are "too busy." Do you do any of these things: Cover your mouth? Scratch your head? Rub your eye? nose? neck? Tinker with your jewelry, coins in your pocket? Tug at your tie or belt? Then try this weight-holding exercise: Practice your speech while holding a book in each hand; this will remind you to keep your hands at your side. Practice a chunk of your speech with the weights, memorizing the feeling of the weights. Now practice several trials without them. Each time your hands start to tinker, recall the heaviness of the books and let the relaxation soak into your hands and arms.

Many speakers ask, "What should I do with my hands?" My answer is always, "What do you normally do?" Most folks don't know. Why we are unaware of our hands offstage, whereas onstage they become three feet long is a curiosity. A way to use your hands more appropriately is to practice a part of your speech that describes an event or process or things in a series. Then say the words silently as you pantomime with your hands those events, processes, things. "Place" one event to your right, another to your left with your hands. You'll feel like a ham, but you'll soon get the hang of it. After a couple of silent run-throughs, practice your speech aloud with the gestures. Loosen up. Have fun with your pantomime and experience how pantomiming the events, and so forth, can help you remember these facts more easily. Practice in everyday conversations, too, in order to make gesturing a more natural part of your style.

POSTURE AND MOVEMENT

Distracting mannerisms communicate timidity, restlessness, or lack of confidence, and they distract your listener. Body language can speak more powerfully than words, so rehearse it at least as carefully as you rehearse your words.

Shifting feet? Stand still and "nail" your feet down with heavy books. You will notice your "shiftiness" when the books slip off your feet. Pretty soon you'll catch yourself before you shift weight, and your problem will be over.

Pacing aimlessly? Play the "solid footing" game. Set two chairs (or four) around yourself. Feel safe and protected, and memorize the good feeling of standing still in your special space.

Awkward moving? If you feel (and look) clumsy try these exercises: First put your weight on your *right* foot; then *move right* with your *left foot*. That should feel awkward. To change your feelings of awkwardness and to move gracefully, try this: Put your weight on your *right* foot, then *move left* with your *left foot* while looking left at the same time. Now your head and feet move in the same direction at the same time. You are not at cross-purposes, with your body going in every which way. Practice shifting your weight and moving your feet with an economy of movement. That's gracefulness.

Not moving? If you feel like a statue when you stand in front of an audience, experiment with these loosening-up exercises: Bounce a tennis ball as you say your introduction. Move the ball around, throwing it in unusual ways, under a leg, behind your back, and so on. Use a silk scarf to "paint" the room as you move your arms gracefully around in circles, above your head, or down to the floor. To move onstage, practice a sport offstage, or join a dance class. People who move easily while speaking before a group are people who do so in private life.

Vocal-Expression Exercises

To assess your voice quality, use a tape recorder or ask your friendly critic to check your strong and weak points.

VOLUME

You probably know that you need air to make a sound. To make good, loud sounds, you need plenty of air and you need to ration it as you speak. If you run out of breath and end up sounding shaky and weak, you can work yourself into a first-class case of jitters.

Short of Breath? Do you have trouble catching your breath as you speak? Try this calm-breathing exercise:

> *Stand erect and put your hand flat against your diaphragm, that large muscle below your rib cage. Take a deep breath without raising your shoulders and notice what happens when you breathe* in. *If your chest expands, your diaphragm will move down and your hand will move* out *when you breathe in. That means you are breathing correctly. If the hand on your diaphragm is* not *moving out as you inhaled, you are very likely having breathing problems.*
> *Again—inhale as you push your hand out.*

Practice this short exercise many times daily until you can move your muscles "out" to make room for large quantities of air in your lungs. Without good breathing, you can't keep your train-of-thought moving smoothly. A voice teacher, who will work with you privately, can help you correct bad breathing habits. Your voice and your health are worth the small investment.

Can you be heard? Some people have enough volume, but they wear out their throats trying to get their voice projected to the back of the room. Here's an exercise that will help you "throw" your voice without shouting:

> *Take a deep breath (push diaphragm muscle* down) *and then say, "Ahhhhh" for as long as your breath lasts. How many seconds can you say, "Ahhhhhh"? Repeat the "Ah" exercise several times every day. Then try the exercise with other vowel sounds like $\bar{e}, \bar{i}, \bar{o}$, and their variations. Record your time for sustaining these sounds and try to exceed your previous record. This exercise will help you build stamina and at the same time relax the throat.*

PROJECTION

Is your message aimed toward your listener, or do you seem to be swallowing words or dropping them right on the podium? If so, you need to work on projection. Here is an exercise to help you feel what it's like to project your voice:

> *Find a partner who will play "voice tennis" with you (or throw the ball at a wall or garage door, which will return it to you and serve as a partner). Stand five feet from your partner and toss the ball underhand as you say, "Helllllloooooo," for as long as the ball is in the air. (Make sure you open your mouth, drop your jaw, and let go with a relaxed throat.) Take turns throwing the ball and Helllllllooooooos back and forth. Memorize the feeling in your*

throat muscles as you throw your Helllllloooooo. *After five or six* Helllllloooooos, *move to about ten feet apart and repeat the toss with the* Helllllloooooo. *Work back gradually until you reach twenty or thirty feet.*

Move together again, throwing the ball and your Helllllloooooo *at closer distances. Always notice how your vocal muscles* feel *and your voice* sounds *at different distances.*

When you rehearse your speech, ask your critic where your voice sounds best. Five feet? Ten feet? Always ask for a microphone if you are likely to strain your voice, because when the voice has to strain and gives out, anxiety usually occurs.

ARTICULATION

Do you mumble? If an audience must continuously figure out your words, they will grow restless and irritated. Sloppy sounds give the impression of a dumb and careless person. Correct such mistaken impressions by changing your articulation. Think what miracles Henry Higgins performed by coaching Eliza Doolittle to speak like a lady in *My Fair Lady*. Like Eliza, you may have to change the way your tongue and lips move in order to change your speech—and your image. Check your articulation:

Pucker your lips and sound a p *and* t *as in* pet *at a piece of paper held six inches away from your mouth. Does it flutter as you sound the* p *and* t*? No? Then increase the air behind the quick explosion.*

Increase the strength and agility of your tongue, so that it moves easily and quickly, shaping the sounds beautifully and correctly. A good speech teacher can help you articulate better.

Do you lisp? If you place your tongue inaccurately, you will distort *s* sounds. For example, *mister* comes out *mither, sane* comes out *thane, mess* comes out *meth.* A lisp can make you sound babyish, weak, and ineffectual. It is difficult to correct a lisp by yourself. Seek help from a speech correctionist if you think you have too soft an *s* sound.

PITCH

Can you express emotions? Many people do not communicate their feelings adequately because they do not vary the *pitch* and *rhythm* of their voice. They sound flat and monotonous. If your voice has a steadily high pitch, you will make a flighty impression on your listeners; if you don't vary your rate of speaking you will sound dull and boring. You can improve your emotional expression. Try these exercises to help you vary your vocal pitch.

Do you speak too high (or too low)? Superior speakers have a wide pitch range. Measurements show that the average pitch for outstanding speakers is close to C below middle C for men and close to G sharp below middle C for women. To discover your own average pitch, say a sustained *Ohhhh* and find the matching key on a piano.

Is your pitch no more than two or three tones (notes) away from the ones typical of superior speakers? Good. Then it is within normal limits. If your pitch is four or more tones lower or higher than the averages of the superior men or women speakers, you may be using your voice improperly. Consider taking voice lessons.

Is your voice thin? Do you sometimes talk through your nose? If you allow air to pass through your nose on vowel sounds, your voice will sound raspy and irritating. Do you sound vowels correctly?

> *Pinch your nose and say* bee, let, father, rutter, booth, row. *Now say those words with your nose open. (They should sound the* same *in both trials. If they don't, direct more air out your mouth.) Continue sounding each word, first with a closed nose, then with an open one, until the quality of the vowel is clear and the words sound the same with your nose open or closed.*

All good speakers learn to communicate content, but exceptional speakers also express feelings with their message. If you think your voice lacks expression, enroll in an "oral expression" course at your local college, or take singing lessons. You can learn vocal expression through expert coaching. You may need to "tune in to your voice."

RATE OF SPEAKING

Can your listeners keep up with you, or do they fall asleep? How fast or slow should you speak? It depends on the complexity of your subject, the size of your audience, the size of the room, and how clearly you articulate your words. Listeners can get bored if you speak too slowly or too quickly. Disfluencies such as "ah," "anda," "uh," and repetitive fillers distract an audience. Instruct your critic to raise a hand whenever you stall with a disfluency. Silence is better than *ums* and *ahs*.

Probably the best way to improve your rate of speaking is to eliminate all the disfluencies that break your rhythm. I have observed that most people with disfluencies (such as repeating two or three words while they find their next thought) are helped by practicing the Progressive Relaxation Exercise in Appendix 1 every day for two to three weeks. In addition, you can instruct your critic to raise a hand each time you utter an "um" or "ah." That kind of signal stops most disfluencies almost immediately.

Decide how you might deliberately vary your rate of speaking at different points in your speech. Analyze and mark your entire speech outline for pauses, words to be stressed, and words to receive pitch inflections. You may want to pause slightly before or after important words and slow down for complicated phrases or important words that carry meaning. After marking your note cards with your own personal symbols, such as — for "pause" or / for "raise the pitch," or ==== for emphasis, practice the pauses, stresses, and inflections chosen. Edit and correct your markings until you get the emotional tone you want. The markings will alert you to alter your expression.

SUMMARY

It is impossible to have a good public-speaking voice without having good, everyday breathing habits. Likewise, if you mumble in private conversations, you'll find it difficult to be clear in public; if you never look people square in the eye while you converse, you'll avoid audience eye contact. But you can change, and it doesn't take a lifetime of experience. It does take a plan of action:

- ☐ Check out your weaknesses and admit what they are (don't excuse them). Enlist help from your friendly critic and develop behavioral objectives.
- ☐ Consider professional help with your voice (singing and speech teachers, especially for improving breathing and articulation).
- ☐ Practice chunks of your speech in front of a mirror or with a tape recorder—replay, retape, replay—and keep going until you achieve what you want.
- ☐ Show more enthusiasm and expressiveness in everyday conversations by improving your pitch variation.
- ☐ Practice moving your body in new ways: Learn a new, active sport, or take a dance or improvisational acting class.

The important thing is free up your body and voice in daily life and you'll stand a better chance of feeling, looking, and sounding good when you are speaking before a group.

12

Avoid
Last-Minute
Panic

It makes little sense to have a good speech and then sabotage it with careless oversights and last-minute jitters. Instead, take precautions against those devilish little things that could go wrong and upset your newly found confidence. Suggestions in this chapter will help you stay calm and organized before you perform.

THE WEEK BEFORE

Relax

The major part of your self-improvement program is already underway. Early in this book you were urged to start your daily program of progressive relaxation and to practice systematic desensitization. I hope you have used these training exercises to get your body and imagination in shape for performance. If you have put off such training, then begin immediately by doing the relaxation exercise in Appendix 1 and the desensitization exercises in chapter 8. They are easy to do, require little time, and can help eliminate excess muscle tension and mental fatigue. Continue with these exercises every day, including the day you speak. With ample practice, you can learn to relax your muscles, feel less uptight, and plan for your success.

Breathe Correctly

Many beginning speakers fear they will lose control of their voices and sound shaky and high-pitched. Others fear they will not speak loudly enough or else they will run out of air and will not be able to speak at all. Fears about running out of breath are well founded, because without breath a person cannot utter one sound and with too little breath a person strains the vocal cords and ends up with a shaky, raspy, high-pitched voice. These breathless speakers end up feeling defeated before they reach the podium. Although proper breathing is a skill few people have, you can get better. You can strengthen a weak, shaky voice by practicing the breathing exercises on page 157.

During the last twenty-four hours it is easy to slip into a pattern of shallow breathing, using mainly the upper chest. If done long enough, this shallow, frequent breathing can create hyperventilation. When this occurs, you feel that you can't catch your breath or get a deep breath. Quite understandably, you get very self-conscious about breathing when you can't breathe! Practice the progressive relaxation exercise, as well as the calm breathing exercise. Hyperventilation seems to be a fairly common symptom of stagefright. Some people who have difficulty regulating their breathing report that reducing their caffeine intake helps. Others say that an easy jog (if you're used to it), a leisurely walk, or a swim helps regulate breathing. Another way to regulate breathing is to do the entire progressive relaxation exercise once or twice a day before your performance.

It makes good sense to relax before each practice session. Right now try a series of routine warm-up exercises, which you can repeat twenty or thirty minutes before each rehearsal and performance (see Appendix 1).

Write Your Own Introduction

If you speak often enough, the time will come when you are embarrassed by a poorly organized, excessively long, deadly boring, and irrelevant introduction. The way to avoid such embarrassments is really very simple. If you want to make sure that you are presented to your audience in the best possible way for the occasion, write out, word for word, your own introduction.[1] Double-space it on good-quality paper (make extra copies to keep in your file and to carry along with you). Keep in mind certain rules, which can be used when you introduce a speaker. A good introduction

1. introduces your topic
2. tells why you are qualified to talk on your topic
3. reveals your humanness
4. repeats your name and speech title

First, *introduce your topic*. Good beginnings require that you gain audience attention by arousing their interest in your topic and by meeting their needs. An audience will be attracted by a quotation, a startling statement, an unusual story. Furthermore, they need to know how listening to you will benefit them. With a good appeal you can show the relationship between your speech and their needs. Finally, state the title of your speech.

Second, *tell why you are qualified to talk about the topic*. Briefly outline your experience, and emphasize those aspects of your experience (both work and educational) that qualify you as an expert on your subject. Do not use initials, such as MBO or APA without explaining what they mean (respectively, Management by Objectives and the American Psychological Association). Avoid lists of qualifications, such as the enumeration of every civic, fraternal, social, and philanthropic group you belong to. Name a couple of major organizations or awards that distinguish you.

Third, *make yourself personal and human*. Is there some personal story or anecdote that reveals a nonfactual you? Make sure that the personal anecdote, habit, or observation qualifies you as an unofficial expert of your topic. It should be light, humorous, and never embarrassing to your audience (that is, not too personal).

Finally, *repeat your name and title of your speech*. Repeating this information gives a ring of finality to the introduction.

In any kind of speech, you should aim for short sentences and active verbs. Read the introduction out loud to check for ease of reading. Eliminate long words with many syllables, clumsy phrasing, difficult sounds. It should sound conversational, so avoid stuffy words such as *heretofore* (*before* is better) or clichés such as "without further ado . . ." (say: "I am delighted to present _____," or "I welcome _____"). Make it simple. Make it short.

You can send in your prepared introduction any time after you have agreed to speak, but usually your introducer will appreciate receiving it a week before the speech. That way the person has time to practice it.

Check Out Your Speaking Environment With Your Host

It has been said that happiness is doing one's utmost under good conditions. Besides preparing and practicing your speech, you will need to check out details that will help you get those good conditions where you can do your best. A good speech can turn into a flop if it's not delivered in the right setting and under good conditions.

Make sure that the conditions regarding format and setting, which you discussed when you agreed to speak, still stand (see pages 32–33). Before you call your host to firm up these details, consider the following items, too.[2]

AUDIENCE ARRIVAL TIME

- ☐ What time will your audience arrive? Will coffee be served?
- ☐ When should you begin? Knowing this helps to set your arrival time. You will want to be done setting up when the first people arrive.

PARKING

- ☐ Where should you park? Most companies have visitor lots. Ask for directions.
- ☐ Who will meet you to unlock doors a half an hour early? Avoid irritating yourself. If you plan to arrive early, make sure that your host, the janitor, or an assistant can let you in.

DIRECTIONS

- ☐ What are the exact directions to the place where you will speak?
- ☐ How long should it take to get there? Ask your host to send a detailed map with a marked route, indicating estimated time to travel there and the building and room numbers.
- ☐ Double-check the room color so that your clothing won't clash with it or you won't blend into the woodwork.

PODIUMS

- ☐ Both tall and short people have trouble with standard podiums. If you are short, you can have one built or carry along your own small platform to stand on. If you are very tall, you might consider bringing your own extra-high table podium. Of course, you can ask for special podiums if you are a superstar, but most speakers will have to arrange for their own conveniences.
- ☐ Tell your host what kind of podium you prefer. Some podiums are false-fronted and your legs won't show; others are on a pedestal and will allow the audience to see every turn of your ankle, every shake of your knees.
- ☐ Place your podium as close as you can to your audience, optimally four to eight feet from the front rows. Distances create formality and make it difficult to project not only your voice (unless you have a mike) but your personality as well.
- ☐ If you feel awkward standing alone, ask for a table with a table podium; however, podiums are out of place when you are speaking to a small audience.

MICROPHONES

- ☐ Ask for a Lavolier mike that fits around your neck and will allow you to move without the audience losing your voice. (Stationary mikes confine a speaker but sometimes can't be avoided.)
- ☐ Arrive early so you can check out the workability of a mike.
- ☐ Practice your final run-throughs with the same restrictions that your podium or mike will impose.

LIGHTS

- ☐ Arrange for someone to help you light the audience and the podium appropriately. It can be unnerving to start speaking in a sun-streaked room and then see your audience's faces fading as twilight falls.

- Will you need someone to dim lights for slides? Arrange signals for "down" and "up."

LENGTH OF TALK

- Double-check how long you are expected to talk.
- Will some of your time be taken up by announcements? Hosts often neglect to mention announcements. If you have a thirty-minute speech and ten minutes are taken up with announcements, you will be running a race with the clock.
- How long will the introduction be? Adjust the length of your speech accordingly. Prepare your own introduction to ensure accuracy.

TIME SIGNALS

- Prearrange a time signal with your host, who can signal from behind the audience. For example, five fingers spread wide means, "You have five minutes left"; holding both arms straight up means, "Hurry up—two minutes left"; "T" with hands forming the *T* means, "Time's up. Stop." If your host can't do this, ask for a stand-in.
- Still, use your own big watch on the podium to keep you on time. It's good to have double reminders, because one or the other may fail.

QUESTIONS AND ANSWERS

- Ask your host to help you solicit questions from the audience by suggesting that he or she help "plant" questions or promise to ask a question if no one else does. Or you might suggest that your host collect questions from the audience on pieces of paper. (See pp. 173–174 for other techniques.)

VISUAL AIDS AND HANDOUTS

- Ask your host to hand out printed material at given signals from you. Or distribute them yourself before or after your talk.
- Does your slide projector have a remote control? Do you want to control it, or do you want an assistant to do it?
- Who will regulate lights to accommodate slides?

TAPE RECORDER

- Will someone tape your talk? Do you want a recording to review? Many conventions hire recorders who sell your speech. You have a right to deny this privilege if you choose.

WATER

- Will your host provide you with a big pitcherful of water? Inquire!

The following checklist is a guide to use when you phone your host. It helps you to collect all pertinent information on one piece of paper. When you are organized about details, you'll feel less harried and anxious. The form can be reproduced and used for other engagements.

Checklist for Arranging Good Conditions

Estimated audience size: _____

Description of room: size _____ color _____

Audience arrival time: _____

Who will unlock doors early for you: _____ when? _____

Parking facilities: _____

Exact directions to room: _____

Length of talk: _____ Coffee first? _____

    Announcements? _____ for how long? _____ When should speech begin? _____ End? _____

    Audience seating arrangement: _____

Kind of podium: _____

Kind of mike: _____

Question and answer period? _____ for how long? _____

Method to ensure questions? _____

Who will introduce you? _____

Who should receive your prepared introduction? _____

Visual aids:_____slide projector   16-mm film:_____

    _____overhead projector   printed handouts:_____

    _____screen   blackboard, chalk, eraser:_____

    _____flip charts, pens

Assistant to help with visual aids? _____ time signals? _____ water? _____

Assistant to help with running of projector? _____ running of lights? _____

Assistant to help with distributing handouts? _____ when? _____

Assistant to time speech? _____

Tape recording made of speech? _____

A COUPLE OF DAYS BEFORE

Think About Your Audience[3]

During your practice you have concentrated on your speech—how to remember it and how to polish your delivery. That is the way it should be. But now you must think about your audience again. The twenty-four hours before you speak is a good time to imagine your listeners in a favorable light.

Simply visualize the room and see a few people coming through the door. Are they looking forward to hearing you? Are they coming of their own free will, or are they required to attend your speech? Presumably, you have prepared your speech with their mood in mind; now prepare your emotional reaction. Tell yourself, "I will make them glad they came. I have something interesting to tell them that will benefit them. I'll do my best."

Where have these people been and what have they been doing? If they have come from work, they may be momentarily "let down." You can start by entertaining them and gradually lead them into more serious issues. On the other hand, a banquet audience poses a particular challenge for a speaker with a serious message. You may want to shorten your remarks, because such an audience's concentration is less predictable than that of a working group. Certainly you can remind yourself not to expect their full concentration and can therefore avoid being disappointed or distracted if their response is short of ideal. An audience that has been drinking is usually on edge. Be especially careful not to light their fires with innuendos and put-downs, or you'll have a grouchy, hostile audience to contend with. Besides, put-downs are out of place anytime. These people are really your guests, no matter what their disposition. However, you don't need to take mean, aggressive, snide remarks either. Simply refuse to talk if conditions get out of hand.

Are there going to be other speakers before you? What are their topics? How can you get yourself into the mood, the flow, of the day? Often it is a good idea to listen to the speaker who immediately precedes you, so that you can familiarize yourself with the audience's reaction. You may decide to arrive early to watch the audience. Is the speaker's delivery too fast? too slow? too soft? too loud? What can you do to convey your message with better clarity? If the other speakers are Bruce Jenner or Gloria Steinem, don't dismay. Audiences do not expect you to be them, but they do expect you to give your all—and they are right.

Are some people likely to arrive late or leave early? What would be their reasons? Could they have been caught in traffic or have mistaken the room number? Also, make up your mind now that you will not assume that because some people leave early, they are bored. These people may have a headache or indigestion or another commitment. Instead tell yourself, "It is unfortunate that they have to miss a good speech!"

What will people be doing after you speak? Do they have time to ask questions afterward, or are they in a rush to get on to a party or back to work? Sensitive speakers realize that most audiences have other things to do besides listening to them. It is a good idea to remind yourself now that you are one event in the lives of your audience, not *the* event.

Also, consider any unusual local happening that might affect the mood of your audience. Have there been national and international events, such as earthquakes, assassinations, recessions, and the like? Just remember that people come to you with many things on their minds. Your sensitivity to their cares will help you be less judgmental and critical of them—as well as of yourself. View your audience right now with compassion and humanity. Say to yourself, "I can't solve all the worries of my audience, but I can focus on a particular concern they have by taking my expertise to them."

Think about Yourself

As your audience arrives, what will you be doing? Distributing handouts? Sitting in the front row or on the dais? Imagine yourself at the scene. Look pleasant! Relax your hands. Move but don't squirm around. Start right now visualizing what you will do after the speech. Will you answer questions? What must you do after that? Collect your slides and notes, shake hands with your host, and walk out the door? What then? Do you have something to look forward to after your speech? Nothing is worse than doing nothing after a big effort like giving a speech. Plan now to do something that you find personally rewarding. It may be dinner out with family or friends, a good movie, a game of tennis, or a good book. Right now anticipate that reward by seeing yourself doing it!

Last-Minute Imaginings

- □ See yourself waiting for the first arrivals.
- □ See your audience coming into the room.
- □ See yourself making eye contact, smiling, greeting your audience.
- □ See yourself being introduced and walking to the podium.
- □ See your audience as you give your speech.
- □ See yourself sitting down after you speak.
- □ See yourself fielding questions or greeting people who come up to speak to you after the speech.
- □ See yourself leaving the room after your speech, enjoying your planned reward.

THE DAY BEFORE

What is the purpose of such detailed planning? Simply this: When you are trying to sleep, you don't want to worry about the mechanics of getting yourself and your paraphernalia to the speaker's hall the next day. Instead, use your energy productively and tend to details before the day of your speech. Most people find it relaxing to do these mechanical, countdown tasks. By staying task oriented these last twenty-four hours, you can feel fully prepared in mind and body.

Know Your Route

If you have any doubts about your route, phone your host for additional instructions the day before the speech. Stake out your exact path on a map. (If you are unsure, take a possible drive to the speaking location.) Know where you're going the day of the speech and how long it takes to get there. Anxiety can build fast if you don't know where you're going.

Prepare Your Clothes

It is helpful to get clothes in order, right down to lining up shoes, stockings, accessories, and personal-grooming aids. Check clothes for missing buttons, tattered hems, or unseemly wrinkles before hanging them separately from the rest of your wardrobe a couple days before speaking. A friend who was giving a speech entitled "Color and Self-Esteem" grabbed a gray jacket in the early hours of a winter morning. Not until she was in the light of a big audience did she notice that her gray jacket was inappropriate for her brown skirt. Avoid last-minute grabs.

Check Your Visuals

Double-check the sequence of your notes and number of handouts. Put slides into your own carousel and check whether they project correctly. Collect the other equipment you are supplying, such as a slide projector, flip chart, felt pens, chalk, and handouts. Does everything work? Take along extra pens and light bulbs for projectors.

I suppose that this detailed preparation can be carried to an extreme, and I may be a prime example. After I practice with the equipment one last time, I lock all my paraphernalia in my car and check the gas gauge.

An expert party giver I know never cooks during the day of the party. I've decided that similar advice is good for a speaker: Don't put yourself and your equipment together on the day of the speech. Any preparation you would ordinarily do tomorrow, do now.

THE NIGHT BEFORE

Most of us feel more anxious the closer we come to performance. Some people attempt to overcome their mounting anxiety by practicing their speech another ten times; others try to escape it all by going out to the movies, watching TV, or jogging themselves out of their minds. Because muscle tension of any kind produces fatigue, jogging ten miles when you normally run a mile is probably not going to relax you. Nor is watching TV all evening (eyeballs get tired too). Walking miles around a golf course or traipsing out to a movie isn't the answer either. And you won't produce a stress-free evening by practicing a speech until you are ready to collapse.

You aren't alone if you resort to extreme remedies, however. Under stress, people often do peculiar things. One time I was unusually anxious about a speech, and I felt compelled to do *something,* anything, to keep busy and distracted. To ease my panic, I started cleaning my closet at ten o'clock the night before my speech, and by midnight, clothing, shoes, and purses were strewn everywhere. Both my bedroom and I were in such complete disorder that I had to close the door and sleep on the living room couch. I slept fitfully until sunrise in the unfamiliar and uncomfortable setting. Quite naturally, I looked awful, felt worse, and dreaded speaking. From that day on, I vowed to plan my life carefully the night before a speech.

Plan Moderation

To meet stressful situations with all your wits about you, plan your activities to provide maximum rest and minimum stress. You can beat nervousness if you *plan moderation*. Use an activity as a way to unwind but not undo yourself. Reward yourself with easy activities that are rewards, not punishments. Don't clean a closet. Keep to your normal pattern of sleeping. Avoid sleeping pills, liquor, tranquilizers— try milk instead. Eat lightly, so that your body doesn't have to work overtime. Drink lots of liquids and avoid decongestants, such as cold tablets, which can make a dry mouth go drier under stress.

Practice One Last Time

Next I suggest that you take the phone off the hook, lock your bedroom door, and practice your speech *one last time* in front of a mirror. Do not rerun your slides, simply note when you will switch them on and off. Practicing alone will supply you with the bedtime security of knowing you can do it. Before you perform your last relaxation rites, put your briefcase with your precious notes by the front door. Finally, you might even prepare the coffeepot and set the breakfast table, so you won't have to think about anything except your speech. The idea is to tend to details *now* so that you can put yourself on "automatic" the day of the speech.

Slow down with a leisurely bath and a cheerful book. Choose one for its happy, relaxed mood. (A spellbinding mystery may keep you reading far into the night, much to your detriment the next morning.) After turning off the lights, put yourself through an abbreviated progressive relaxation exercise, letting yourself float off on a carefree cloud. There you can enjoy a very good feeling of accomplishment and confidence, not to mention a good night's sleep.

Countdown Checklist for the Last 24 Hours

- ☐ Check out your departure time, destination, and route.
- ☐ Check out your clothes, shoes, and accessories and put them aside from your other clothes.
- ☐ Count your handouts and put them in your car.
- ☐ Gather your equipment (check slides in carousel, felt pens, flip charts, and so on) and put it in your car.
- ☐ Set up your breakfast.
- ☐ Rehearse one more time in front of the mirror.
- ☐ Take a leisurely bath.
- ☐ Read a funny book.
- ☐ Turn off the lights and go through your relaxation exercise in bed.

THE DAY OF THE SPEECH

It is important to pace yourself slowly the day you speak. For example, allow an extra half hour to travel to your destination, so that you will have ample time to check out the room where you will speak. You may find that your request for a particular seating arrangement has not been met or that equipment is not working properly. If you arrive first, you can deal with the emergency—or ask someone else to deal with it. If you find a two-foot-high speaker's platform situated only a foot or two away from the front row, you can change the arrangement and avoid "looking down" on your audience.

Likewise, if the room is too hot or too cold, you will have time to locate a maintenance man. If it is too light or too dark, you can arrange shades or have burned-out bulbs replaced. Chairs can be rearranged, podiums moved, PA systems tested. You can put your house in order the way you want it. Even when you cannot change the environment, you can acknowledge its limitations and share your concern with the audience. Most audiences will accommodate you by listening if you ask for their attention in spite of the environmental obstacles. If you can also add a bit of humor about anything which is not working properly, then you can share laughter, the great elixir for tension.

Do a "Dry Run"

Arriving a half hour early gives you a chance to familiarize yourself with the room, the podium, the audience arrangement, and the acoustics. Sometimes in checking out your course to the podium you'll notice wires that you could trip over or a step leading up to the platform. Practice your walk to the podium so you can appear graceful in spite of such obstacles. Before your listeners arrive, practice—unhurriedly and in a relaxed manner—those first minutes of your speech, thereby testing the acoustics and composing yourself for those opening lines. Finally, pretend that you are a member of the audience and sit in their seats. As you sit there, imagine yourself standing and speaking up at the podium.

When you make a positive first impression, you are helping your audience relate to you quickly, and when audiences respond warmly to your introduction, you can feel more confident and eager to give the rest of your speech. These trial runs help you deal with problems ahead of time, and that experience builds confidence.

Last-Minute Operations

- ☐ Check out the ventilation.
- ☐ Check out the seating arrangement.
- ☐ Clean up dirty blackboards, used ashtrays, coffee cups, and so on.
- ☐ Check out blinds and lights.
- ☐ Check out the microphone.
- ☐ Practice walking to the podium and returning to your seat.
- ☐ Practice the introduction of your speech.
- ☐ Sit in the audience and see yourself up front as the speaker.
- ☐ Sit still, close your eyes, take a deep breath, and relax with heaviness.

Relax Minutes Before You Speak

Refresh yourself during the fifteen minutes before you speak. Find a quiet, private place to do your warmup exercises (see Appendix 1).

Make Contact with Your Audience Before You Speak

Once your audience begins to arrive, take a personal interest in them. Look around you. Is there someone close by to whom you can say hello? Short conversational exchanges can help you get interested in your audience before you talk. If you don't want to talk, you can ease your nerves by simply looking and smiling at three or four people who look friendly and kind. Then, instead of seeing only unfamiliar faces as you begin to speak, you can concentrate on those who look like old friends. This will help you to speak in a more personal, relaxed tone of voice during those first crucial minutes at the podium. Others in the audience will not notice that you are communicating with only three or four sympathetic souls; they will only see you behaving in a warm, personal manner. As a speaker, you will create a mood of liveliness and enthusiasm.

While you are being introduced, look at the speaker most of the time. You want an audience to hear the good things being said about you, so don't ham it up by distracting them from your introducer. Once you have been introduced, rise quickly, move to the podium with purpose and shake hands (extend your hand as you approach the person who has introduced you, so that he or she will anticipate your action). Take your time by arranging your notes, scanning the audience, and counting 1-2-3. Then begin.

AFTER THE SPEECH

Succeed with the Question and Answer Period[3]

Face it. The question and answer period is often a time of letdown for a speaker. It can also be a no-win situation. If you have delivered a good speech and a sparkling performance, you probably would like to end while you are ahead. Conversely, if the speech was difficult and the audience hardly responded at all, you probably would like to head for home and a hot bath. What, then, can be the purpose of a question and answer period? Two things: It gives the audience a chance to inquire and challenge, and it gives you a second chance to complete your explanations. If you honestly welcome the chance for a continued dialogue, then you will have come a long way in reducing your anxiety about this part of your performance.

Here are some of the reasons speakers fail in the question and answer period:

- □ They don't know what to do when no questions are asked.
- □ They don't know what to do when they don't understand a question.
- □ They get defensive when someone asks a question they can't answer or catches them making a mistake.
- □ They are afraid that people will ask personal questions.
- □ They are afraid that they will make a stupid mistake because they don't know all the facts.

Obviously any of these hazards could occur. If you face a difficult personality, how can you assert yourself so that you won't appear stupid, defensive, fearful, unsure, unclear, and downright mean?

Get Questions

First, make sure that you get questions. Being asked no questions at all is almost as unnerving as being asked a hostile question. Here are some action plans that will ensure a lively question and answer period:

□ *Plant questions in the audience*. Write out a few questions you want to be asked and enlist your friends to ask them.

□ *Ask a question*. "Would anyone like to know some guidelines for deciding 'Should I assert myself'?" Someone will nod or say, "Yeah, sure," which is your cue to answer your own question.

□ *Ask your host to solicit questions* from the group before the meeting. This often works for very passive and very hostile, aggressive groups, the former being too shy to speak and the latter being too angry.

□ *Attribute a question to others*. Say: "Many of my students want to know about . . ." or "Shy people usually ask: . . ." or "Yesterday, I overheard a customer say, 'If you don't give me my money back, I'll never shop here again.' Do you think he gave her money back? Why? Why not?"

□ *Ask directly*. For example, "Would you like to hear how our moods affect memory?" (Be sure to choose a very popular aspect of your topic, or you may get some No's.)

You may get questions all right, but you may have a hard time figuring out what the questioner is saying. What can you do assertively to control feelings of irritation or stupidity? First off, realize that most people—like ourselves—have stage fright, and asking a question is a brave act. Isn't it understandable that they don't say things clearly? Practice compassion. What can you do to get clarity? to keep on track? to refuse put-downs? Here are some examples:

REPHRASE COMPLICATED, LOADED, OR UNCLEAR
QUESTIONS

Q: *"Do you think men and women are really equal?"*

A: *"I believe you are asking me if I think men and women are different and if I support ERA. Is this right?"*

Q: *"Yes."*

A: *"I believe men and women are different, but I also believe all people—even those who are different from men—should have equal rights under the law. Therefore I support the Equal Rights Amendment."*

KEEP QUESTIONERS ON TRACK

Q: *"I have this friend who is always interrupting me and I feel so angry. Don't you think interrupters are rude?"*

A: *"The words rude and interrupter are words we all use frequently. They are good examples of how our observations of other people's behavior are not truly objective descriptions but rather value judgments. Let me illustrate this important point by . . ."*

DO NOT ALLOW OTHERS TO PUT YOU DOWN WITH
NEGATIVE LABELS, SUCH AS "DEARIE" "YOUNG
LADY," AND SO ON

Q: *"Look, my dear little lady . . ."*

A: *"My name is* _____. *Please call me by my name"* or *"I like to be
called* _____."

Admit Your Mistakes

As a speaker, your first obligation to an audience is to be truthful. Scientific subjects
require objective, observable data for proof, whereas topics about moral issues rely
heavily on an emotional appeal to needs. Whether you are presenting a scientific
paper or a moral "truth," you need to be honest. That means you must get your facts
straight and from reliable sources (see chapter 6). If you don't know an answer,
admit, "I don't know that fact, but I can get it" (only say this if you can).

If you make up statistics, testimony, or untrue examples, you deserve to be put
on the spot. In cases where you have made an honest mistake, do not interpret benign
questions as hostile. Remarks such as "Would you document that statistic?" Or "I
have read the whole quotation. You are leaving out the part where the president says
. . ." may turn your face red or unnerve you, but get hold of yourself. If these seem
hostile to you, then you are not distinguishing reasonable disagreement from vicious
slander. If you have made an honest mistake, swallow hard and admit it—"I'm
wrong" or "I am at fault." Answer quickly and get on to the next question. Be
grateful that someone has helped you so that you will never make that mistake again.
At least you won't discredit yourself with your next group.

Understand Techniques of Arguers

Understand that some people ask a question and proceed to answer it by arguing with
you. Perhaps they ask questions to release tension, but do not spend all your time with
one arguer. Others will ask questions clearly without pet editorializing. Spend time
with them. They are not arguing; they are clarifying.

If your subject is controversial, prepare for the worst. That way you won't be
caught off guard. First of all, to know how to answer, you must recognize how
arguers may confront you. Arguers have at least four characteristic ways of presenting their views:

1. Arguers cite "new evidence." Often it is unheard of, and frequently it is not
   from a reliable source. (See chapter 6 for a review of what constitutes evidence.)
2. Arguers attempt to disqualify you by questioning your credentials: "You're a
   professional woman; how can you talk about being a housewife?" (Always be
   able to say in a few choice words why you are an expert.)

3. Arguers attempt to dismiss your facts by telling about one personal exception to your facts and examples. Make sure that your facts are reliable and your examples are representative (see page 84).

4. Arguers attempt to dismiss your conclusions by showing inconsistencies in the data or in your line of reasoning. It is very important that you be able to explain your reasoning. Also, you will need to identify the fallacious reasoning (if there is any) of your arguer. (See pages 85–88 to check out the soundness of your reasoning.)

ASSERTIVE-REPLY TECHNIQUES

It is useful to identify the kinds of assertive replies that can be made to difficult audience members. The following replies are taken from the author's book *Asserting Yourself,* chapter 8.[4] These replies are adapted here to answer audience questions and statements that attempt to put you down or discredit you. Use them judiciously, because excessive reliance on one-liners is aggressive and can cast you in an unfavorable light. Nevertheless, these assertive replies can serve to equalize the balance of power in a humane way when you feel that a listener is clearly abusive and taking advantage of you.

Persist	Repeat your main point, the object of your speech. Usually this is your central thought or a main point of your discussion. (''I wish to emphasize the main idea here: . . .'')
Disagree	Make a straightforward, direct statement. (''I don't agree.'')
Emphasize Feelings/Thoughts	Stress your feelings or thoughts about the arguer's behavior. (''It is important to me to keep our exchange on a nonpersonal basis. Therefore, I wish to stick to a discussion of the subject, not of my personality.'')
Agree . . . But	Agree with the other person's right to have certain feelings and draw certain conclusions, but disagree with the idea that you must hold the same feelings or draw the same conclusions. (''You may feel that way, but I have different feelings and, therefore, I draw different conclusions.'')
Dismiss	Ignore a rude or detouring comment completely, or—better—quickly deny its relevance to the problem under discussion. (''That's not the point here.'')
Redefine	Don't accept someone's negative label for your behavior; redefine your behavior in positive terms.

	(Q: "You sure are sensitive." A: "I'm sensitive to the facts" or "You may call me sensitive, but I call myself aware.")
Answer Quickly	Sometimes it's best to answer with a simple yes or no or with some other brief, direct reply, so that you can get on with your central concern. (Q: "How can you know about being a homemaker when you're a professional woman?" A: "I'm both.")
Ask a Question	Instead of accepting vague criticism, ask for clarification. ("In what ways do you think I'm presenting a biased view? Do you have other information that would change my mind?")
Stipulate Consequences	When pushed to the limit of your tolerance or when you feel threatened, consider promising realistic, negative consequences if the offensive heckler continues. Beware of this approach, because it may backfire. ("I'll not continue unless the officials of this gathering ask the heckler to leave" may be coming on with too much too soon.)

Here's how you could use these assertive replies for typical, hostile questions. Notice that aggressive (hurtful) arguers get at the speaker with put-downs and innuendos, whereas assertive replies get at the problem with neutral, objective language.

Arguer:	*"Where in the world did you get that statistic? You are way out of it!"*
Assertive reply:	"I got it from ＿＿＿＿ (answer quickly), *and they are timely and accurate*" (redefine and emphasize a thought).
Arguer:	*"I don't see how you can quote Ms. X. She's a pervert."*
Assertive reply:	"I quote Ms. X because she is an expert physicist and a member of many respected academies (redefine) *and therefore, highly qualified to support my point*" (emphasize a thought).
Arguer:	*"I can give you a hundred examples that prove the opposite point of view."*
Assertive reply:	"Perhaps you could—although "a hundred" must be an exaggeration (emphasize a thought). *But would they all be as accurate, appropriate, and honest as mine?*" (Ask a Question).
Arguer:	*"I really don't get your point. How does 'I think it's important' differ from saying, 'I feel it's important'?"*
Assertive reply:	"I realize this is still puzzling you (emphasize feelings), *but I have explained it twice in the last hour* (emphasize a thought). *I must move on to other topics* (persist), *but I'll be glad to talk to you at break time*" (emphasize a thought).

Delivery Points for Question
and Answer Period

- □ Keep up your speaking style. Do not change your style drastically when you field questions.
- □ Maintain eye contact with the whole audience, not just the person who asks the question.
- □ Repeat every question before you answer it.
- □ Don't protest with a hostile arguer for too long. Give an accurate but quick answer.
- □ Keep yourself on track. This is not the time to explain the point or tell the story you forgot to tell during your speech.
- □ Keep questioners on track. Resist *their* agendas. Ask them to clarify their question if you don't understand it, or say, "Let me make sure I understand your question . . . " (and repeat it).
- □ Never put down your questioners, even if they appear dumb, rambling, and irritable. Instead, use assertive replies, which get at the problem, not at the person.

Now get ready to deliver your train-of-thought. If you have assembled your thoughts so that they come one after the other in a reasonable order, if you have practiced carefully session by session, and if you have arranged for a favorable setting, then I think you'll find excitement and enjoyment in this trip to the podium. Stand straight. Speak superbly. Experience the joy of knowing that you have something important to say and that you know how to say it. That is painless public speaking!

13

Speaking Up
In Meetings

Do you know anyone who looks forward to meetings? Have you heard anyone anywhere say, "I'm so excited! I'm a member of my organization's problem-solving committee, and we get to discuss problems and decide solutions for the entire group?" Probably not. Most people associate committees with tiring sessions filled with continuing irritations. When the hour grows late and the solution grows longer, haven't you seen perfectly normal, cooperative people turn into brutal beasts incapable of reasonable talk? When frustration and fatigue take over, group members become divided and vicious, and the problem-solving group has become a problem to itself. Even when factions don't develop as a result of long, rambling meetings, people are clearly exhausted and their spirit and enthusiasm for the organization are seriously diminished.

How do meetings fall apart? Why do people give up? What can you do about it? That's what this chapter is all about. It is intended as a useful, short guide for democratic-minded people who want to be less intimidated and overwhelmed by groups and more assertive and influential.

It is important to distinguish one kind of group from another. This chapter does not include groups such as existential therapy groups, where the format is to forgo momentarily normal social habits of cooperation and politeness so that members can report their thoughts and spontaneous reactions freely. Encounter groups, T-groups, sensitivity groups, and therapy groups are relevant to clinics and hospitals and possibly to industry and governmental agencies, and "growth" groups where the purpose is to enable participants to express feelings about themselves and each other. This chapter does focus on many other groups, such as volunteer and civic organizations, school and church committees, political committees, and special interest groups such as environmental and social change groups, as well as many "skills" groups, which are directed to both student and nonstudent populations. For example, many high school and college students participate in group guidance courses, such as "How to Overcome Shyness" or "How to Choose a Career," task groups on planning school events, or small group instruction, such as improving study skills. The leader is there to help students learn a body of information, but instead of lecturing to the group, the leader uses group discussion to reveal the information.

Very broadly speaking, in skill *guidance* groups, information is emphasized, whereas in *counseling* groups, feelings are highlighted. Obviously both groups deal with both information *and* feelings, and the group dynamics and the way they are led depend not only on the emphasis (content or feelings) but on the personality of the leader. Because leadership style is particularly important in counseling groups, you should be very assertive in questioning leaders about their philosophy of groups, their orientation, and their goals for the group before you join one. Jonestown is a tragic reminder of the diabolical power an unethical leader can have when he promises ethical rewards. Will your leader deliver what he or she says? Ask and be skeptical.

At the onset, it is important to understand that a group experience is unlike any other experience. There is nothing like it in our everyday life. In ordinary day-by-day living, we do not automatically pick up the skills for being a useful member of a group. Not even experience, acquired from being a member of your local civic or church group is a surefire way to becoming effective. Practice as a member of a discussion group may help reduce your nervousness with a group; it is possible to learn slowly, through trial and error, how to become involved in the uniqueness of group work, but trial and error takes time, insight, and opportunities. While group members cast about trying to find their way, productive interaction and solutions to problems are delayed. If you want to help and not hinder your group's progress, it makes good common sense to identify and practice very specific speaking skills that will help you interact quickly and productively.

HOW YOU CAN INFLUENCE A GROUP
AS A LEADER

Be a good model for people in your group. Seem like a vague prescription? Not when you consider that a group draws its definition from its leader. Group members often resemble their leaders. Be authoritative without affection—and notice how people will react in hostile, resentful ways. Be disorganized—and see how members become scattered too. Be partial and play favorites—and watch people take sides. Be indecisive about ending discussion and taking a vote—and see how members grow unsure of themselves. A depressed, hostile, unskilled leader can radiate ineffectiveness throughout the group; a nourishing, optimistic, skilled leader thrives on interaction and radiates a positive attitude that is contagious and enriching for the group.

If you are a leader, you have special responsibilities. Good meetings occur when forward-looking leaders plan for success. Assertive leaders take the initiative and do the following tasks:

1. *Set a specific, realistic goal.* The goal is stated at the top of the agenda and emphasized at the beginning of the meeting. Vague, unfocused goals confuse groups. Also, it is difficult to cover a broad topic in a short time. Here are two examples of stated goals:
   Broad: "Our goal is to become a better publishing house."
   Specific: "Our goal during the next two hours is to provide management with specific solutions to meet our editing needs."
2. *Contact key people before the meeting.* Get their ideas and concerns. Incorporate their input into the agenda as much as possible. If feasible, get back to key people to explain omissions on the agenda.
3. *Organize the agenda* (the proposed step-by-step discussion outline) and send it to all participants at least one week before the meeting.
4. *Arrange the time carefully.* Choose a time and place where people can work under good conditions. Here are some guidelines:
   a. In order for people to sense completion of a task, present only a few agenda items in a long time slot. Discussion takes time.
   b. Decide when people are most alert and, if you can, schedule the "heavy thinking" and the most controversial items when people are least likely to be fatigued—in the morning or after a break.
   c. If participants will be discussing important controversial matter, provide some time for socializing and talking about noncontroversial items first. When people can meet socially under pleasant conditions first, they tend to be more cooperative and less hostile later.
   d. Consider entertaining participants the night before an important meeting. Entertaining is a way to provide for a group's affiliation needs, to identify with each other and have fun. Money spent creating a short and pleasant encounter can improve the *esprit de corps* and quality of interaction later. Avoid long drinking hours and heavy foods. Excess liquor and food does not quiet nerves.
   e. Provide a variation of activity in the schedule to avoid fatigue and boredom. If participants are being asked to work more than two hours without a break, many will grow restless, bored, or hostile. If you can't afford the time to break, consider serving a glass of lemonade or iced tea. Even a round of peanuts or lemon drops can provide a little relief for a tired group.
5. *Choose the setting carefully.* The meeting place should help set the psychological tone. Both room size and lighting affect people. Light, airy rooms generally

help people feel "light" and free to respond; dark, somber rooms create a "heavy" feeling, often weighing people down and making it difficult for a leader to get contributions. Although some groups need space to write and spread out papers, leaders often pay attention only to space needs and neglect the lighting requirements. Most leaders agree that groups are generally more successful in small but well-lighted rooms rather than in large but darkly lighted ones. Just as a gloomy room can cast people into a dark mood, so can a glaring room put people into a tense one. Avoid the extremes of dark and light, big and small, by choosing a room that is comfortable both visually and spatially for your size group.

Other considerations about the setting include formality or informality. Cozy homes and forest retreats can prevent a group's systematic problem solving. A room away from the office can provide a safe environment from the usual demands of the office and prevent participants from dashing back and forth to their offices. If your group is an ongoing group, change the setting once in a while to provide the group with a new orientation. Variety in setting may not answer a dull group's needs, but it can be a welcome relief for an active group.

6. *Ask for or appoint a note taker before a meeting*. Even experienced leaders often find it difficult to take notes, attend to the group's train-of-thought, and summarize points throughout a meeting. Instead, divide the labor. Some note takers can summarize periodically throughout a meeting; however, ensure your safety (and sanity) by checking that the note taker is capable of both note taking and summarizing and *has agreed* to do both tasks *before* the meeting.

7. *Navigate the meeting:* (a) summarize frequently; (b) ask questions for clarification; (c) connect one item of the agenda to the next with smooth transitions; (d) ask for volunteers or assign tasks; and (e) get verbal agreement to do the tasks. Here is a leader using all four techniques:

"We have now finished item one on the agenda. We have talked about methods for assessing a potential author: reputation in their field, former books written, and personal characteristics." [*summary*]

"Let's proceed to item two, which is, "What can the publisher do for the author to make the publishing house attractive?" [*transition*]

"So far I have heard that X and Y are the favored proposals." [*summary*]

"Is there another?" [*question for clarification*]

"Which proposal seems more workable?" [*question for clarification*]

"We need to do X, Y, and Z tasks by the first of next month" [*summary*]

"Who will volunteer?" [*question for clarification*]

and/or

"I'll assign the following people to these tasks: Joe to task X; Betty to Y; and Ted to Z [*assign tasks*]."

"Do you agree? Is there any objection?" [*get verbal agreement*]

"We have agreed to do X Y Z this month. Now let's take up the second item: What do we do next month?" [*transition*]

8. *Use assertive confrontation,* if necessary, to create a nonabusive atmosphere in which negative individuals are not allowed to obstruct problem-solving tasks (see pages 185–196).

HOW YOU CAN INFLUENCE A GROUP AS A PARTICIPANT

While leaders are responsible for setting up a good meeting by preparing a specific question, as well as a logical outline called an agenda, discussants have responsibilities too. As an assertive participator you can make a difference in the success of your group.

Inform Yourself

Study the agenda carefully and make pertinent notes, then study the issues and do some serious research. Power lies in information. If you want to influence a group, there is no substitute. Not only must you know what you are talking about, but often you must know more about the question than anyone else.

Articulate Your Ideas

It is useless to have the information and not communicate it. If there is a particular point that you want to make, prepare and practice a very short one-point "speech" ahead of the meeting (a mini train-of-thought).

Be Sincere

Be aware of your own hidden agendas. Do you want to *look* bright, or do you want to shed light on a topic? Keep in mind that it is pretty hard to look sincere about a topic if you are full of opinions but empty of facts.

Remain Flexible

Discussants who are able to withhold their opinions until they gather enough facts either on their own or from others will appear "open." Also, it is no crime to change your mind and admit it openly when new facts change your opinion. We all know people who hold tight to their opinions. They appear self-righteous, stubborn, and inflexible to others, and rarely influence anyone except themselves.

Show Support For Others

This characteristic is demonstrated when you use objective language and do not call a fellow member "stupid," "insensitive," "ignorant," or other such negative labels. Also, reinforce others for their good ideas: "You really clarified that issue succinctly" or "I think you presented the idea clearly" or "I like the way you summarize a complex issue" or "Thank you for shedding light on a big problem." Show your support to the person who is talking: look at the speaker, nod, inject a yes or "I agree" quickly at appropriate intervals in the speaker's presentation of an idea.

Get Active by Listening and Taking Notes

If you feel inadequate and are silent because you think you have nothing to say, you can still be active by asking appropriate questions, summarizing ideas, and keeping people on track. If you can't do one thing, do another to get into the action.

Develop Creativity

Most people agree that it's very difficult to think of creative solutions if you don't think about the problem before the meeting. Homework provides the seed for little ideas to grow into creative solutions. On-the-spot thinking is usually just that—spotty.

Act Friendly

People who glare and scowl are not popular. Assertive listening is listening without glares, scowls, frowns. Assertive speaking up is speaking without judgmental, put-down statements that get at another person, such as, "I don't think you've thought about this matter." Instead, introduce your point with neutral, assertive language that gets at the problem: "Another way to look at the matter before us is . . ."

Show Purposefulness

Probably the most important thing you can do as a discussant is to stick to the point. Most everyone wanders in thought, but check out those tendencies. Is the point you want to make *really* necessary? Will it add important cargo, or will it be excess baggage? Will your message add information and develop a necessary line of argument? If so, think a minute. How can you make the point quickly and succinctly? Most folks who get to the point have gotten there in their *own* heads first.

Listen

Speakers are not always careful about stating their main ideas. Interrupt and ask for clarification if you don't understand. Besides listening for the main idea, listen for new ideas, jot them down, compliment the discussant for his or her unique contribution. Listen for details, too, because many speakers sound good talking about general concepts but are miserable with details regarding implementation of their idea. In this regard, suspend judgment about the worth of an idea until you question for details.

HOW TO CONFRONT DIFFICULT PERSONALITIES

It is helpful to remember that most "difficult" people are probably not interrupting or wandering off the point deliberately. You may know people who are perfectly normal, nice human beings outside of meetings, but inside the meeting room, they appear to change personalities. Their fear of groups results in long silences or excessive talking. These annoying behaviors should be seen as ineffective coping mechanisms for people with fears and anxieties about groups. Besides anxiety, a second reason for inappropriate behavior is a lack of communication skills necessary for solving problems with a group of people. Of course, some folks may *like* to bully and upset the group's train-of-thought for the sheer purpose of gaining personal power, but, in the words of Anne Frank, it is best to consider that "People are good at heart" (but bad at group skills). Nevertheless, a nonproductive climate occurs when people habitually behave in irritating, stereotypical ways.

When and how can you confront a difficult personality without being disagreeable and hateful yourself? First, it is helpful to identify behaviors that complicate the functioning of a group. Here's a list that describes some of those difficult personalities:[1]

Who Are the Difficult Personalities?

- □ *Wanderer:* gets off the track and brings up irrelevant information.
- □ *Attacker:* attacks another person's intelligence, judgment, honesty, personal appearance.
- □ *Procrastinator:* does not do prescribed homework, makes excuses for non-productivity.
- □ *Socializer:* converses with another discussant.
- □ *Orator:* talks excessively and for long periods of time.
- □ *Debater:* debates another member by asking, "Why do you feel that way?" The "why?" affects others by forcing them to justify their feelings about their position, thus putting them on the defensive.
- □ *Jokester:* makes jokes whether or not others appreciate it.
- □ *Body-Language Manipulator:* shows disinterest or hostility by remaining silent and doodling or reading, or displaying negative body language, such as no eye contact, slouched posture, nervous tapping of fingers or shaking of foot. The negative body language indirectly controls others.

□ *Pacifier:* smoothes over conflict with mothering (or fathering) phrases, such as, "You don't really disagree with each other" or "I'm sure we'll all work together." The pacifier appears to be afraid of open conflict.

□ *Complicater:* compulsively brings up every little objection to a proposal. This person is seen as nitpicking. Very often the person is afraid to take even reasonable risks until every possible objection is answered to his or her unreasonable satisfaction.

□ *Simplifier:* glosses over details, ignores serious arguments against proposals, and constantly presents "the grand picture." This person may be anxious about details and lack skills in logical thinking. Being neither patient nor calm, the Grand Simplifier ignores incongruities and differences in order to make life easy. His or her anxiety about making decisions is solved by action—any action reduces the tension produced by indecision.

□ *Disputer:* argues unintelligently with grandiose clichés that may sound good on the surface but are really a subtle form of put-down. Disputers are often considered narrow-minded and boorish.

□ *Interrupter:* jumps into a discussion before another has finished. This person has not learned the fine art of timing that enables one to get into the discussion discreetly and persuasively.

When and Where You Can Assert Yourself

What can you do to deal effectively with difficult personalities? Decide *when* and *where* to speak to offending individuals. Some problems are solved better before a meeting, during a break, or immediately after a meeting; others need to be dealt with in the meeting itself. If you have one or more of these nonproductive types in your group, decide now when and where you could speak to them. Later you'll have an opportunity to plan what you will say to those whom you identify here as problem types for your group.

How You Can Assert Yourself

While leaders should do something about these difficult disrupters, many leaders are too passive to confront a difficult person. As a group member, what could you assertively say to help? The idea is to plan what you will say to the difficult personality without sounding like a nag or a dictator. Remember, try your best to get at a *problem* with neutral, objective, assertive language and not at a *person* with hostile, offensive, aggressive put-downs. In other words, how can you disagree without being disagreeable?

In *Asserting Yourself,* I present a four-step model for developing an assertive (not aggressive) message called **DESC**. Essentially, you write out and then practice aloud a few short sentences that do four things: Describe behavior and situations objectively → Express feelings and thoughts without blaming → Specify behavior changes → and spell out positive and/or negative Consequences. Here's how the DESC method can work for you when you want to confront a difficult personality.[2] You would

1. DESCRIBE the offensive behavior and/or the situation using objective, not subjective words. For example, assertively say to an orator, "Are you aware that you have continued to speak after I have asked you twice to wind up your remarks quickly?" (Avoid making an aggressive judgment: "Do you know that you monopolize the time by talking too long?")

2. EXPRESS your feelings and/or your thoughts to the person about his or her behavior in the group without blaming the person. For example, assertively say, "I am having a hard time getting others to talk." (Avoid aggressively saying, "You make me mad because you don't give a damn about anyone else.")

3. SPECIFY to the person exactly what you want him or her to do from now on. Be objective, be reasonable in your request, and ask for behavior change, not attitude change. For example, assertively say, "Next time I ask you to wind up, please just finish your sentence." (Avoid aggressively saying, "Change your superior attitude; stop thinking that you are a modern-day orator and that everyone is dying to listen to you.")

4. Spell out one of three CONSEQUENCES, depending on the person's agreement with your request for behavior change:

   a. If the person agrees to your Specify request, say something like this: "Thanks a lot. I appreciate your help on this matter." *(positive consequence)*

   b. If the person gives a reason for his or her excessive talking, such as, "No one else talks. Someone has to carry the ball," you could assertively say, "If you talk less, I will call on others to help you carry the burden." *(positive consequence)*

   c. If the person continues to blame others for his or her excessive talking, you could assertively say, "If you continue to talk after I have asked you to wind up, I'll ring a bell!" *(negative consequence)*

   Be sure you can carry through. (Is it appropriate to ring a bell and do you have a bell to ring?) Be careful of negative consequences, because you can gain an enemy. However, if you are pushed to the limit, a *mildly* punishing negative consequence can often let the person know you mean business. Put negative consequences in brackets [   ] to remind yourself *not* to use them unless absolutely necessary.

DESC is a useful way to organize your train-of-thought for speaking up. Assertive DESC messages have helped many thousands gain courage to voice their opinions in group situations with difficult people.

You, too, can learn to plan, write, and practice assertive DESC messages. Next time you need to assert yourself with a group member either in a meeting or privately, think about your words. Will your message assertively get at the problem and not at the person? The following sample DESC messages are not meant as blueprints which you should copy word for word; nevertheless, they should be helpful in providing some ideas for your own assertive DESC messages.

Sample DESC Messages for Difficult Personalities

Type of Difficult Personality	When and Where Will You Assert Yourself?	A Sample DESC Message
Wanderer	Beginning of the meeting	D— "I prepared an agenda that was mailed to you two weeks ago."
		E— "I think it is a good way to keep us from wandering off track."
		S— "Will you vote to accept the agenda?"
		C— "Thank you. I will appreciate your remarks that speak to the point we are discussing on the agenda." *(positive consequence)* and/or ["If I'm unsure of how your statements relate to the agenda, I will ask you for clarification."] *(negative consequence)*

Setting up expectations of what you as a leader will and will not do when individuals get off-track can reduce anxiety within a group. Speak up to all potential Wanderers at the very beginning of a meeting. But if a member starts digressing after an initial warning, you can assert yourself quickly by saying, "I'm not sure how x relates to topic y on the agenda, which is what we have scheduled ourselves to talk about now. Will you clarify, please?"

Attacker	During the meeting immediately after the attack	D— "You are calling Joe 'stupid' and Pete 'fuzzy-headed.'"
		E— "I am intolerant of personal name calling."
		S— "Please attack issues, not people."

Type of Difficult Personality	When and Where Will You Assert Yourself?	A Sample DESC Message
		C— "If you do, I'd like you to stay." (*positive consequence*) and/or ["If you continue name calling, I will insist you leave this meeting."] (*negative consequence*)

Group members can be intimidated by people who use negative labels to keep others in their place. Whether you are a leader or a participant, take immediate positive action to stop this downright mean practice.

Procrastinators	Directed to an entire group of procrastinators early in a meeting	D— "You have told me that the work which you promised to do is not done."
		E— "I am irritated that we have met now when you do not have the necessary information ready."
		S— "I suggest that we adjourn until everyone has the necessary information. Will you let me know?"
		C— "I'll look forward to getting together when you have everything together." (*positive consequence*) and/or ["I will not call a meeting until you call me."] (*negative consequence*)

Some leaders are too lenient with volunteers who promise to do work and then don't. Set up some way for procrastinators with a thousand and one excuses to be responsible. Consider a plan where they must call you or some group member if they haven't started their homework by an agreed-upon date. If only one person is holding up the group, he or she should be approached privately.

Socializers	After a minute or less of the annoying behavior	D— (If it's obvious what's going on, omit the Describe step this time; otherwise, tell them which behaviors are annoying.)

Type of Difficult Personality	When and Where Will You Assert Yourself?	A Sample DESC Message
		E— "I'm distracted from my train-of-thought.
		S— "Please give your attention to the meeting."
		C— "I appreciate your help." (*positive consequence*) and/or ["I will dismiss the meeting."] (*negative consequence*)

It's difficult to understand how people can talk and talk when a meeting is in progress. There is a tendency to think, "Oh well, their discussion must be urgent and they'll be done in a moment." Oftentimes it *is* done in a few seconds but then starts again a little while later. Leaders, speak up! If your leader doesn't, you can—and should. The socializers, not you, are the social outcasts in the eyes of the group.

Orator	During the meeting	D— "Jim, you've been talking overtime for three minutes."
		E— "I must firmly enforce time rules."
		S— "Please sit down."
		C— "I will recognize you again after others have spoken." (*positive consequence*) and/or ["I will remind you of the time rules."] (*negative consequence*)

Long-winded people can start dominating a group, because people who talk longest often get the power. You can equalize the balance of power by speaking up about this misuse of power and asking for equal time.

Debater	After a member asks, "Why do you feel this way?"	D— "You have asked Mary why she feels that *x* is important."
		E— "I think she explained her reasons for her conclusion last time, and we are not asking people to describe or explain their emotional feelings in this meeting."

Type of Difficult Personality	*When and Where Will You Assert Yourself?*	*A Sample DESC Message*
		S— "Please do not ask people to justify their emotional feelings here, only their reasoning method."
		C— "I'll appreciate your eliminating any 'why?' questions that aim at emotional justification." *(positive consequence)* and/or ["I'll remind you of their right not to have to justify their emotions."] *(negative consequence)*

Debaters are people who confuse the purpose of a problem-solving group. You are not there to justify your feelings, but to present a point of view.

Jokester	Privately, at the first break	D— "I counted five times that you stopped the meeting with your joking asides."
		E— "I am irritated by these irrelevant asides, because the group becomes sidetracked."
		S— "I want you to stop all comments you think are smart remarks." and/or
		C— "I know that you can contribute ideas rather than these distracting comments." *(positive consequence)* and/or ["I'll ask you to leave the group if you continue with these remarks."] *(negative consequence)*

Joking is a way for some individuals to reduce anxiety. A good joke appropriate to the occasion is welcomed; three or four "cute" comments constitute distraction. Sometimes ignoring one or two comments dissuades jokesters. Other times, you will need to ask for their attention in the meeting. The above message is for the persistent joker; therefore, it is easier to deliver it privately.

Type of Difficult Personality	When and Where Will You Assert Yourself?	A Sample DESC Message
Body-Language Manipulator (nonproductive body language)	In private, during a break	D— "I am aware that you are reading the newspaper during the meeting." E— "This signifies to me that you are not interested in our discussion. Are you?" S— "I would appreciate your not reading while the rest of us are working." C— "That way we won't be distracted." (*positive consequence*) and/or ["I will become increasingly irritated with your not joining in to help us."] (*negative consequence*)
Body-Language Manipulator (nonverbal disagreement)	During the meeting	D— "Harry, I see that you are shaking your head." E— "I think that means that you disagree." S— "Is that interpretation correct?" C— "I'd feel better if you all speak your piece when you disagree, because I may not see your head shaking." (*positive consequence*) and/or ["I am not going to acknowledge shaking heads anymore."] (*negative consequence*)
Body-Language Manipulator (the smile can be cover-up for disagreement)	During the meeting	D— "Sarah, I see that you are smiling." E— "I think that means that you agree with Kim." S— "Am I correct?" C— "I feel good as a leader when people speak up." (*positive consequence*) and/or

Type of Difficult Personality	When and Where Will You Assert Yourself?	A Sample DESC Message
		⎣"I can easily misread body language."] *(negative consequence)*

It is important to ask people who show negative body language to speak out. Get a verbal commitment from these silent people. At the beginning of a meeting you could say to participants, "Actions do not speak louder than their words, and therefore I will interpret silence as agreement."

Pacifier	During a break; however, in counseling groups, this would be said during the meeting, since their purpose is to talk to each other about communication patterns.	D— "Rhonda, you have just told Rita that she shouldn't be hurt by Jerry's comment." E— "I realize that you mean well, but I believe that it is important for Rita to express herself to Jerry if she wants to, without your trying to smooth things over." S— "Please let Rita speak for herself." C— "That way each person gains experience in expressing his or her own feelings." *(positive consequence)* and/or ["Otherwise, we will become passive and rely on others, not ourselves, to express our feelings."] *(negative consequence)*

While the pacifier is most often heard in encounter or counseling groups, where feelings are emphasized, discussion groups occasionally have a motherly (or fatherly) type who tries to smooth over feelings by saying, "Don't worry" or "He didn't mean that. . . ." and so on. As a leader, you can clearly call the shots. Do not let people take jibes at each other. If someone attacks another, assert yourself (see sample script for attacker) with the offender. Often the pacifiers are gentle, unknowing types, and it is most kind to speak to them during a break. In counseling groups, they are usually unaware of how "doing good" is undoing the group process.

Complicater	During the meeting	D— "Harry, you are speaking about C and D, but we only need to consider A and B. C and D are not the business of our agenda."

Type of Difficult Personality	*When and Where Will You Assert Yourself?*	*A Sample DESC Message*
		E— "I am eager to talk only about the most critical issues that affect us."
		S— "Please do not talk about the matters you are bringing up now."
		C— "We'll get done faster sticking to A and B." (*positive consequence)* and/or ["If anyone gets off A and B, I'm going to remind everyone again."] *(negative consequence)*

If you are an ongoing group, talk to the complicater privately. Note several specific incidents when the person has complicated an issue, argued, and disputed irrelevant points. Be firm. Express your feelings *without* saying, "The whole group is restless with your constant disputing." (Bringing in the group to make your point is generally perceived as aggression.) Sometimes strong negative consequences need to be stated, privately: "If you continue to dispute every point without evidence, I am going to ask the group what they think about your contributions."

Simplifier	During the meeting or privately	D— "Tom, you have told us not to worry several times,
		E— "but I feel uneasy with your optimistic advice, because we are not paying attention to critical arguments and details."
		S— "Please stop telling me not to worry. I want to look at several solutions, not just the one you propose."
		C— "I'll be less anxious if I know I'm not asked to gloss over serious problems." (*positive consequence)* and/or ["I'll be even more persistent with my questions if you continue to tell me not to worry."] *(negative consequence)*

Type of Difficult Personality	When and Where Will You Assert Yourself?	A Sample DESC Message

Often the simplifier should be talked to privately. This person needs to be told about the problems involved in arriving at any solution, and he or she needs to be assured that only through a deliberate, careful process will the group arrive at the best decision. This person is often nervous about indecision and cannot tolerate the anxiety of not knowing the answer to a problem. Because group decision making is often anxious business, a leader must be very much aware of the simplifier who promises a rosy ending to any solution. He or she can sway a group simply because people like the thought of quick solutions that hold no complications.

Disputer	During the meeting	D— "You have told us that 'this sort of thinking' will lead us to ruin."
		E— "I am unsure what you mean by 'this sort of thinking.' "
		S— "Will you clarify that phrase?"
		C— "I will appreciate every group member's effort to refer to specific rather than vague criticisms like 'this sort of thinking.' " *(positive consequence)* and/or ["I'll always ask members to clarify vague terms."] *(negative consequence)*

A disputer is one who sounds good, even reasonable, until you carefully analyze the words. Listen for hackneyed terms and vague references, such as "this sort of thinking," "that way of life," "their way of putting things," "like that." It is a more subtle form of put-down than outright negative labels, such as "bleeding heart," "red-neck," "hardhat," or "pussy-footed officials," but the objective of the disputer is clear: to dispute the value of a solution by associating it with the perceived negative elements in society. Of course, the negative side is opposite the disputer's point of view.

Interrupter	Immediately after the interruption	D— "Mike, Janet is talking."
		E— "I regret that I didn't hear all of what she said."
		S— "Please let her finish now before you start talking."
		C— "Thanks." *(positive consequence)* and/or

Type of Difficult Personality	When and Where Will You Assert Yourself?	A Sample DESC Message
		C— ["I'll remind you if you interrupt again."] *(negative consequence)*

If you are being interrupted, assert yourself by saying, "I want to finish." If that doesn't work, keep talking without looking at the Interrupter. The second method is less assertive than speaking openly and directly about what you need in the situation, but it is a last resort when it is very important to make your point for the written record.

Ethical Use of Assertive Techniques

I have emphasized that ethical people use techniques to get at problems, not at people. They have learned to use persuasive and facilitating techniques in ways that help people solve problems; however, these same techniques are also available tools for unethical, self-serving leaders who misuse a group for their own welfare. In fact, the nature and philosophy of the leader often will determine whether these tools are used for the betterment of people or for their belittling. One way to contain unethical misuse of power is to assert ourselves early when we see unjust and undemocratic practices destroy the effectiveness of a group. Many times difficult personalities (including those of leaders) can obstruct a group's progress. It is important to confront these annoying behaviors in others—and in ourselves—so that important problems can be examined and workable solutions can be proposed.

METHODS FOR PERSUADING GROUP MEMBERS

This chapter has suggested several ways you can influence a group positively so that you can work together productively. However, when you want to persuade a group to adopt your idea, it is often not enough to be a positive influencer; you will have to double your influence by becoming a persuader. At the outset you'll have to distinguish persuasion from manipulation and coercion. Manipulation means getting people to do things by devious means, such as appealing to their guilt or inferiority or greed in such a way that they cannot resist your offer. A manipulator can calculate, dictate, bully, judge, or use an irresistible personality to get another to agree. On the other hand, one can use honest and reasonable arguments as the basis for persuading another person. In any case, it is important to identify the methods of persuasion, because even if you choose not to use them, others may, and you should recognize what they are doing.[3]

1. *Contact and pressure members individually prior to the meeting.* Use information, reason, and arguments to convince people one by one, not lavish lunches or presents, which look like bribes. Honest talk, face to face, with one person is time-consuming, but generally more effective than meeting everyone head-on at the group's meeting.

2. *Make your proposal at the most advantageous time.* When a vote is called for, experienced persuaders delay proceedings until they have the necessary support. Delaying tactics are used until enough people have been contacted on a one-to-one basis.

3. *Start at a level where you know you can win.* Suppose you have to go through a number of committees to gain support or approval. Approach the most positive committee first, so that you can point to its approval when trying to gain subsequent approval from another.

4. *Have more information on the subject than anyone else in the meeting.* Before the meeting, write out all questions with reasoned answers on 4 × 6 cards. Research every aspect of the problem and know exactly how you will answer each objection.

5. *Recognize where your support is.* During the meeting, be alert for signals from others that lend support to your ideas. Some members may comment or nod in agreement with you. Ask for their comments first, immediately after you speak, so as to build up a "bandwagon" effect.

6. *Refer to similar programs that have been successful.* Arguing by precedent lends credibility to your proposal. Where else have your ideas worked? The problem in arguing by precedent is that no two situations are the same, so arguing by example often is not very convincing. It helps to have many details about the other program and to have names and addresses of people whom members can contact for verifying your details.

7. *Work on the people who are "on the fence."* The die-hard opposers are difficult to persuade, but the likely abstainers are people to contact one by one. Try to discover why the abstainer cannot or will not vote decisively and attempt to overcome the apathy.

8. *Speak in a persuasive tone of voice.* Shouting down the opposition is not recommended as a persuasive technique; rather, emphasize detail, use pauses to let ideas sink in, accent important nouns and verbs. The vocal tone should be impassioned but not emotional, that is, emphasize with force but don't let the variations in volume, pitch, force, and rate get so extreme that your voice lacks a reasonable, commonsense quality.

9. *Have a concrete proposal that is ready immediately.* Do not allow argument to go on so long that any proposal is in doubt. Introduce your solution in a detailed course-of-action approach: First, lay out the solution; second, outline the course of action; third, suggest what each member can do individually. If they agree, end the meeting quickly before dissenters start arguing all over again.

SUMMARY

In summary, assertive people plan for success. They do their best to set up good conditions under which they—and others—can solve problems effectively. Techniques for persuading others, like any skill, can be misused by unethical people. If you notice the misuse of techniques in meetings, meet the challenge and correct the unfair practice by asserting yourself. The best way for you—or anyone—to assert yourself is to know how to deliver a persuasive train-of-thought that gets right to the problem without getting off the track. Those who know how to get through with a problem by offering the best solution are generally those who can sell their ideas with the least commotion. Persuasive techniques can ease your group's task and make the whole enterprise less frantic and hectic.

This chapter has briefly outlined some of the things you can do to promote goodwill and progress when people come together to solve problems. They are assertive techniques useful for equalizing the balance of power among discussants. They aim to help shy, intimidated individuals find their way in the unique experience called group discussion. Probably nowhere else in the world can group discussion be used more often to contribute to the betterment of us all. If we are to continue relying on group decision making in the democratic process, it is essential to learn how to be effective and ethical leaders and discussants.

This entire book has urged you to prepare carefully, and then do the best you can to speak out about your ideas and your feelings. Develop the ability to make your ideas clear to others individually and in groups. You'll find that when you do this, you'll assert yourself—your real self—and your ideas will make a difference, an impact, on people such as you never made before.

You will notice your self-confidence growing as you speak to others, and your whole personality will grow warmer and more personable. Because you'll have faith in your ability to express yourself, you'll feel better off emotionally and physically, too. But do not wait for a public audience for an opportunity to deliver your train-of-thought. Speak when you can, to one or many, and you will find in yourself new life, a new sense of being whole and happier. You will have a new feeling of well-being that comes when you know that you can express ideas and feelings without crippling anxiety. And who knows? Very soon you may *enjoy* speaking before a group!

APPENDIXES

Appendix 1: Relaxation Exercises

We can agree that good posture makes people look younger, more enthusiastic, and lively. However, are you aware that poor posture can contribute to your feeling awkward, unattractive, and even afraid? Suppose your throat is tight as a wound-up top and your knees are pushed back in locked position. Not only will your uptight body reveal to an *audience* that you are a nervous wreck, your tense muscles will tell *you*. A tense throat strains with a high-pitched voice, and wobbly knees vibrate under pressure. Tight muscles create physical pressure that restricts the blood supply necessary for a good, easy performance.

Likewise, tense stomach muscles alter our natural breathing pattern, so that instead of breathing abdominally, we start heaving our chests up and down. Chest breathing, often called thoracic breathing, causes us to inhale too much oxygen too fast. Once that happens, the heart is forced to beat faster in order to carry off the excess to the rest of the body. Since other muscles are restricted with tension, they cannot absorb the oxygen at a proper rate, which in turn causes the brain to signal for more oxygen. Thus, heaving our chests and gasping for air, we begin hyperventilating, upsetting the oxygen–carbon dioxide balance in the lungs, until the excess oxygen causes dizziness or light-headedness. Once the lungs have too much oxygen, other symptoms occur, such as a fear of fainting. Now the body responds by tensing other muscles to prevent passing out, and we end up a quivering wreck. But something can be done to prevent this unnecessary spiraling.

HOW THE PROGRESSIVE RELAXATION
EXERCISE CAN HELP YOU

The following instructions will tell you to tense and relax certain muscles one at a time. As you do the exercise, notice which muscles are most tense. Study the tension levels in various parts of your body. This will help you identify where you are likely to feel the most tension when speaking before a group. You can learn to relax muscles before they can seriously restrict the flow of blood through your body to your brain. By learning how to turn off tension early, you can prevent the tremors, sickness, and dizziness of stage fright from happening. Many people, including Gerald Rosen, have described the progressive relaxation method.[1]

To illustrate what you will be doing as you exercise, let's start now with your right hand and forearm. Make a tight fist, but do *not* tense so hard that it hurts. Instead, make a vigorously tight fist. As you hold it for 5 to 7 seconds, feel the warmth come into your knuckles, thumb, fingers, the back of your hand, and wrist. Perhaps you are feeling the warmth creep up your arm. Relax quickly now all at once. Feel the tingly sensation for 10 or 20 seconds as the tension creeps out of your hand and fingers.

Now, a word about tension and relaxation. First, it is important to concentrate, to take careful notice of how your muscles *feel* when you tense them and how they feel when you relax them. Second, when you tense a muscle, quickly monitor the rest of your body for tension. If you find that your stomach, or tongue, or big toe is tense when you clench your fist, quickly let go of all the tension in the rest of your body and keep only your fist tense. If you move a muscle you shorten it and also tense it. However, if you simply let the tension "drop" or "go down" into your resting place, you allow the muscle to elongate, smooth out, and relax.

HOW TO PRACTICE THE PROGRESSIVE
RELAXATION EXERCISE

1. Read through the-exercise instructions in order to understand the sequence or progression of muscle tensing and relaxing. Then, either do the exercise as someone reads the instructions to you, or tape record the instructions for your own use. A third way to use the exercise would be to memorize the muscle sequence in item 9 below and simply tense and relax each muscle as you think of them one after the other.

2. Don't "hurry up and relax;" instead, plan to spend thirty minutes each day (or twice a day) learning exactly what you must do to relax your muscles one at a time.

3. Practice in a quiet setting: take the phone off the hook and darken the room.

4. Lie on a carpeted floor or sit in a comfortable lounge chair or on your bed.

5. Keep warm. Use a lightweight blanket if you chill easily.

6. Tense vigorously for 7 to 10 seconds but don't exaggerate tension because a muscle may cramp.

7. When you tense one muscle group, deliberately relax every other part of your body.

8. Focus on how tension feels in *one* muscle group and then concentrate on how relaxation feels in that same muscle group. Practice tension and relaxation in each muscle before moving on to the next. Learn to discriminate between tension and relaxation.

9. Memorize the order for relaxing those muscles most directly involved in speaking:

   □ fist

   □ arm

   □ forehead

   □ eyes

   □ mouth

   □ jaw

   □ lips

   □ neck

   □ shoulders

   □ chest

   □ stomach

   □ calves

10. If you practice only one thing, then practice correct breathing (see following exercise). Often it can produce an immediate change in reducing your speech fright.

THE PROGRESSIVE RELAXATION EXERCISE

(Note: Do not say the words in parenthesis when giving instructions or recording.)

Now is the time to let go—just feel your body pressing against the place where you are lying. Just sink into it. Now take a deep breath of air. Hold it for a count of 1, 2, 3, 4, 5, and let it go. Let your whole body relax into easiness. (Pause.) Starting with your right arm, make a fist tight enough to feel the warmth coming into it. Study that tension. Hold it—1, 2, 3, 4, 5, 6, 7, 8, 9, 10. Let it go all at once and feel the good feelings of tingling relaxation as the tension goes out of your right arm. (Pause for 15 seconds.) Now try clenching both fists vigorously and again hold the tension to at least a count of 7. As you tense your fists, locate knots of tension in other parts of your body. When you find them, just let them go down. Do not move. Just let go of those muscle knots wherever you find them. (Pause silently to a count of 10.)

Next, with your arms at your sides, twist your arms outward, turning your elbows inside out. Feel the tension in your arms. Hold it to a count of 7, then let it go all at once. Relax. (Pause.) Repeat.

Now close your eyes tightly. (Pause.) Release the tightness and just let your lids rest gently over your eyeballs. (Pause.) And again, roll your eyes—to the right–down–left–up. And again—right–down–left–up, then relax your eyeballs and see nothing. (Pause.)

Next, tense your forehead by raising your eyebrows and wrinkling your forehead. Again, hold it to a count of 10. (Pause.) Let it all go, all at once. Notice the tension flowing out of your forehead. Enjoy the good feelings of relaxation. (Pause.)

The next exercise involves your jaw and the powerful muscles that open and close it. Because many speakers feel a lot of tension in their jaw, lips, tongue, and throat, repeat these exercises two or three times. A relaxed head and throat help reduce feelings of speech fright. Right now, clench your jaw and grin broadly. Feel those powerful jaw muscles that extend on up to your temples. (Pause.) Now release and notice the feelings of relaxation as they spread around your lips and jaw area. (Pause.) Repeat the jaw exercise. Next, pucker your lips. Hold it. (Pause.) And release. (Pause 10 seconds.) Repeat the lip pucker exercise. (Pause.)

The tongue, together with the lips, are the important muscles responsible for clear articulation. If you want to speak clearly and distinctly, exercise your tongue now to get it in good shape. Press your tongue hard against the inside of your upper teeth. Then, pull it back tight across the roof of your mouth. And relax your tongue. Just let it go limp in your mouth. (Pause.) Repeat this exercise for the tongue. (Pause.)

Take a couple of deep breaths now. (Pause.) Just let everything go as you let out the air. Feel yourself become more and more relaxed. Enjoy the good feeling of doing nothing.

Now, touch your chin to your chest. Stretch those muscles running down the back of your neck. Hold it to a count of 7 (pause) and release. Enjoy the warmth of relaxation for 10 to 20 seconds. (Pause.) Repeat this exercise. (Pause.)

Next, relax your throat by swallowing. Just notice the wave of relaxation that follows the wave of tension down your throat as you swallow. Memorize this feeling of relaxation.

Next, push your shoulder blades together. Try to make them touch behind you. Hold them close for a count of 7 (pause). Release. Let the tension flow out of your shoulders for 10 to 20 seconds. (Pause.) Repeat the shoulder blade exercise. (Pause.)

This time try to touch your shoulders in front of you. Hold the shoulders together for a count of 7 (pause), and relax all at once. Just let your shoulders fall back and relax. (Pause.)

Now pull in your stomach vigorously. Hold it for a count of 1, 2, 3, 4, 5, 6, 7, and let go. Again, pull in and count to 7 (pause). Let it go. Notice how your stomach feels when it is relaxed. (Pause.) Try this exercise once again. (Pause.)

Now spend a few minutes tensing and relaxing your legs. Point your toes away from your body. Notice the tension running along your shins? (Pause.) And relax. (Pause.) Repeat. (Pause.) Next, point your toes toward your nose and feel the tightness all along the calves of your legs. Hold it. (Pause.) Relax now for 15 or 20 seconds as you notice the tension flowing out of your legs. (Pause.)

This is correct breathing: put your hand on the muscle below your ribs: as you take in a deep breath of air, you will be pushing your diaphragm muscle *down and out;* now *expel* the air: you will be pulling that muscle *up,* forcing the air out of the lung sacs. So now, practice deep breathing. Keep your chest and shoulders relaxed as you take a deep breath way down deep, and when you get to the top, hold your breath to the count of 7 (pause). Now let it go all at once. Relax. (Pause.) Try this deep, deep breathing exercise again: Breathe in and hold it (pause) and release it. Let the release of air be like a sign of relief and your signal to relax a little bit more each time. (Pause.) Repeat the deep breathing exercise several times. If you notice any knots of tension developing just let them go, one at a time. Continue to relax by breathing deeply. (Pause one minute.)

Now, relax each part of your body beginning with your toes: Relax your toes– arches– calves– knees– thighs– stomach– chest– shoulders– neck– arms– wrists– hands– fingers– jaw– tongue– eyelids– eyebrows– forehead– scalp.

Let all the tension sink down into the bed or floor right now as we count backwards from 10 to 1: 10–9–8–7–6–5–4–3–2–. (Continue to relax for a few minutes, growing heavier and heavier.) So now, if you want to, go to sleep. If you want to get up again, then gently move an arm or leg sometime later and treat yourself to a gentle arousal.

ROUTINE WARM-UP EXERCISES FOR PERFORMERS

Each person must be responsible for his or her own exercise routine. If you have a health problem, consult your physician about these exercises. After testing these exercises over a period of years, I believe that they can prepare the normally healthy person to cope more adequately with the stresses of public performance. Athletes practice routine exercises to prevent injury. Joggers know that tight muscles can produce bum knees and tight hamstrings. Speakers learn that tight muscles produce debilitating fatigue and fuzzy thinking, resulting in low energy and distracting thoughts. Below are some exercises students have found particularly satisfying and relaxing.[2] Do them before your final practice sessions, as well as a few minutes before you perform. Find a place where you can relax all alone. These exercises can help you redirect your stage fright into stage presence.

□ Take a deep breath, hold it to the count of 5, then let it all out at once. As you exhale that sigh of relief let all your shoulder, neck, and facial muscles completely relax. Repeat four or five times.

- Close your eyes. Let your lids rest gently on your eyeballs. Now let your head drop forward, relax your tongue, and slowly rotate your head in a circular fashion—first to the right, then to the left. Work it slowly until the crackling sound diminishes. Feel the sensations of relaxation spread through you.

- Stretch your arms out to the sides as far as you can and rotate them in increasingly larger and larger circles. Go easy. Keep your neck loose and enjoy the feeling of loosening up your shoulders.

- Hug yourself by folding your arms across your chest, stretching to touch your finger tips in back of you. Gently pull (go easy). Feel your arms and upper back relax.

- If you have no back problems, you can bend forward from the waist and hang limp like a Raggedy Ann or Andy. Bend your knees to release tension in your back.

- Reach high with your left hand, then your right hand. Let go. Repeat. Let your arms hang limp by your sides.

- With arms at your sides, loosen your hands and fingers. Then clench your fists tight. Hold a tense position for three or four seconds and then let go. Repeat the clenching–relaxing exercise three or four times.

- Play opera singer by holding your fingertips together in front of you, much as an opera singer would, and inhale deeply as you extend your arms out to your sides. Then, simultaneously, say ''ahhhh'' and bring your fingertips together again in front of you. Repeat this exercise four or five times. It works wonders for releasing tension in the throat as well as in the chest area.

- Loosen your jaw, lips, and tongue by yawning–stretching and then relax. Just let your jaw hang slack and let your tongue rest loosely in your mouth.

206

□ Then warm up your articulators by reciting a tongue twister, using various rhythms, pitches, and volumes throughout. Say "Sister Sally at the seashore" or "Peter Piper picked a peck of pickled peppers." Here is a version of "Betty Bottah" that many performers use: "Betty Bottah bought some butter but she said, this butter's bitter. If I put it in my batter, it will make my batter bitter. But if I bought a bit of butter better than my bitter butter and I put it in my batter, it would make my batter better. She put this butter in her batter, thus she made her batter better. So t'was better Betty Bottah bought a bit of better butter."

□ Practice a ballet kick to relieve tension in your legs; kick your leg up to reach your hand. To do this, grab hold of a chair, table, or kitchen counter with one hand and extend the other hand out to your side. Go slowly as you move your foot up to reach your hand. Most people can't touch their foot to their hand, so go easy. Do the best you can. Repeat this exercise several times for each leg.

□ Imagine your "comfort zone" as you lie or sit down, hands by your sides, eyes closed. Picture a place in your imagination where you are completely free and without any responsibilities or fears. Perhaps you are sitting under a shady tree, relaxing in a hot tub, or lying on the beach. Choose a place that helps you to escape! Just rest as you imagine yourself in your comfort zone for a few minutes. Finally, take another deep breath, hold it, and let it go.

□ Enjoy your relaxed body as you walk to your practice room or speaking destination, repeating the first lines of your speech over and over.

Appendix 2: Suggested Topics for a Train-of-Thought Speech

1. What makes a novel (or a play or a film) great for you?
2. Follow a few basic principles and you can travel light.
3. What are the demands of women's lib?
4. What are some of the new prison reforms?
5. What are some of the remedies for our "backed-up" courts?
6. In what ways have the media kept minorities stereotyped?
7. My favorite pastime (hobby) is . . . (and why).
8. My pet peeve is . . . (and why).
9. The most significant book I ever read was. . . .
10. My greatest fear (or delight) is. . . .
11. Ten years from now I see myself as. . . .
12. This is the way this _____ (object, gadget) works.
13. Is modern music sense or nonsense?
14. Drugs—their use and abuse.
15. Should the government take steps to regulate birth control?

16. Where should we begin to clean up our world?

17. Should the federal government provide free drug clinics?

18. Is the new sexual freedom good or bad?

19. What good are encounter groups?

20. Should the federal government support our Olympic athletics? our artists? our theater? our symphony orchestras?

21. Should the arts be censored?

22. Are the present censoring laws realistic? practicable?

23. What foreign policy should the United States pursue in Asia? in Africa? in the Middle East?

24. What would be the best way to teach public speaking?

25. Who is the failure—the student or the teacher?

26. Should every woman have the right to legal abortion?

Appendix 3: References

Depending on the topic of your speech, here are listings of where you can find more information.

For information appearing in the more popular periodicals, such as *Time, Newsweek,* the *Saturday Review of Literature,* see *The Reader's Guide to Periodical Literature.*

For information appearing in the professional journals, see *The Social Science and Humanities Index.*

For information about aspects of education, see *The Education Index.*

For information about current affairs, see *The New York Times Index.*

For information about people, see *Current Biography, American Biography, Who's Who, Who's Who in America, Who's Who in American Women.*

For general background on historical or scientific topics, see *Collier's Encyclopedia, Encyclopedia Americana, Encyclopedia Britannica, Encyclopedia of Associations, Encyclopedia of Social Sciences.*

For political information, see *Congressional Quarterly and Statesman's Yearbook.*

For statistical information, see *Statistical Abstract of the United States, Facts on File, World Almanac.*

For current humorous anecdotes, see *The New Yorker, Reader's Digest,* your daily newspaper, or any of the numerous books on humor in your local library.

For quotations, see *Bartlett's Familiar Quotations, Oxford Dictionary of Quotations,* or *Stevenson's Home Quotations.*

These are not the only references, so ask your reference librarian to help you if you can't find the information you need to develop a good speech.

SUGGESTED READING

Books on Public Speaking

DALE CARNEGIE. *The Quick and Easy Way to Effective Speaking*. Revised by Dorothy Carnegie. New York: Pocket Books, 1977.

JOHN HASLING. *The Audience, the Message, the Speaker*. 2nd ed. New York: McGraw-Hill Book Company, 1976.

JOHN HASLING. *Group Discussion and Decision Making*. New York: Thomas Y. Crowell Company, Inc., 1975.

ROBERT C. JEFFREY and OWEN PETERSON. *Speech: A Text with Adapted Readings*. New York: Harper & Row, Publishers, Inc., 1971.

MARVIN KARLIN AND HERBERT I. ABELSON. *Persuasion*. 2d ed. New York: Springer-Verlag New York, Inc., 1970.

ROBIN LAKOFF. *Language and Woman's Place*. New York: Harper Colophon Books, 1975.

ROBERT L. MONTGOMERY. *A Master Guide to Public Speaking*. New York: Harper & Row, Publishers, Inc., 1979.

RICHARD PARKS. *How to Overcome Stage Fright*. Freemont, Calif.: F-P Press, 1979.

BEVERLY POTTER. *Turning Around: The Behavioral Approach to Managing People*. New York: AMACOM, 1980.

GEORGE RODMAN. *Speaking Out*. New York: Holt, Rinehart & Winston, 1978.

GERALD ROSEN. *The Relaxation Book*. Englewood Cliffs, N.J.: Prentice-Hall, 1977.

RAYMOND ROSS. *Speech Communication*. Englewood Cliffs, N.J.: Prentice-Hall, Inc. 1980.

DOROTHY SARNOFF. *Speech Can Change Your Life*. New York: Dell Publishing Co., Inc., 1970.

JANET STONE and JANE BACHNER. *Speaking Up*. New York: McGraw-Hill Book Company, 1977.

ANN TAYLOR, TERESA ROSEGRANT, ARTHUR MEYER, and B. THOMAS SAMPLES. *Communicating*. Englewood Cliffs, N.J.: Prentice-Hall, 1980.

PHILIP ZIMBARDO and EBBE B. EBBESEN. *Influencing Attitudes and Changing Behaviors*. Reading, Mass.: Addison-Wesley Publishing Co., Inc., 1969.

Articles on Speech Anxiety

A. BANDURA. "Self efficacy: Toward a unifying theory of behavioral change." *Psych. Rev.* 84 (1977): 191–225.

D. J. COOKE. "Hyperventilation: its treatment and relation to anxiety." *Behav. Ther.* 2, no. 5 (1979): 32–33.

S. B. Fawcett and L. K. Miller. "Training public speaking behavior: An experimental analysis and social validation." *Jour. of Appl. Beh. Analy.* 8 (1975): 125–135.

W.J. Fremouw. "A client manual for integrated behavioral treatment of speech anxiety." *Catalog of Sel. Doc. in Psych.* 1 (1977): 14.

W.J. Fremouw and M. G. Harmatz. "A helper model for behavioral treatment of speech anxiety." *Jour. of Consult. and Clinical Psych.* 43 (1975): 652–60.

W. J. Fremouw and R. E. Zitter. "A comparison of skills training and cognitive restructuring and relaxation for treatment of speech anxiety." *Beh. Therapy* 9 (1978): 248–259.

F. D. Glogower, W. J. Fremouw, and J. C. McCroskey, "Assessment procedures and treatment manual." *Cog. Therapy and Res.*, in press.

M. R. Goldfried and C. Trier. "Effectiveness of relaxation as an active coping skill." *Jour. of Ab. Psych.* 83 (1974): 348–55.

J. J. Horan, "Coping with inescapable discomfort through 'In Vivo' emotive imagery." In *Counseling Methods,* edited by J. D. Krumboltz and C. E. Thoresen. New York: Holt, Rinehart & Winston, 1976.

M. E. Jaremko and G. R. Walker. *Treatment and Assessment Manual for Speech Anxiety Workshop.* Richmond Va.: University of Richmond, 1978.

I. Kirsch, M. Wolpin, and J. L. Knutsen. "A comparison of In Vivo methods for rapid reduction of stage fright in the college classroom: A field experiment." *Behav. Ther.* 6 (1975): 165–71.

D. H. Meichenbaum, J. B. Gilmore, and A. Fedoravicious. "Group insight vs. group desensitization in treating speech anxiety." *Jour. of Consult. and Clin. Psych.* 36 (1971): 410–21.

A. Mulac and A. R. Sherman, "Behavioral assessment of speech anxiety." *Quarterly Jour. of Speech* 60 (1974): 134–43.

B. D. Sanders. "Behavior rehearsal and imaginal desensitization in reducing public speaking anxiety." Ph.D. dissertation, Stanford University, 1968. 28, 3065–66B. University Microfilms no. 67–17, 474.

R. Suinn and F. Richardson. "Anxiety management training: A non-specific behavior therapy program for anxiety control. *Behav. Ther.* 4 (1971): 498.

L. D. Trexler and T. L. Karst. "Rational emotive therapy, placebo, and no treatment effects on public speaking anxiety." *Jour. of Ab. Psych.* 79 (1972): 60–67.

Assessing Speech Anxiety

M. E. Jaremko and G. R. Walker. "The content of coping replacement statements in the cognitive restructing component of stress inoculation." Paper presented at the Association for the Advancement of Behavior Therapy Meeting, Chicago, 1978.

M. E. JAREMKO and W. W. WENRICH. "A prophylactic usage of systematic desensitization." *Journal of Behavior Therapy and Experimental Psychiatry*, 1973, 5,
102–105.

A. MULAC and A. R. SHERMAN. "Behavioral assessment of speech anxiety." *The
Quarterly Journal of Speech*, 1974, 60, 134–43.

M. ZUCKERMAN and B. LUBIN. *Manual for the Multiple Affect Adjective Checklist.*
San Diego: Educational and Industrial Testing Service, 1968.

Appendix 4: Turning an Article into a Train-of-Thought Outline

Instructions: read this article and compare it to the Train-of-Thought outline which follows it.

ADVANCE FOR P.M. RELEASE THURSDAY, SEPT. 7, 1972

STANFORD—Stanford University researchers today (Sept. 7) announced plans to launch a new, community-based program to help prevent heart disease, using mass media campaigns in an attempt to persuade people to change high risk habits.

The project represents the first time that newspapers, television, and radio will be employed in a behavior-change effort at the community level. It also marks the first attempt by scientists to evaluate critically whether or not the media can be used successfully for this purpose.

An interdisciplinary research team headed by Dr. John W. Farquhar, associate professor of medicine at Stanford's School of Medicine, will begin implementing the program next week in the community of Watsonville. Several other Northern California towns will be involved during the next few months.

Watsonville and Gilroy will receive the initial mass media, behavior-change campaigns for a period of one year, Farquhar said. To determine the success of the campaigns, a random sample of 500 individuals per town will be selected for before-and-after comparison of heart disease risk factors such as blood pressure, body weight, and levels of blood sugar, fats, and cholesterol.

Along with the media campaigns, virtually concurrent one-year research studies related to the causes, prevalence, and risk factors of heart disease will be conducted in Tracy and the communities of San Mateo County.

Farquhar stressed that all planning for the project was done in close cooperation with local heart associations and medical societies, and civic organizations in the involved communities. "Their input was solicited from the beginning," he said, "and they've been very enthusiastic about the project. Without their cooperation and interest, we simply couldn't have gotten off the ground."

The program has been in the planning stage since it was established a year ago with the support of two grants from the National Heart and Lung Institute. The grants, due to run at least five years, totalled over $750,000 the first year and are projected at nearly $4 million for five years.

In the next several years, the researchers plan to conduct further studies and behavior change campaigns in other California towns.

Farquhar said the Stanford project represents the type of preventive efforts needed to help stem the "epidemic" of heart disease in this country, which claims the lives of over 600,000 Americans per year.

"Most of the deaths of people under 65 in the United States due to coronary heart disease are preventable," he said. "We believe that success in achieving substantial behavior change at the community level lies at the root of any future national campaign to reduce premature mortality from heart disease and stroke."

Farquhar identified several high risk habits which will be targets of the media campaign, including smoking; physical inactivity or lack of exercise; gaining excess weight; and consuming increased amounts of cholesterol, saturated fats, sugar, salt, and alcohol. Physicians have long associated these habits with heart disease.

"We're not advocating that people make massive changes in their lifestyle, just small but significant ones," said Dr. Henry Breitrose, associate professor of communication and a member of the research team.

"Our message will be a simple one—minor changes in a person's daily activities can significantly reduce his heart disease risk factors."

The campaign, which will be conducted in both English and Spanish, will utilize radio and television spots, press release, recipe columns in local newspapers, a "cooking for your heart health" cookbook, and possibly other media.

A subgroup of certain high risk individuals will receive an intensive follow-up campaign, Farquhar said. These "triggering" sessions will consist of frequent meetings of the high risk group with "change agents" from the Stanford research team in an encounter group atmosphere.

Preliminary testing of the individuals in the random sample will begin next week in Watsonville and in Gilroy in mid-October. The data-gathering efforts in Tracy and in San Mateo County communities are due to begin in November.

Initially, home interviews will be conducted with individuals in the random samples to explain the nature and goals of the project, Farquhar said. Then, a survey center will be established in each town, where those in the sample will be given physical examinations and tested for prevalence of heart disease risk factors, including body weight, blood pressure, and levels of blood fats, cholesterol and sugar.

"At the end of a year, we'll come back to check the same things in these same people," Farquhar said. "In addition to behavior change, we'll be looking for beneficial changes in attitude, motivation, and information."

In obtaining these data, tests and examinations at the survey center will be supplemented by detailed written questionnaires.

The before-and-after aspect of the Stanford project distinguishes it from previous behavior change efforts, Farquhar noted.

"Money has been spent in the past on media campaigns to change behavior and get people to do the right thing,'' he said, ''but no attempt was made to find out whether they worked.''

Involved in the planning of the project and the production of the media campaign has been a research team consisting of physicians, behavioral scientists, journalists, television and film specialists, dieticians, exercise physiologists, and statisticians.

Dr. Nathan Maccoby, professor of communication, is co-principal investigator of the project with Dr. Farquhar. The media campaign is directed by Janet Alexander of the Department of Communication. Dr. Peter D. Wood, senior scientist at the Medical School and deputy director of the program, will supervise testing for levels of blood lipids (cholesterol, fats, and other compounds).

Farquhar noted that the Stanford project, initiated last June with the establishment of a Lipid Research Clinic and Specialized Center of Research (SCOR) in arteriosclerosis, reflects a new federal commitment to the prevention of heart disease. Fifteen SCOR centers and 12 Lipid Research Clinics focusing on arteriosclerosis detection and prevention have been developed nationwide since the National Heart and Lung Institute began the program last year.

A vast number of civic organizations, medical groups, and individuals in the involved communities have worked closely with the Stanford researchers in the development of the project, including: county medical societies, health departments, and comprehensive health planning agencies; local heart associations; community hospitals; chambers of commerce; mayors' offices; city councils; and local newspapers, radio, and television stations.

Introduction (Engine)

 500 Watsonville and Gilroy residents are going to be subjects in a new research project that's already been tested in northern California.

 With 600,000 Americans dying of heart disease every year we are well on the way to an "epidemic."

 A Stanford research team is planning to find out if a mass media campaign can change people's old behaviors and improve their chances against an early death from heart disease.

⊐⊏ Physicians, behavioral change specialists, dieticans, exercise specialists and statisticians plan to do these things: first, . . .

Discussion (Boxcars and Cargo)

 The campaign will target in on those high-risk habits associated most often with heart disease:

⊏⊐   ⌈ Smoking
           | Physical inactivity
           | Excess body weight
           | Increased consumption of cholesterol, saturated fats, sugar,
           ⌊ salt and alcohol.

⊐⊏ While you might think the project is aimed at changing life styles,

🚃 it is advocating that people make small but significant changes in their
behavior, such as changing their habits of

smoking
inactivity
overweight
eating the wrong foods

⊐⊏ The campaign will not only be scientifically controlled,

🚃 it will be waged in English and Spanish using:

TV spots
Press releases
Recipe columns in local papers

⊐⊏ Another important feature of the campaign is that . . .

🚃 it will conduct home interviews with the sample 500, explain the goals of
the project 500 and do a follow-up one year later to measure changes.

These will go to survey centers to be tested for all those nasty
things like cholesterol, sugar and fats, weight and blood
pressure before and after the one year campaign.
A before and after questionnaire will be given to measure
behavior and attitudinal changes.

⊐⊏ In conclusion, impressive goals are being set, so, as you can see . . .

Conclusion (Caboose)

This class is not only the only group interested in changing its attitude and
behavior.

Moreover, our class in behavior change won't cost the money that the one
year project in Watsonville and Gilroy will cost, which holds a $750,000
price tag but any price is cheap if . . .

ⒸⓉ these Stanford physicians, communications experts, behavior change
experts may be able to reverse the "epidemic" of heart disease in this
country, which claims over 600,000 lives a year.

1-4 Essentially the project aims at recording habits, weight, blood pressure,
and so on, both before and after a media campaign is waged in both
English and Spanish.

A year from now we will hear the results of this heart disease project
aimed at changing people's bad habits. Hopefully, in *this* class we will
see our own behavior change in some small but significant way, too, and
we won't need to wait a whole year!

Appendix 5: Notes

Introduction

1. The discussion of coping with emotions has been adapted and partially excerpted from chapter 3, "Coping with Stress," of *Asserting Yourself* by Sharon A. Bower and Gordon H. Bower, © 1976. Reprinted by permission from Addison-Wesley Publishing Co., Reading, Mass.
2. AMPS is adapted to public speaking from *Instructor's Manual for Asserting Yourself* by Sharon Anthony Bower and Beverly Potter, © 1976. Reprinted by permission from Addison-Wesley Publishing Company, Inc.
3. A standard reference is Edmund Jacobson, *Progressive Relaxation* (Chicago: University of Chicago Press, 1938).

Chapter 1

1. Research supporting this idea is reported by Gordon H. Bower, "Analysis of a Mnemonic Device," *American Scientist* 58, no. 5 (Sept.–Oct. 1970): 496–510.
2. From Janet Stone and Jane Bachner, *Speaking Up* (New York: McGraw-Hill, 1977, pp. 60, 64–72). Copyright © 1977 by Janet Stone and Jane Bachner. This section is adapted and expanded from this volume.

Chapter 2

1. These methods for defining central thoughts are adapted from pp. 398–402 in *Public Speaking: Principles and Practice* by Giles Wilkeson Gray and Waldo W. Braden. Copyright © 1951 by Harper & Row, Publishers, Inc.

Chapter 4

1. Some of these attention-getting techniques are from an interview with Philip Zimbardo, psychologist, author, and professor at Stanford University, Spring 1980.
2. David Walechinsky, Irving Wallace, and Amy Wallace report this statistic in *The Book of Lists* (New York: Bantam Books, 1977). Reprinted with permission.

Chapter 5

1. See Philip Zimbardo and Ebbe B. Ebbensen, *Influencing Attitudes and Changing Behaviors* (Reading, Mass.: Addison-Wesley Publishing Co., Inc., 1969).

2. The two outlines for "compulsory health insurance" are from Lawrence Mouat, *A Guide to Effective Public Speaking* (Boston: D.C. Heath & Co., 1959).

Chapter 6

1. The speech outline is adapted from one prepared by UCLA student Nancy Archibald.
2. Some of this section is adapted from Taylor, Rosegrant, Meyer, and Samples, *Communicating,* 2nd ed., © 1980, pp. 129–31, 134–36, and Ross, *Speech Communication,* 5th ed., © 1980, pp. 314–16. Adapted by permission of Prentice-Hall, Inc., Englewood Cliffs, New Jersey.

Chapter 7

1. This categorization of transitions is adapted from pp. 364–66 of *Public Speaking: Principles and Practice* by Giles Wilkeson Gray and Waldo W. Braden. Copyright © 1951 by Harper & Row, Publishers, Inc.
2. Chart adapted from p. 366 of *Public Speaking: Principles and Practice* by Giles Wilkeson Gray and Waldo W. Braden. Copyright © 1951 by Harper & Row, Publishers, Inc.

Chapter 8

1. This chapter is largely adapted and partially excerpted from chapter 3, "Coping with Stress," of *Asserting Yourself* by Sharon A. Bower and Gordon H. Bower, © 1976. Reprinted by permission from Addison-Wesley Publishing Co., Reading, Mass.
2. The systematic-desensitization technique is usually credited to Joseph Wolpe, in his *Psychotherapy by Reciprocal Inhibition* (Stanford, Calif.: Stanford University Press, 1958).
3. The efficacy of this technique was demonstrated in research by Patricia L. Garfield (née Darwin), "Effect of Greater Subject Activity and Increased Scene Duration on Rate of Desensitization," unpublished doctoral dissertation, Temple University, 1968. (See *Dissertation Abstracts,* 30, no. 3, 1969.)
4. Al Bandura proposes the theory of self-efficacy in "Self Efficacy: Toward a Unifying Theory of Behavioral Change," *Psychology Review* 84 (1977). 191–225.
5. From "The Clinical Potential of Modifying What Clients Say to Themselves," by D. Meichenbaum and R. Cameron. In M.J. Mahoney and C. E. Thoreson (eds.), *Self-Control: Power to the Person.* Copyright © 1974 by Wadsworth, Inc. Reprinted by permission of the publisher, Brooks/Cole Publishing Company, Monterey, California.

Chapter 9

1. Research supporting this idea is reported by Gordon H. Bower, "Analysis of a Mnemonic Device," *American Scientist* 58, no. 5 (Sept.–Oct. 1970): 496–510.

Chapters 10 and 11

1. Some of these exercises for improving your speech delivery were originally used in the author's "Self-Control of Speaking Anxiety" course, Foothill College, Los Altos, California, and later adapted to assertiveness training in Chapter 9 "Looking and Feeling Assertive" of *Asserting Yourself* by Sharon A. Bower and Gordon H. Bower, © 1976. Reprinted by permission from Addison-Wesley Publishing Co., Reading, Mass.

Chapter 12

1. The material on introductions is adapted from Malcolm E. Lumby, "Presenting the Do-It-Yourself Speaker's Introduction," in *The Toastmaster* Magazine, 2200 N. Grand Ave., P.O. Box 10400, Santa Ana, Ca., May, 1979.
2. From Janet Stone and Jane Bachner, *Speaking Up* (New York: McGraw-Hill 1977, pp. 60, 64–72). Copyright © 1977 by Janet Stone and Jane Bachner. This section is adapted and expanded from this volume.
3. *Ibid.*
4. Assertive replies illustrated here are for speaking up in group discussions. For speaking up in other situations, see chapter 8 of *Asserting Yourself* by Sharon A. Bower and Gordon H. Bower, © 1976. Reprinted by permission from Addison-Wesley Publishing Co., Reading, Mass.

Chapter 13

1. Adaptation of "Qualities of the Group Member" (pp. 34–36) in *Group Discussion and Decision Making* (Thomas Y. Crowell) by John Hasling. Copyright © 1975 by Harper & Row, Publishers, Inc. Reprinted by permission of the publisher.
2. DESC illustrated here is for speaking up in groups. For speaking up in other situations, see *Asserting Yourself* by Sharon A. Bower and Gordon H. Bower, © 1976. Reprinted by permission from Addison-Wesley Publishing Co., Reading, Mass.
3. List adapted from "Methods of Persuasion" (pp. 129–131) in *Group Discussion and Decision Making* (Thomas Y. Crowell) by John Hasling. Copyright © 1975 by Harper & Row, Publishers, Inc. Reprinted by permission of the publisher.

Appendix 1

1. See Gerald Rosen, *The Relaxation Book* (Englewood Cliffs, N.J.: Prentice-Hall, 1977).
2. Richard Parks illustrates some of these exercises in his book *How to Overcome Stage Fright* (Freemont, Calif.: F-P Press, 1979), pp. 50–56.

Appendix 4

Reprinted with permission of the Stanford University Medical Center, from a news release of September 6, 1972.

Index

JOKES, QUOTES AND ONE-LINERS FOR PUBLIC SPEAKERS

Herbert V. Prochnow and Herbert V. Prochnow Jr

Stuck for words? Never again! From the author of *The Public Speaker's Treasure Chest*, here is a treasury of quotations for all occasions.

- ★ over 4,000 entries, each one keyed to a full subject index

- ★ witty one-liners

- ★ thought-provoking anecdotes

- ★ proverbs, toasts and verses

a must for anyone who is called to speak before an audience or who wishes to add sparkle and interest to their conversation.